THE GUERRILLA FACTORY

THE MAKING OF SPECIAL FORCES OFFICERS, **THE GREEN BERETS**

TONY SCHWALM

FREE PRESS

New York | London | Toronto | Sydney | New Delhi

*f*P
Free Press
A Division of Simon & Schuster, Inc.
1230 Avenue of the Americas
New York, NY 10020

First Free Press hardcover edition November 2012

FREE PRESS and colophon are trademarks of Simon & Schuster, Inc.

For information about special discounts for bulk purchases, please
contact Simon & Schuster Special Sales at 1-866-506-1949 or
business@simonandschuster.com.

The Simon & Schuster Speakers Bureau can bring authors to your live
event. For more information or to book an event, contact the
Simon & Schuster Speakers Bureau at 1-866-248-3049 or
visit our website at www.simonspeakers.com.

Designed by Julie Schroeder

Manufactured in the United States of America

10 9 8 7 6 5 4 3 2 1

Library of Congress Cataloging-in-Publication Data

Schwalm, Tony.
The guerrilla factory : the making of Special Forces officers,
the Green Berets / Tony Schwalm.—1st ed.
    p. cm.
1. Schwalm, Tony. 2. United States. Army. Special Forces—Officers—
Training of. 3. United States. Army. Special Forces—Officers—Biography.
4. Commando troops—Training of—United States. 5. Guerrilla warfare—
United States. I. Title.
  UA34.S64S37 2012
  356'1675—dc23
  2012017015

ISBN 978-1-4516-2360-4
ISBN 978-1-4516-2362-8 (ebook)

In memory of my son, Philip McKinley Schwalm.
Here's what you never got to see.

THE GUERRILLA FACTORY

THE WORLD TRADE CENTER was smoldering, and the nation had joined together in one voice demanding retribution. "Find who did this. Make them pay." Gathered from Special Operations Forces across the Department of Defense, we sat in a windowless room at U.S. Special Operations Command in Tampa, Florida, discussing what our brothers would need to satisfy that demand. The Navy SEALs and Army Special Forces officers gathered with me that day would be sitting out the first phases of Operation Enduring Freedom. We were going to miss the big dance in Afghanistan scheduled for the fall of 2001.

For most of us, our war-fighting days were behind us. We no longer endured the wet and cold until our jaws and abdomens ached, or the crunching of bones after parachuting out of a night sky. The days of chasing black rubber boats on a dark sea and letting our kids grow up without us were gone.

Now we would suffer a different feeling of absence: watching through a telescope from Tampa, focused on Afghanistan ten thousand miles away, as our brothers in the teams we had left fought the war we had all trained to fight, in the land that was home to Al Qaeda. Our job as staff officers was to man the mother ship and make sure they didn't lose.

In early October 2001, Dov Zakheim, the comptroller for the Department of Defense at the time, gave U.S. Special Operations Command (or SOCOM) around $1.8 billion to fund the fight in Afghanistan. My group's mission was to prioritize the spending of that money.

All of SOCOM's elite units, from Fort Bragg, North Carolina, to Coronado, California, had put in their requests. Their wish lists included everything they might need to infiltrate Afghanistan and destroy the Taliban government that had facilitated the terrorist strikes of September 11, 2001. No request would be denied; nothing was too expensive. Our only limiting factor was time: We couldn't buy everything fast enough. The units had what they really needed: a big chunk of ground, a mission that allowed for the maximum latitude of action at the lowest level, and a mouth-watering number of targets. I was one of the Army Special Forces officers at the table and, ostensibly, the leader of the group, though I often felt like a hood ornament on a race car.

My fellow Green Berets would join up with friendly Afghan warlords and call in air strikes that would hopefully pulverize Taliban strongholds. Other Special Operations units would sniff the air for signals betraying the location of influential Taliban or Al Qaeda members. Then our specially trained and exquisitely armed athletes would pile into black helicopters and disappear into the night to hunt these men down.

Our job was to make one master list from all the wish lists sent by the components. The men who would be working on the ground in Afghanistan took top priority. As we went through the possible outcomes of the situation, our list evolved. But in the rush to deliver justice in a remote part of the world and make life difficult for those who parked airplanes in office towers, one thing was easily overlooked: the need to preserve the legitimacy of our mission.

How would the world judge our actions? Right then, none of us cared. We were heady with the sense that we had absolute license to do anything we wanted to in order to kill whoever had destroyed so many lives in a single horrific day.

The world was watching, and most of its nations were cheering the United States on, memorializing those lost by lighting candles and laying flowers at our embassies. But how long would that attitude endure? I would hazard that no one anywhere in the Department of Defense, probably in the entire U.S. government, was worried about a potential loss of rapport with the world. The United States had been cut and wounded, humiliated. The global community rallied behind us, and the mandate from the American people to her war machine was simple: "Go get them. Get them all. Make them pay." No one in the Department of Defense needed any prodding, and such enthusiasm was particularly intense among the Special Operations Forces, or SOF, the elite units funded by SOCOM.

For the sake of clarity, Special Forces (like the word *paraphernalia*, never written in the singular) are only those soldiers who have successfully completed the Special Forces qualification course and have a very specific purpose in life: unconventional warfare. The broad banner term, Special Operations Forces, or SOF, encompasses the Navy SEALs, select Marines, Army Rangers, Air Force pararescue (or PJs, as they are known), select Army Psychological Operation and Civil Affairs personnel, and a cadre of highly trained pilots with an exquisitely equipped fleet of airplanes and helicopters. I will focus on the SOF that operate on the ground, and of that set, the ones who famously wear green berets. That said, the uninitiated—which is everyone outside of the SOF community—require some background.

Broadly speaking, there are two types of SOF: Daniel Boone and Superman.

Superman is what most Americans believe the SOF soldier to be: a barrel-chested freedom fighter capable of bench-pressing twice his body weight and wielding lethal gadgets with an easy expertise. He practices martial arts to the point of being lethal in a fistfight. Those guys exist, and they have my unfailing respect. But of the fifty thousand people who fall within the purview of Special Operations Command in Tampa, Florida—the mother ship, if you will—fewer than five thousand meet that description.

The Superman of SOF is without equal in the world, probably in history. Collectively, these men, with their training and equipment, are a killing machine *sine pari*. To illustrate, when Superman arrives, he usually says, "I'm here to kill somebody. Where is he?" If you are that carbon-based life form and identifiable to Superman, you are probably going to die at his hands. People standing near you at the time of the hit are not going to fare well either.

I have heard it said, and seen it borne out in the real world, that efficiency is the enemy of effectiveness. In other words, if you have to ask how much Superman costs, you don't understand the nature of what he does. Superman performs and consumes like a Ferrari race car. If you're driving a Ferrari, you probably don't care about the cost of gas or the impact of your exhaust on the planet. It's a Ferrari. It doesn't just go fast. It goes fast well. Likewise, Superman doesn't just kill the enemy. Superman kills the enemy well with an alacrity and precision bordering on the preternatural.

Most Army Special Forces soldiers, on the other hand, are more like Daniel Boone and they move very differently. We're a group numbering around sixty-five hundred, and our *primary* mission is entirely different. That mission is unconventional warfare, or UW. Unlike Superman, when we show up we might say, "Hello, and how is everyone today? Good. So, we're here to train you to use your stuff more effectively and maybe bring in some American air power if we need it. But hey, while we're waiting, how's everybody feeling? Huh? Anybody sick or wounded? Got a pregnant wife? Girlfriend? Both? No problem. We're here to help." And so we begin our encounters with questions focused not on the enemy but, rather, on those we are sent to train. We are sent to train and fight alongside what we affectionately refer to as the "indig" (short for "indigenous forces"). The idea behind SF is that other countries should fight their own wars unless U.S. national interests are directly at risk, in which case we need to send Superman and maybe a cast of thousands for a conventional ground fight.

That requirement to dialog with foreign nationals compels SF soldiers to know languages and possess communication skills capable of transcending cultures. When I say "transcend cultures," I mean more than not showing the bottom of your foot to a person from the Arabian Peninsula or refraining from patting a person from South Asia on top of his head. I mean understanding that when you're talking to a military officer from Saudi Arabia, keep the conversation away from anything having to do with the Palestinian Territories. I mean knowing when you're talking to a Turkish colonel the mention of a Kurd in anything but a pejorative context may close doors.

While SF may on occasion appear to act like an armed version of the Peace Corps, we are, at our core, soldiers, which means we are killers, and no less killers than Superman and crew. But where Superman intends traumatic amputation, SF brings cancer. We make the body, the host, kill itself. As amputation usually kills faster than cancer, unconventional warfare is unfortunately time consuming. As Superman devours money and equipment, Daniel Boone demands time, and this temporal reality hurts the cause of UW.

The reality in the twenty-first century is that Superman is always the first choice when the guy in the White House decides to employ U.S. armed forces, SOF or otherwise, and the decision is always predicated on a timetable. One word defines that timetable: elections.

Superman promises to get wherever the geopolitical fire is burning, put it out, and get back before anyone knows he's gone. Daniel promises to get to the fire, enter the house, find a corner not immediately threatened by the conflagration, and begin an assessment process, the length of which may cost him his marriage.

From that UW skill-set, we learned how to help a body heal itself. The other side of the UW mission is counterinsurgency, or COIN. (Actually, there was another term, Foreign Internal Defense, but the U.S. government forgot how to spell it after Vietnam.) Since we understand how to foment insurgency, we know how to quell insurgency. Like check forgers and computer hackers who work for the Justice Department, just so, Green Berets can advise governments on what to do in the face of a violent insurgency.

Superman goes, does, and leaves. Daniel Boone goes, does, and stays and stays and stays. In the end, both come to the same place: killing somebody. The question then becomes who pulls the trigger.

Killing people, breaking things (the euphemism for "making war"), and then leaving quickly the destruction thus created are the organizational focus of most SOF units. In the Army Special Forces community, we perform these kinds of missions, but we also spend a lot of time thinking about how America's actions affect the locals.

Popularly known as the Green Berets—the guys with the ballad by Barry Sadler (number one for five weeks in 1966) and the headgear shared with the British Royal Marines and the Girl Scouts—the Army Special Forces were established in 1952. President Kennedy christened us with the signature headgear in 1962, and we strive to live our motto, *de oppresso liber* (roughly, "liberate the oppressed") and put into practice the one thing we do better than any other arm of the U.S. military: wage unconventional warfare.

Conventional warfare is the traditional, symmetrical, large-scale fight, conducted with tanks, warships, large formations of aircraft, an endless supply of cruise missiles, and hundreds of thousands of men and women in uniform. Unconventional warfare is categorically different. It is the art of using another country's indigenous forces to fight in support of U.S. national interests. It is messy, asymmetrical, and can be very expensive in ways that reach far beyond money. If you mishandle this type of warfare there is hell to pay regarding reputations and lost relationships. Think of the Bay of Pigs in 1961.

But this fall day in Tampa, I noticed that there was no budget for unconventional warfare operations in Afghanistan. People in the halls of SOCOM were talking about UW, like a big party that someone was going to have because her parents were out of town. But no one had considered how such an approach would be paid for. There was no budget for arming guerrilla forces. I had heard of something called a Northern Alliance, a group of indigenous fighters that battled the Taliban. And I knew that the 5th Special Forces Group, the Green Berets from Fort Campbell, Kentucky, were in the lead to go to Afghanistan with pallets of equipment packed and hundreds of men waiting for the green light to commence the reckoning. The SOCOM leadership, generals and admirals, kept discussing a UW campaign, but no one addressed funding such an approach. I decided I needed to bring it to the table of my group.

"How much will it cost to do UW in Afghanistan?" I asked. The responses around the room were telling. The SEALs looked around at each other blankly. Though they knew what I was talking about, they couldn't care less about it. They don't train for unconventional warfare, nor are they meant to conduct it. But the Special Forces guys enthusiastically embraced the need to carve out funding for UW. This difference in reactions speaks volumes to the difference between SF and the rest of SOF, the rest of the Defense Department.

Conventional warfare is like a bayonet, designed to kill directly. The Special Operations component, or the SEALs, can be equally lethal, but they're like scalpels. Unconventional warfare is a Swiss Army knife, with many modes, some of them subtle and indirect. Yes, there is a sharp blade, but it's far from being a bayonet, and it comes attached to a screwdriver, a tiny pair of scissors, a corkscrew, a toothpick, and a multitude of other devices not intended to do any serious cutting.

By design, Army Special Forces conduct combat operations arm in arm with men and women from other countries. The only other organization in the U.S. government with this nonstandard design feature of playing well with others is the CIA, and this part of the CIA is very small, numbering in the hundreds.

Other branches of the U.S. military can do some of this, but not by design. And the return on investment for SEALs, Rangers, and others of the SOF doing what SF is capable of is not worth the effort. Imagine removing the cork from a wine bottle using a scalpel. Sure, it's possible. Now imagine using a bayonet. Not pretty.

Green Berets get to know the people of other countries where we train (and fight) and do so intimately. Our goal: to ensure legitimacy and win rapport among people that our military is unaccustomed to worrying about very much. Our success in pursuing our interests anywhere in the world can be measured along these lines. When we have legitimacy and rapport, our folks can walk freely without body armor among the people—and rip the very heart out of the enemy's ability to operate there. Legitimacy brings intimacy, and intimacy brings understanding—and victory. Like lovers, we get to know the people by way of an intimacy born of wanting to help. Once we have their trust we often find that we didn't know what we were getting into.

Our training during the six-month-long qualification course hammers home the value of waging war this way. An SF team of ten to twelve guys may be the only Americans the local people will ever meet. They make a small footprint and work in relative isolation. They live or die on their talent for unconventional warfare.

In 2001, sitting around that table in Tampa, the challenge of finding and killing the violent radicals who were bent on bleeding the United States through a thousand cuts was so immediately compelling that it was perhaps easy to overlook the principles of unconventional warfare that we in SF consider so important. Today, those principles, founded on an indirect approach, should be front and center anywhere America seeks to bend the shape of the world in line with its interests. I learned their power years ago. I earned my green beret in 1993 and went on to serve as the commander responsible for training officers at the schoolhouse in Fort Bragg, North Carolina, training known as the Army Special Forces qualification course. We call it the "Q course."

My purpose in telling the story of my journey into the Special Forces is to show how, more than ever, the principles and ideas of unconventional warfare deserve to emerge from the shadows and inform our security policy at the highest level. Though our brand of war fighting is but a niche in the Department of Defense, it deserves to stand as the model for U.S. engagement abroad. As we draw down our large conventional forces and rely increasingly on firing Hellfire missiles from drone aircraft piloted remotely from sites in Nevada, it is critical that we remain in contact with the people on the ground. Without the people accepting us and our cause, we are occupiers, at best tolerated and at worst despised. The British during the American Revolution, the French in Spain during the time of Napoleon, and the Soviets in Afghanistan in the last century are lessons in the result of losing the favor of the people. The people are the prize unless you plan to obliterate them.

Gone is the spirit that moved people around the globe, in the days following 9/11, to light candles in memory of our dead. There are no crowds cheering us as liberators. We have buried thousands of Americans and have broken the bodies of thousands more. We'll never know how many noncombatants died and suffered as collateral damage. In a war for hearts and minds, the number of enemy dead becomes irrelevant. Our legitimacy as a guarantor of peace without fear, and stability without tyranny, must be the new metric of victory. My own journey taught me to regard one tenet of war as sacrosanct: The most powerful army is useless in the pursuit of peace if the world regards it not as a policeman, but a bully.

Through this book, I aim to show that America's stunning success in Afghanistan in 2001 and our equally remarkable success in western Iraq in 2003 were not flukes but the product of our deft application of a mode of warfare discounted in the days of a twenty-four-hour news cycle. Unconventional warfare derives its power from a sophisticated blend of diplomacy and shocking violence—drawn from principles and behaviors that should guide our decision-makers before they ever again send the bayonet, the scalpel, and the Swiss Army knives into battle. I came to understand these principles the hard way. This is one Green Beret's story.

TWO

I HAVE HEARD IT SAID among leaders from every profession that success is a habit. It took me quite some time to form that habit. My first attempt to climb out of the pack and join the ranks of the Special Operations elite began with a catastrophic failure. It happened in 1985, at the U.S. Army Ranger course.

Rangers have long been known as the Army's elite light infantry. Never shy to say "Rangers Lead the Way," they served with distinction in World War II, leading the charge up the heavily defended cliffs at Normandy's Pointe du Hoc. From the American Revolution to the present day, Rangers in combat are the stuff of Hollywood legend, and they have certainly earned it.

In January 1985, with seven months on as a second lieutenant beginning his army career, I signed into Fort Benning, Georgia, at a place known as Harmony Church. My wife drove her twenty-two-year-old second lieutenant, fresh from the Armor officer basic course in Fort Knox (a six-month gentlemen's course intended to introduce new officers to the Army and show them how to command tank units) and dropped him off near a long line of nearly bald men waiting to begin the two-month Ranger course. As she drove away, the men in the line looked at me and snickered.

My coiffed hair—that is, long enough to be coiffed, though within regulation—made me stand out like a beacon in an environment where anonymity was highly prized. As I joined the line, the men at the end turned and took my full measure. Unimpressed, they were moved to pity.

"Damn, LT," said one man, pulling a knife from his belt. "Why are you wearing all this shit?"

"What?"

"You don't wear rank here, sir." That was the last time I heard "sir" for several weeks. I knew we went through the course without rank, but I hadn't been instructed to remove the marks that told the world who I was before this moment. The soldier started cutting my gold bar and tank insignia from my collar. Another man cut the stitches on my other patches with the tip of the knife. My fellow students worked quickly, and soon I was wearing the appropriate uniform. I had a pocket of mangled cloth with frayed threads and an ego in a similar state.

At the front of the line, a gigantic man in a long-sleeved black sweatshirt loomed in the doorway, peering out over the heads of the students in front of me.

"What the fuck are you studs doing?" he inquired.

"Squaring this Ranger away, Sergeant," came the reply.

The man eyed me hard. "See if you can do something about his hair." He turned and disappeared into the building. Comments about my hair would continue throughout the evening.

I thought we would be given the opportunity to get a haircut upon signing in, likewise to remove patches and generally get ourselves ready to go. With the clarity of a slap across the face, I began to understand how grossly I had underestimated what I was attempting. Additionally, I realized I was a lightning rod in a storm where God was slinging down the heavy stuff. As we continued to draw equipment and fill out paperwork to begin our Ranger training, the Ranger instructors (famously known as RIs) let me know I was unwelcome. I understood this to all be the result of my hair. When we were finally released to sleep, I walked into the latrine and shaved my head with disposable razors. It took about twenty minutes. When I was finished, I was bald, safe, and, for the moment, legitimate.

Such was the beginning of my sad effort to separate myself from the pack of Army officers who didn't attend Ranger school.

Designed to test one's ability to think and plan while under conditions of extreme duress, the Ranger course is the first taste of what life might be like in the world of Special Operations, a term that I could not define at the time. In 1985, that duress was induced through food and sleep deprivation while conducting small-unit missions, specifically patrolling. Ranger school taught and then assessed small-unit tactics, albeit in a remarkably stressful setting and with little ambiguity. But as everyone around me seemed to know what was coming, I felt clueless. And this ambiguity was born of my own ignorance.

So why did I attempt Ranger school at all? Why not just be a good Army officer, regardless of special training, and go about my merry way? I, like most people uninitiated with a world defined as elite by those who speak with authority, was enamored with the thought of being special.

Early on as an ROTC cadet, I learned that all *real* leaders in the Army had Ranger tabs. Including the most senior generals in charge and all the senior NCOs around them, everybody who was anybody had the coveted "black and gold," as the Ranger tab in its color form is called. One had but to watch the actions of soldiers in a group to see that a Ranger tab conferred alpha male status to the bearer. Once, during a six-week summer training exercise at Fort Bragg, the importance of a Ranger tab was explained objectively. As several hundred ROTC cadets looked on, all the officers who were Ranger qualified were brought before us, and the merits of having successfully completed the fifty-eight days of hell were explained. With eyes wide open and mouths agape, we officer-wannabes learned that the men standing before us were Rangers, embodying all that was good in Army leaders.

Thus my thoughts ran: I was to be an officer; officers are leaders in the Army; all good leaders in the Army have Ranger tabs; ergo, in order to be a good Army officer, I needed a Ranger tab.

Though Ranger school was famously difficult, I was twenty-two years old, still immortal, and fully believed that it would be hard but not *that* hard. I was relatively fit and had completed all the training scenarios the Army had ever thrown at me. I believed that it would all come together, and that I'd pass Ranger school. *Maybe not honor grad, but hey, who knows. It can't be that hard, right?*

But boy was I wrong. I was mentally and physically unprepared to be trying what most people consider the most intense leader-training course in the world. To think I was still smoking cigarettes as I prepared for Ranger school defies all logic, unless one considers my ignorance at the time. The Marine Corps even sent men to the Army Ranger course—it was that good as a leader-development tool—and I had the idea I might just breeze right through it.

Over the course of the forty days I survived Ranger school, I came to understand what it meant to have nearly apostolic devotion to the Army. In the early days of training, a Ranger officer pulled the other officers in the course into a small circle and explained to us that it was acceptable to the Army if we died during training, that student deaths were understood to be the cost of making the men who populated the Ranger battalions. I listened to a man fall down in the dark on the side of Hawk Mountain in north Georgia and remember the blue pallor of his face under the glare of flashlights when we could not revive him. The medics told us later his core body temperature was ninety-four degrees. Conversely, I watched men fake injury in order to terminate training. Ranger school was designed to not just test endurance but commitment, honor. In order to quit, to just raise one's hand and say "enough," a soldier had to sign a letter of lack of motivation. An LLOM (each letter pronounced in the saying of the acronym) was tantamount to confessing to being a pedophile. No one, not any officer or soldier in any branch, would ever embrace a man who signed an LLOM. The Army made it so by the esteem shown those who had earned the tab. If the best leaders had Ranger tabs, then those without might be good, maybe, but those who had tried and quit—not failed, *quit*—they were bad. While quitting occurred to me almost immediately upon arrival, the thought was repugnant.

Actually, I made it through the hard stuff. But thanks to a bad ration and the accompanying food poisoning, I was misdiagnosed with a ruptured appendix about halfway through the course. When I came to after the surgery, I was lighter by the weight of a healthy appendix and had a six-inch incision bisecting the front of my stomach. The following day, the doctor who had called for the invasive procedure dropped by to see how I was doing and apologized for making the bad call. I blew into a plastic tube, raising a small ball up a scale, thereby ensuring I would not contract pneumonia, and listened as my attending physician made the following remarks.

"You really didn't need the surgery. But hey, look at this way: You'll never have to worry about your appendix rupturing. And you'll be getting a nice vacation. No lifting anything over fifteen pounds for two weeks, no driving for six weeks, and you're on convalescent leave for thirty days starting today."

"When can I go back to Ranger school?" I asked, contemplating my situation. I had failed the test emotionally, physically, by every dimension. The bad ration was just a curtain call to a similarly bad performance. Even if I had successfully completed the course I would have never been proud of how I had comported myself. But I got it now, where "it" was a standard of conduct I have never witnessed, only read about. I was ready to get ready, to go back with feet like a Sherpa and the mind of an ox if that's what it took to succeed in, not just survive, Ranger school.

"Oh hey, Lieutenant, that's at least six months away. You can't do any strenuous activity until those stomach muscles have fully healed. Yeah, at least six months."

My convalescent leave would be longer than the entire course, and then I would have to start from scratch to prepare my body. The Army was not going to pay me to hang out at Fort Benning waiting to go back. I would be shipped to my first real duty assignment as an armor officer and would arrive gutted.

Upon leaving, the doctor smiled like a kid who just hid a frog in your car's gas tank, and I never saw him again. He who should have diagnosed me with food poisoning had instead ripped my stomach apart and started me down a path of self-doubt. I would now go to my first assignment as a second lieutenant who had failed fabulously at trying to earn a Ranger tab. I would walk into rooms with other officers who sported the coveted black and gold and see their eyes go to my left shoulder looking for the sign that I was part of the club, the club of alpha males, the guys who had endured two months of the most severe training. Without actual combat as a measure of an officer's mettle and propensity to lead, there was Ranger school. And the door had been slammed and riveted shut.

The notion of chasing the doctor down the hall and beating him to death with my IV stand did occur to me, but it vanished as I tried to sit up. For my entire tenure as a commissioned officer (twenty years), my incision, my Ranger tab as I came to refer to it, oozed due to the shoddy stitch job the good doctor gave me. It served as my constant reminder of the failure that began my military career, a failure I swore never to repeat. I have a collection of brown Army underwear stained in the front at the waistband with blood. I came to know that I needed to lose weight when it didn't bleed, as I was packing a layer of fat over it.

———

Following that sixty-day convalescent leave (thirty from Ranger school and another thirty from the hospital at Fort Benning), my first assignment was to an armor battalion in Wildflecken, West Germany, beginning in April of 1985. Somehow, everyone had heard of my failure. My first company commander welcomed me to the unit, and during the course of the initial interview he explained that I was due to take the Army physical fitness test. I was still on profile with a note from the doctor saying what I could and could not reasonably be expected to do. Before I could begin the embarrassing story of how my stomach was still seeping blood and that I wasn't supposed to strain harder than one might experience during a particularly difficult bowel movement, my commander explained that officers don't have profiles and that no officer in his command would ever hide behind a piece of paper delivered by some medical idiot in order to avoid leading by example.

The next morning, after seventy pushups followed by seventy sit-ups and as I started the two-mile run, the bottom of my shirt darkened with blood as the muscles strained against nondissolving sutures.

Welcome to the Army.

I spent three years in Germany, leaving in May of 1988, having led a tank platoon, a reconnaissance platoon on the now-defunct East-West German border, and finishing as the executive officer for a tank company, the second-in-command to a captain. Dogged by my failure at

Ranger school, I was determined to show that I could perform with the best the Army had, that the Department of Defense had. While I couldn't go back to Ranger school for a second shot as an armor officer, I could change branches and volunteer for Special Forces, the Green Berets.

I had not yet met anybody who was Special Forces qualified, and my view of the shadowy world of Special Operations stood solely on popular icons of movie fame. I wasn't sure exactly what SF guys did, but I knew it had to be physically demanding. I wanted to succeed at something really difficult. I quit smoking and took up running, training for a marathon, just because it seemed like the right thing to do. Undaunted and ignorant of what I was trying to accomplish, I began to take all the lessons I had learned at Ranger school and prepared for a radical departure from the path of a normal armor officer, along a course that would take me to a table surrounded by Green Berets and SEALs at a time when our nation would eventually be desperate and grateful for what we had learned to do.

At least, I thought I was going to follow that path.

THREE

I FOUND MYSELF DETOURED from the path I chose in 1988. A baby girl arrived and put a magnet on my compass. The imagined path of what SF may have held seemed less than the ideal of being a conventional Army officer, leading tanks in mock battle in West Germany or the desert expanse of southern California. I envisioned coming home at night to play with this happy, healthy little girl who really seemed to like me. Being a dad felt important, and staying on my tank felt safe, safer than falling out of airplanes at night wearing a hundred pounds of "lightweight" equipment.

As if to affirm my decision to play it safe, my wife delivered a son on July 26, 1990. While I was on leave in Fort Riley, Kansas, enjoying this little man, Iraq invaded Kuwait.

Fast-forward to February 1991.

Our orders were simple: Go north, kill everything. I was twenty-eight years old and had 124 men watching and following me as their commander. Thankful they could not read my mind, I was certain they would follow me only out of curiosity had they known my self-doubt. We were living the moment we had waited for our whole lives, whether we knew it or not. We were soldiers in a war, living on machines that rumbled through the tabletop-flat desert of the Saudi Arabian peninsula, and waiting for the signal to attack.

The leadership above me, generals and colonels, bequeathed to us, the First Infantry Division of Fort Riley, Kansas, the distinction of being part of the vanguard that would invade Iraq and displace the Iraqi forces. A thousand years ago, in the previous August, Iraq invaded

Kuwait and had been preparing for our arrival ever since. We communicated through the free press that we, the U.S. armed forces, were coming; the Iraqis watched and believed what they heard on the news, and they dug miles and miles of trenches laced with mines. I spent that time reluctantly hopeful that we, my team of leaders, were forging an ensemble of competent soldiers and lethal equipment into an effective killing machine, part of the blunt tip of a juggernaut set to launch.

Many times during Desert Storm, I sat on the turret of my tank, considering how I had come to be part of the initial wave of ground forces that would soon wash over the Iraqis like an armored tsunami. In an effort to play it safe, to avoid the uncertainty of SF, I stayed on my tank in 1988 after successfully completing the Special Forces Assessment and Selection course.

SFAS was born out of the Army's desire to save money and the desire of Special Forces to weed people out before wasting training resources on someone who wanted a green beret for the wrong reasons, like looking good in uniform. Before 1988, anyone could volunteer if he met the basic requirements and then move to Fort Bragg for training. Throughout the years, more than a few individuals had gamed the system, moved to Fort Bragg, failed training (intentionally or not), and then sought assignment in the storied 82nd Airborne Division. Additionally, SFAS was designed to establish a base physical requirement that all of us would have to meet. Until then, the only requirements for SF were a laughable passing grade on the Army physical fitness test and the infantry requirement from Fort Benning to march twelve miles with a forty-pound rucksack in less than three hours. SF had no specific standards peculiar to the branch except language training. But SFAS was changing all that. I was going into the third such class. It was all very new, even for the cadre, the group of anointed practitioners taken from the ranks and entrusted with making more of themselves.

A three-week gut check to see if one had the physical and mental capacities required to earn a green beret, SFAS was a crucible of contrived hardship that mixed physical exhaustion and mind numbing tasks in a slurry of ambiguity. Those volunteering for SFAS were already in the Army. The candidates, as we were called, came from every specialty: infantry, tankers (like me), artillery, mechanics, cooks, chaplain's assistants, and just about everything else except musicians. (I never met someone from the Army band trying to be a Green Beret.) Though we came from all the different branches of the Army, we had no idea where each person was from. We wore the same sterile uniforms worn at Ranger school. No saluting, no saying "sir," except to those running the course. While among Ranger students this absence of military courtesy engenders a sense of egalitarianism, at SFAS it added to a sense of uncertainty as we were being assessed, not trained. Ranger school is training followed by testing. SFAS is testing only.

My friend dropped me in front of a building that had housed troops bound for Germany during World War II, and I fell into a line with others beginning the quest. No one snickered at me this time. Following predictable military bureaucratic processes, we signed our names dozens of times, received old kits, like canteens and ammo pouches intended solely for training, and moved to barracks built before any of us were born. Inside, we found rows of metal bunks and dilapidated wall lockers. We were given the evening to move into the barracks and square away our stuff. Among the stuff we had to square away were four heavily used Vietnam-vintage olive green uniforms and a stack of eight white cloth strips measuring approximately two by four inches. We were instructed to sew, using dental floss, one of the strips on each leg of the pants under the cargo pocket. On the strip, each of us wrote his roster number in large block characters. My new identity was now Roster Number 186 and would remain so for the next eighteen days.

At 0430 the next morning, the lights came on and we were informed of the day's activities. The first test for assessment was a simple aquatic event: swim fifty meters while wearing uniform and boots. Following breakfast and a short bus ride, a class of over a couple of hundred candidates made a line that snaked around the deck of an indoor pool. While we were waiting for instructions, the senior noncommissioned officer, the command sergeant major, jumped into the water.

"Everybody look at me," he commanded, as if we hadn't noticed the oldest guy on the deck step into the pool fully clothed. He swam the length of the pool and back, hoisted himself out, and ran a hand over his thinning hair. He had executed a solid freestyle-form swim about as fast as anyone could while wearing a full set of fatigues and leather combat boots.

"That's how you do it," he said. "Any questions?" The gauntlet had been dropped. A man old enough to be a father to most of us had just set the bar high.

Most made the swim look easy. Some, like me, struggled to the end but made it. Still others failed and usually by a wide margin. A few had to be rescued.

At the end of the swim test, about sixty men were told to pack their gear. They could reapply for SFAS at a future date.

That was it. Game over. Go home, loser. Those men had signed in to start the Green Beret pipeline and couldn't last twenty-four hours.

The failures would go back to deserted barracks and empty their wall lockers filled only the night before. Equipment recently drawn would be returned. Phone calls would be placed asking wives or girlfriends to pick them up at the airport.

It was now time for the Army physical fitness test, which was composed of three events: pushups, situps, and a two-mile run. Passing the test was not a milestone that called for heavy celebration. But still, achieving a maximum score was not easy. As future Green Berets, most of us expected to max it or at least do very well. While a perfect score was 300, below a 290 indicated (to us SF wannabes at least) a character flaw, perhaps something genetic. Passing was a 180.

On this day, around forty students failed, and I remember thinking their failure was borderline immoral. Later, I found out that some of the candidates had come from assignments in Turkey and Korea; they were running on less than four hours of sleep in the last two days. One man had lost a bag to the airline coming over from Europe. He was doing all the events in borrowed clothes and shoes.

That night we were told to pack our stuff for movement out to Camp Mackall, where the assessment would begin in earnest. The next morning, after a breakfast of eggs, bacon, hash browns, toast, a doughnut, coffee, juice, chocolate milk, and anything else I could cram into my maw—we didn't know when we would eat again—we loaded trucks and left the main reservation of Fort Bragg. After an hour, we arrived at the small gated community known as Camp Mackall.

If Fort Bragg is the Mecca of Special Forces, Camp Mackall is the Qa'aba. In 1988 it was a small cantonment area of nondescript aluminum buildings set on 7,900 acres. Approximately five hundred yards square, the cantonment area had barracks for roughly five hundred students, two cavernous classrooms, a mess hall, a miniature exchange store that sold junk food along with various forms of tobacco, and a latrine facility known as the "million-dollar shitter." Like the Qa'aba, what Camp Mackall lacked in appearances it exceeded, by several orders of magnitude, in significance to those who found themselves walking around it.

Set apart from the new aluminum structures were six decrepit buildings, each about twenty by thirty feet and sheathed in black tar paper. These were the last of the "tar paper shacks" and were famous among the old hands as the buildings that had housed them as they prepared for Vietnam, Laos, and Cambodia in the early sixties. Scheduled for demolition, they looked forlorn and abandoned, and I've never forgotten them. They seemed out of place among the new construction, yet they had produced the very men we all sought to join, to follow in a type of war that had not changed since the Maccabean revolt against the Greeks 150 years before the time of Christ.

We jumped off the back of military trucks and, with duffel bag and rucksack, shuffled past the old and into the new. The irony of the name "million-dollar shitter" became apparent as we observed a long row of portable latrines that lined the road we walked to get to our new barracks. The newly completed massive facility meant to service the hygienic needs of hundreds of men training at Camp Mackall did indeed cost a million dollars but as yet could not handle the waste produced by over two hundred soldiers. We could shave and shower in it, but biological functions were to be performed in the fiberglass less-than-a-million-dollar units. We were directed by name into one of seven large buildings, and each man looked for a bottom bunk, as midnight trips to any latrine made negotiating the rails to the ground an unwanted adventure.

We stowed gear on the bunk that would be home and talked of what we thought was coming while waiting for the next set of instructions. That night, we filled one of the classrooms to take a series of tests—one on math and two on our psychological makeup. One question stood out: Do you torture animals? Years later, the question about torturing animals was dropped because guys were answering yes due to a sense of guilt born of hunting.

We were put to bed around 2100 (nine o'clock). Muffled chatter and the occasional nervous laugh floated through the darkness of the open bay between row after row of metal bunks. My hearing locked on to a distinctly Hispanic voice describing the moonlighting exploits of a male dancer. The speaker's engagements had audiences with members of the officers' wives' club, and his story transported me to a high-school gym locker room and the exaggerated conquests told to the rapt attention of the uninitiated. Still, his story rang true, and I feel asleep as he described how a general's wife had demanded a picture of him in his thong while she put her tongue in his ear.

The training cadre, all noncommissioned officers, entered the sleeping bays the next morning with the air of policemen walking into a bar looking for trouble. Though we had all been to basic training and had served for at least two years (many of us four or more), we were trying to gain access to their world, and they were the gatekeepers. Walking quietly among us as we swung out of the bunks and started dressing, they wore black sweatshirts, pressed camouflage trousers, and low-cut black hiking boots, and most had their lower lip protruding from snuff. There was no yelling or screaming as they turned on the lights at 0500, and they moved among us like smoke.

"Formation at zero six, candidates," one of them said, as if announcing the arrival of a plane at the gate. "We're going to do some running this morning. Fall out in PT gear. And make sure you grab three rations."

Boxes of MREs (meals ready-to-eat) were stacked by the door.

Without pausing to choose, each of us shoved three of the slick plastic bags into our rucksacks.

The space we filled with bodies and bunks took on the air of a football locker room on game day. As the clock ticked to six, some of the men shaved with electric razors; others sauntered off to the million-dollar shitter. At the door, the chatter was light between spits of toothpaste and large gulps from green canteens. The uniform for the day was T-shirt and shorts with running shoes. By 0545, everyone was standing outside. At 0600, five rectangles of forty-plus men stood ready to receive whatever instructions might come.

"Right, face," barked a sergeant, obviously cadre. In unison, we pivoted to the right ninety degrees. "Forward, march." We marched out the gate of the cantonment area and down a dirt road. I admit there was relief in the certainty of being told what to do. But that vanished quickly.

"Halt." We came to a stop.

"Left, face." We were now looking at cadre members. They stood with the same detached indifference one might expect from ranchers appraising a new herd of cattle. Holding flashlights and clipboards, they formed a line along the road, like a gauntlet.

One walked up to my group. "When I call your roster number, sound off," he said, loudly but dispassionately. He called our numbers, and each responded, "Here, Sergeant." Two numbers called received no response. Our new leader, who never identified himself, walked over to another anonymous member of the cadre and conferred. When he returned, he informed us that two of our group had quit during the night.

"Nothing wrong with that. Better here than in the Q course," he said.

As the sun was coming over the pines, we toed a line drawn on a dirt road. Like a mass start at a marathon, we waited for the signal to go. But unlike a race, we were never told the distance we were going to run. When asked, the cadre would only say, "Until you're told to stop."

At the word "Go," we took off like horses on a racetrack. The sand alternated between soft and hard. I tried to keep what I estimated to be about a seven-minute-per-mile pace. After the first mile, the pack had become a line of men in gray running clothes strung along a dirt track flanked by tall pines with shafts of golden sunshine dancing on their backs. Our breaths made jets of steam in the cold morning air, and we were pouring sweat by the time we rounded a corner an hour later and were told to stop. A cadre member was sitting next to a pickup truck listening to a radio station, and upon announcing that this was the finish line, he noted our roster numbers and times. Based on how fast some of us had run and the time it took for completion, the run had to be over seven miles.

Afterward, we marched back into the gated area to do physical training. In teams of eight or nine, we performed every manner of calisthenics known. By the end, my arms and legs were involuntarily twitching like a horse's after a race.

A cadre member then told us to clean up and assemble in classroom number two in duty uniform with a writing instrument. We jogged back to the barracks and headed en masse to the million-dollar shitter. The chatter in the shower was punctuated by nervous laughter.

"What do you think the time standard for the run was?"

"I saw one of the cadre write down my roster number. I don't think I had done anything wrong though."

"This place is just a giant mindfuck."

We ate our MREs and headed to the classroom. At the entrance and hanging in simple black frames were black and white photos of those who had gone before us and the trophies they had bagged. Most memorable of them was the one of Che Guevara, taken just after he was executed by commandos in Bolivia. Legend has it that a team from 8th Special Forces Group was advising the commandos when they captured him, and that a U.S. government Skilcraft pen taken from the revolutionary's pocket still adorns the wall of a Green Beret. Che was not looking so good in this picture.

A very slight (by U.S. soldier standards, anyway) sergeant with the carriage of a gymnast told us to take our seats as quickly as possible. We winded our way on a sloping concrete floor between long tables and steel folding chairs. On the tables were maps and thin hard plastic squares—protractors for measuring distance on the maps and plotting grid coordinates.

Cadre members, gargoyles in crewcuts, lined the back wall, silently eyeing us.

The NCO at the front of the class encouraged us to move with a sense of urgency and explained that for the next several days we would be executing land navigation, what the civilian world commonly referred to as "orienteering." This was 1988, and we were years away from the global positioning system that would come to be as ubiquitous as leather boots. He further explained that we would navigate on foot with map and compass both day and night, and that we would be measured against time standards. A hand went up among the sea of candidates.

After the NCO instructed us to keep all questions until the end, he paused and then said something that stuck with me. "By the way, there are such things as stupid questions. Like, a train leaves New Jersey going west at seventy miles per hour and one leaves Las Vegas going east at eighty miles per hour, then how much does Santa Claus weigh?" He watched us for a reaction, which was dead silence. "See, that question has nothing to do with the speed of trains. So make sure you really have a question and are not looking for a reason to speak when you really should shut up and listen." The confidence pouring off of this guy as he explained life to over two hundred desperate Green Beret candidates left its mark on many of the officers sitting in front of him, as indicated by the comments overheard during our few breaks. He knew there were officers in the crowd, though hidden beneath a roster number on white cloth, and he didn't care.

He continued to describe how we would know what we needed to take each day as we left for training. The packing list for the rucks was simple and included two two-quart canteens or a gallon of water, a change of uniform and boots, socks, food, foot powder, and other sundry goods as well as a safety kit.

He explained the safety kit like this. "If you get out there and don't have a clue where you are, do not walk to Charlotte [a distance of 130 miles]. Just walk until you hit a paved road and sit down. Somebody will be by in a truck to get you. And no, you're not automatically put out for getting lost. We'll take you back to your last point and you can keep trying.

"But"—and here he leered at the class—"if you decide that this Green Beret bullshit is just not for you, grab that red star cluster out your safety kit and pop that puppy. We will come to you, wherever you are, and give you a ride back here. And you're done. No harm."

I'm sure he saw every emotion expressed in the faces staring back at him.

"And please don't shoot it into your head." We chuckled. The star cluster was a foot-long metal cylinder about an inch and a half thick. One end had a removable cap that, when placed over the other end, acted as a firing pin for the rocket housed inside the cylinder. Holding it at arm's length with one hand and smacking the cap into the bottom with the other launched five pieces of burning phosphorous over fifty feet in the air. The power required to launch this phosphorous was easily capable of maiming or killing the person unfortunate enough to mishandle it. I know one officer with a steel plate in his head after such an encounter. (His men called him "Rocket Man" behind his back. He never lived it down.)

"If you decide to kill yourself with it, please leave a note. The investigation will be much easier if we know you meant to shoot this thing into your mouth." Nervous laughter answered him.

He then asked if everybody had a map and protractor, and requested that whoever didn't raise his hand. We all had what we needed.

"Everybody knows how to use these, right?" Silence enveloped us as we exchanged glances. He didn't wait for a response. "The answer is 'Yes, Sergeant.' See, I know that's the answer, because navigating with map and compass is a basic soldier task. And you guys are all soldiers, and you have to have done this before in order to be a soldier, so I'm not going to stand up here and bore you with a class on the five colors of the map, converting grid to magnetic angle, and how to read a scale. Because all you guys already know that or you couldn't be soldiers. Right?"

We stayed silent.

He explained that the cadre was not here to teach us anything. They were here to assess us and then select the best, assuming that we all met the standards (though we would never know what the standards were even after we completed the course). We had been here three days at this point and had just found out how SFAS worked.

"Just do your best," he concluded. We were then instructed to take out something to write with before beginning more testing. We took standardized tests and wrote essays about why we wanted to be SF. These mental exercises lasted until dark, at which point we were released to eat one of our MREs.

When we reassembled in the classroom, we were missing a few people. More had quit. A pickup truck carrying several candidates and their gear had left Mackall, headed back for Bragg.

I remember thinking: *We really have not done anything yet. Why are people quitting?* I discovered later in my career that stress of the unknown is enough to make many people quit what they think they wanted to do before they started, regardless of their previous experiences. SFAS hit some soldiers as too odd to make sense enough to stay.

That night brought something new: debates. Groups of randomly chosen candidates were given a topic to present to the rest of the class. For each topic, two groups were arrayed against each other to present point and counterpoint arguments. All the topics were taken from the daily headlines. A recent headline in December 1988 was the refusal of the United States to grant Yasser Arafat a visa in order to address the United Nations general assembly. The move had prompted calls from the international community to relocate the UN to a more neutral country, like Switzerland. For this debate, it was one-on-one, no team. Each candidate was given a position to support regardless of how he felt (if he felt anything) about the topic. As fate would have it and unbeknownst to the cadre running the "gong show," as we came to call it, the candidate chosen to support the idea of relocating the UN was an officer, fairly conversant on events of the day and (theoretically, at least) capable of critical thinking. The candidate with the ostensibly patriotic position of keeping the UN in the United States was an enlisted man from one of the Ranger battalions. Physically, he looked like a shaved gorilla. Academically, he still looked like a shaved gorilla. After five minutes to think, the combatants squared off in front of over two hundred sleepy soldiers. Thus the battle unfolded.

The candidate who supported the move went first, and as soon as he started speaking, the whole room knew he was an officer. On the fly, he had crafted a reasonable line of logic as to why the UN should move. We all nodded our approval.

The cadre told him to take his seat and then instructed the other candidate to begin.

As soon as this man opened his mouth, we all knew this matchup was lopsided. His words have stayed with me through the years.

"You cannot move the United Nations," he began in a hard, New England streetfighter accent. "It is made of concrete and steel and glass. This building is huge. I have seen it."

At first, many of us thought: *Good on you, buddy. That's the way. Just load this place up with bullshit and let's go to bed.*

But he continued. "It was built by Americans, with American steel and hard work." As he continued in this vein for a few more minutes, he convinced all of us that he was no longer pretending. He really thought the most salient point of the argument was the physical relocation of the thirty-nine-story building.

Among the less compassionate of us arose the hummed strains of "The Battle Hymn of the Republic," provided as a musical backdrop to the hyperobvious pronouncement delivered with the sincerity of a political speech. One guy sitting nearby quipped, "Now we know what the *n* in *Ranger* stands for: *knowledge.*" We muffled our laughter.

"Okay, that's good," the moderator said, cutting the speaker off. "Well done to both of you. Go ahead and take your seats." With a face that was saying "Wow! What was that?" he told us to return to our barracks and stand by for inspection. It was after 2130.

At 2200, the cadre rolled in—not like smoke this time, but more like tornados. As instructed, we were standing by our bunks, some recently vacated, while several NCOs went from bed to bed rifling through our kit, each of which was laid out in accordance with a hand-drawn picture posted on the wall. Every snap, snapped; every button, buttoned; every zipper, zipped. Infractions were noted on the spot and publicly.

To my left, I heard, without turning to look, "You can follow instructions, right?" Again, dispassionate but terse, loud.

"Yes, Sergeant," came the nervous reply.

"Then why are the snap fasteners on your rucksack not snapped?"

"I don't know, Sergeant."

"You don't know? You think someone came in here and undid them?"

"No, Sergeant."

"Then you must have failed to check them, isn't that right?"

"Yes, Sergeant." This was followed by the most unnerving question a candidate could be asked.

"What's your roster number?" The question was intended to intimidate, as we all wore our numbers under the cargo pocket of each leg. The cadre had but to look down.

The scene was repeated throughout our area. Every infraction was noted loudly but without anger.

He came to me and found no infractions. Obsessive-compulsive disorders are rewarded in some circles.

After an hour, the area looked like it had been hit with a hard wind. Canteens, socks, boots, rucksacks were everywhere.

One of the cadre stood at the door and before leaving told us to be ready to go at zero five in boots and uniform. (We turned off the lights at 2300). Someone whispered, "I bet we're doing the obstacle course in a few hours." As soon as my eyes closed, I instantly fell into a deep sleep.

By the time the lights came on 0415, I felt like I had just blinked. Cadre were among us, watching us, not talking, only making notes. Two NCOs were standing over a still-sleeping candidate.

"Anybody gonna help this guy? Or is 'buddy' just half a word with this group?" asked one of them. Several men moved to the bunk, and one shook the guy's feet. "Is 'buddy' half a word" is shorthand for "buddy-fucker," as in letting a guy fail whom you could have helped.

Electric razors whirred. Some men dry shaved with a disposable razor. I made a cup of cold instant coffee and ate part of a meal. My stomach growled.

We did more exercises, this time in uniform and leather boots. When the sun finally appeared, we were camouflaged pillars of steaming sweat. We walked over to the obstacle course, though not all of us. Several more had quit after the morning workout.

When it was light enough to see, we were walked through the course and shown how to negotiate each obstacle. Like with any complicated action, observation and execution are very different.

Each man was given an individual start time, with a minute-interval separation between him and the next guy.

My turn arrived. "Roster Number 186. Go." I shuffled to the first obstacle, a seven-foot vertical wall. No sweat. Up and over. I went through the rest in similar fashion, until I hit the rope climbs.

Climbing a rope vertically requires significant upper-body strength. The secret, however, is to use the legs. One leg wraps around the rope (usually one and a half inches thick) with a portion on top of a boot. With legs bent, trap the rope with the other boot and straighten. The body inches up, and the hands clench, holding on to whatever was gained. Release the rope with the feet and bend the legs. Slow but effective, the inchworm approach allows just about any man of reasonable fitness the ability to ascend a rope.

Or, one can climb using only the arms, as I did, in an effort to mask his ignorance of the aforementioned technique. I did fine on the first rope and thought I had thoroughly impressed the cadre at that station. As I ran down the trail, I congratulated myself on being able to climb thirty feet using my arms alone. I rounded the trail leading to the next event and noticed that the officer in charge of selection, Major Velky, was ahead of me, standing to the side. As I got closer, I saw that he was watching other candidates at the second rope climb. I picked up my pace and sprinted to one of three ropes hanging from a log resting three stories in the air atop two telephone poles. At the top of the rope, the candidate smacked the log triumphantly.

As soon as I grabbed the rope, my arms sent notice that they were done for the day. I made it half way up and stopped. My hands began to slip. To avoid rope burn, I climbed hand over hand back down.

The cadre at the station said, "One-eighty-six, go around." I was stunned and stared at him. "Get out of the way, candidate. People are trying to climb the ropes." I headed out, deflated, thinking the rest of my efforts would be in vain because I had failed to learn how to climb the rope with my legs. I saw Major Velky look at my leg and then write something in a little memorandum book. We knew only a few of the cadre names and had no relationships with any of them. They were assessors. We were being assessed, like mail-order brides.

Resigned to my potential failure, but with the knowledge that I would go down swinging, I negotiated the rest of the course without incident. I ran into the growing circle of heaving candidates, steam coming off of us like locomotives chugging up a hill. I sought solace after my failure at the second rope obstacle.

"I didn't make it up the second rope," I said, looking for a "Don't sweat it" from the crowd.

"You're fucked," came the only response. My heart sank. When we had all finished, we were herded back to barracks to clean our personal areas, shower, and eat.

The afternoon was filled with classes on the organization of various Special Operations Forces and associated missions. Toward the end of the day, the cadre who had warned us about stupid questions explained that our individual movement phase would begin the following day. He instructed us to return that evening with our maps, protractors, and compasses.

That night, we sat at long tables practicing how to use these primitive navigational aids but without instruction. The cadre gave us problems to solve using the tools and then walked among us checking our answers—no yelling, no teaching, just nodding or "Try again." Invariably, another candidate would lean over and try to help the recipient of "Try again." Navigating by map and compass is an art born of science. We were practicing the science: basic geometry drawing lines on the map, converting what our compasses would show to what we would have to do on paper, and learning that looking at the map before we started walking could prevent us from crossing the same creek several times. A straight line may be the shortest distance between two points but not necessarily the fastest route.

This phase of the course was known as the "humpathon," as in humping (or carrying) a rucksack under marathon conditions. We would be trucked out to various start points on federal land around Camp Mackall and navigate with map and compass through the pines and scrub oaks for the next five to six days. From the start point, each man would find his first point and then be given his next one by a cadre member sitting there for him. Each man had his own route to follow, though the same points were used. Members of a previous class estimated they had walked over 250 miles during the eighteen days of SFAS, most of it during the individual movement phase.

Using whatever lesson plan they were following, that night our handlers turned the time screw another turn. We got six hours of lights out.

At five o'clock the next morning, we were outside in the frosty North Carolina air. Ancient Army trucks lumbered through the gate and made a line, like elephants at the circus.

"Truck one," a voice called out from behind us. "When I call your number, sound off and get on." The process continued until we had filled approximately eight trucks with men carrying rucksacks and rubber rifles, affectionately called "rubber ducks." Candidates were quitting every day, and we had just started the hard part.

Day one of individual movement accounted for approximately six miles along a route defined by three points on a map through palmettos, bushes, and swamps. Barely sweating in the winter chill, I was surprised when the cadre at the last point said I was done. Other candidates trickled in throughout the day, and we busied ourselves keeping the fire going.

As night came, our last point became our start point for the night phase. The cadre called us over one at a time, gave us new coordinates, and sent us on our way. This night phase was similar to the day portion in length. We were on the trucks and back at Mackall by ten that night.

Lights out at 2300. Wakeup at 0430. We got five and a half hours. More bunks were empty.

On day two, the distances were longer. We got to the barracks by midnight and dragged ourselves to the shower before crawling into bed. Wakeup was at 0500.

Day three was like day two but with much longer distances to cover. We got back to the barracks at 0100. Wakeup was 0530. We still had no idea what the time standards were.

Have I already failed and don't know it? I thought.

Day four was a blurring repeat of the previous days. When the lights came on, I rolled out of bed, and my eyes felt like they were full of dirt. With legs like lead, I walked to the latrine, washed my face, and shaved. In the barracks, very few of us were sleeping on top bunks. The voluntary withdrawals, or VWs as they were known, had the unexpected effect of opening up bottom bunks. The daily routine of climbing into the trucks became much less of an effort. We were no longer crammed inside. There was plenty of room. During this portion of selection, the candidates did not have a chance to bond as in a conventional military unit or on a Special Forces team. And we were not competing against one another. We were competing against an unknown standard and as individuals, not as a team.

Still, we were all trying to be Green Berets, and we exhibited the natural inclination to be a tribe. One conversation around the fire waiting for the trucks illustrates this point.

Those of us remaining by the fourth day knew why we had trained so intensely to be there. Without weeks and months of preparation, only someone born to this type of life, like a Sherpa, could have made it this far. We recognized in each other a commitment to achieve what we had started, without ever saying it. We knew we had walked close to a hundred miles by this time, and anyone sitting around the fire was a credible soldier. While some men would come to the fire and immediately fall asleep, most would take the opportunity to talk and decompress from the hours of moving as quickly as they could while carrying sixty pounds and a rubber rifle.

"You know the Christmas houses?" asked someone from the edge of the fire. Grunts from the circle indicated that, yes, we were all familiar with the private residences inexplicably located in the middle of the federal lands on which we were training; they had been decorated for the holiday season. The disembodied voice started to describe a scene that stopped all conversation around the fire. This candidate exited the tree line and saw three Christmas houses glowing with multicolored lights that lay astride his direction of travel. Despite racing the clock, he walked up to one house and looked inside the window. At first, he hid and peeked. What he saw brought him to stand and stare, fully framed by the opening. A man, a woman, and several children were watching a Christmas special on television. Dripping with sweat, making steam in the chilled night air, and separated by a quarter-inch of glass, he surreptitiously joined the rear of the family in their den. He turned and continued on his way when the first commercial came on.

"If the window had been open, I could have touched the dad."

As our training area was a vast expanse of sand, palmetto, and pine trees, I wondered what the family would think the next morning when they discovered footprints clearly imprinted in the ground under the window of their family room. A minute of silence followed his story, as each of us considered what the scene must have looked like and how we missed being inside a place like the one described.

With a snort and pointing at the fire, someone said, "We got a TV." The comment broke the silence and made smiles crack our dirty faces. "Ranger TV." Given the primitive conditions under which soldiers in the field live, a fire is always considered a form of entertainment.

The rumble of trucks disrupted our exchange, and soon we were back at the barracks. We got four hours of sleep that night. We were given part of the day to clean our gear and we spent the remainder in the classroom listening to instructors drone on about topics that were immediately forgotten. By this point, we knew that all the classroom instruction was intended solely to keep us awake. That night, the lights were out at 2200. They came back on at 0200. By three that morning, we were scattered across the training area at our respective start points.

With a small flashlight sticking out of my mouth, I plotted my first point on the map. By 0330, I had my first mile behind me. I walked up to my endpoint over seven hours later. As with every other event at SFAS, I discovered I was finished only when someone told me I was, not because I knew the end was near.

Spent, I found a place near the fire and rotated to the ground, coming to rest in a seated position against my rucksack. Men were already lying in their sleeping bags, and the snoring was heroic. A few were awake, and the chatter focused on the likelihood that this was the last night of individual movement.

Back at the barracks, we took stock of who was left. Our number appeared to be around one hundred and fifty; another seventy had quit over the last four days.

We were now at the official halfway mark through SFAS and could enjoy a two-day reprieve from walking with heavy loads while the cadre convened a board to review those who had not quit. Behind closed doors, the Green Berets in black sweatshirts compared notes, deciding who would go forward to the team phase. Less than a dozen were told they could not continue, due to medical reasons. A check of feet by one of the medics revealed men walking on bleeding soles. Others had disclosed a need for painkillers, like ibuprofen, due to tendinitis.

Though the reprieve was truly the eye of the hurricane, we enjoyed sleeping eight hours for two nights in a row and eating hot rations, albeit from cans. I volunteered to help serve the meals and ladled heaping piles of food to my fellow candidates. On the second day, I was serving chocolate pudding from metal trays, each tray meant to serve twenty men. When the last candidate had passed, the tray I was serving from was still three quarters full. The sergeant supervising the mess line told us to eat whatever was left in the trays. I grabbed a large metal spoon, sat down with the tray between my legs, and ate enough chocolate pudding for fifteen men. The next day, the first day of team phase, I was glad that I had.

The cadre organized those of us still standing into squads of nine men. Each squad had a mix of commissioned and noncommissioned officers, with usually two or three commissioned officers per squad.

While the individual phase had been an emotional, physical endurance test built on the premise of isolating each of us while he moved under a heavy load, team week was described by those who had preceded me as intensely psychological and with greater emphasis on strength, like trying to watch and provide an analysis of *A Clockwork Orange* while attempting a personal best in every weightlifting event there is.

On day one of team week, we walked to our first event: Mr. Happy, later known as The Sandman. The lights came on at a decent hour—0530—and we were ready to move with rucksacks and rubber ducks at 0630. A cadre member, Staff Sergeant Rose, collected us from the barracks, and we walked for about thirty minutes until we came to what first appeared to be two men sleeping near a trash pile. There were eight steel pipes ten feet long, each about four inches in diameter, lengths of nylon rope, and a pair of mannequins dressed in olive green coveralls, the arms and pants tied shut at the cuffs, and two cloth litters, obviously intended to be slid over the poles somehow to be used as a stretcher.

"Roster Number186," SSG Rose said, inquiring of the nine men eagerly watching him. I raised my hand. "You're the leader, candidate. Come over here and let's have a chat." I could feel my pulse in my neck.

As officers are supposed to possess the planning and organizational skills within most military units, they were chosen to go first to demonstrate to the enlisted guys, who may have never led anybody. The officers were supposed to show how to execute the improvisational style of planning required for each leader during his turn during team week.

SSG Rose explained the scenario we were in. The two mannequins were injured guerrilla fighters requiring immediate evacuation. The only means of conveyance (a term that would come to strike fear in me) was what I saw in the pile of steel pipes and nylon. He handed me a map and showed me my location.

"You have three hours to get them here or they die," he said, pointing to a spot about six miles away.

"What happens if they die?" I asked.

"You fucking fail. What do you think happens?" he snapped.

"Roger, that."

But that wasn't all.

"Now you're going to meet one of the guerrilla leaders. He wants to personally explain the importance of your mission. Do not look at him and do not allow him to come within ten meters of you. Is that clear?" SSG Rose paused, searching my face. I returned a gaze that I hope did not convey my sense of being a pig considering a wristwatch.

"Is that clear, candidate?" he repeated.

"Yes, Sergeant," I replied, appending my response with the military courtesy by addressing him formally, as if he outranked me. Because right then he did.

"Good. Here he comes." He stepped away from me, like he had just noticed a bomb tied around my neck.

"American GI," said a voice in faux Eastern European accent. I looked at the ground, trying to see the feet of whoever was addressing me without getting closer than thirty feet (or ten meters) as instructed. "You are going to save my comrades, yes?" The speaker was rapidly approaching me. I bent double and began backing up but not fast enough. He was less than ten feet away when I almost fell trying to open the space between us. "Where are you going? Why don't you speak?" I continued back-pedaling, looking only at the ground.

"We will do our best," I replied. I sounded hollow, a little boy telling his teacher the dog ate his homework.

"No! No!" he yelled. "You *will* save them! Tell me now! Are you going to save them?"

My mind was racing but on a treadmill. I couldn't think of anything to say.

"We will do everything in our power to save them," I replied, still backing up, anxiety turning to anger as the speaker was obviously trying to get close to me.

"If they die, we will know that you do not care for our cause, that America has sent us the weak and stupid," he said, more to himself. He turned and walked away.

SSG Rose walked next to me and said, "Didn't I tell you to keep ten meters away from him?"

"Yes, Sergeant." He stared at me and wrote something down in a little green pad.

"Get your people organized," he ordered, looking down at his watch. "Time begins now. Oh, and you have to use everything. Nothing gets left behind."

I trotted back to the group and told everyone my plan, which I had only conceived on my way over to them. I explained that we would build one giant litter for both mannequins. To my team members' credit, they immediately set about the work of organizing the poles, ropes (better known as lashing material), and stretchers into a raft, on which we would place the wounded guerrillas and float them to the designated location on our shoulders. We had been going for about ten minutes when SSG Rose came over, looked at me, and told us to stop.

"This won't work. Just trust me. You're building the *Queen Mary*, and you won't be able to get there from here. Build two conveyances."

Without hesitation, I divided the squad into two teams of four and put a man in charge of each team. Then we started building a separate stretcher for each mannequin. In twenty minutes, we had built two stretchers, each weighing over a hundred pounds. We now had two and a half hours to travel six miles.

When we started to load the mannequins, we understood a nuance of traveling the distances we had been given: While there was a mannequin's head at the top of each set of coveralls, the bodies underneath were sandbags.

"Holy shit!" came as a chorus line when we tried to pick them up. Each one weighed 150 pounds. We started to drag them to the stretchers, but SSG Rose intervened.

"Is that how you treat your wounded? You guys do know how to pick up a wounded man, right?" We nodded and said yes, both confused and embarrassed. "I don't want to be on your team if that's how you treat the wounded." He turned away, seemingly disgusted.

My confidence began to fail.

The team had momentum despite my self-doubts, and I heard one of them say, "You hold his head. Pick up on three. One, two, three." The grunting was audible as we lifted with textbook precision—with one of us holding a mannequin's head in a stable position—and nestled each sandman on his respective platform.

"Let's go," I said, and we picked up our rucks and rifles, the slings holding them from our necks like garish jewelry. Each team surrounded its conveyance and, with two men on each side, hoisted the stretchers into the air to the top of our rucksacks. The straps holding the ruck frames to our bodies groaned and popped with the sounds normally associated with a leather saddle on a horse. I climbed under the one where I could find some room to help—no way was I going to walk to the side offering encouragement without physical assistance. Five under one, four under the other, we headed out on a single-lane dirt road under a beautiful North Carolina sun.

We walked for about thirty minutes, mostly staggering. I called a halt, and we sat the monstrosities in the middle of the road. Our faces red and streaming with sweat, we dropped our rucks and took hard pulls from our canteens. After realizing that we had traveled one and a half miles, we began to worry that we would never make the cut-off time. I checked the map. We could shave two miles off the distance by cutting through the woods, but trying to leave the road might add several hours to the travel time. Our stretchers precluded any off-road movement.

"Let's get it on," I said, trying to sound encouraging. Lifting the stretchers up and over our heads made the log drills seem like a light day of exercise. Once we were moving again, SSG Rose came alongside me and spoke quietly while my shoulders screamed under the steel pipe driving the rucksack into my back.

"One-eighty-six. How we doing? Are you going to make the cut-off time?" he asked absently, without any emotion.

"Yes," I replied. I didn't try to sound convincing.

"Really? Well, that's good to hear," and I could hear his smirk as he wrote something down and walked away.

We went through an intersection of dirt roads, and something inside me said, "Check the map." I would have to stop us to get the map out of my cargo pocket. My mind was telling me to check the map. But my body didn't want to make the moves necessary to stop.

We walked fifty meters through the intersection before I called a halt.

"I need to check the map," I called out. Instantly, we pushed the stretchers up and over our heads to put them down. I unfolded the map and realized I had added one football field to our movement. We should have turned left at the intersection. I looked at the group and saw by their faces that they knew what was coming.

"I fucked up. We have to go back to that intersection and go south." I looked back at the intersection to see that SSG Rose had not followed us. He stood there in repose, waiting. He looked at his watch and back at me.

I yelled, "Can I request an extension on the deadline?"

"You can request anything you like, candidate," he replied.

"I request an extension."

"Denied," he said and smiled.

I turned back to my team. "We have a mile and a half to go," I said. "Almost there." We picked up our wounded guerrillas and struggled back over the last fifty meters we had just walked. Adding one more step to this effort felt like criminal stupidity.

We walked into the designated "hospital area" an hour late. My guerrilla leader from four hours before was waiting.

"You are indeed very weak and stupid," he yelled as we hoisted our cargo into the back of an army truck. "You do not care about our noble struggle. They are dead, thanks to you."

I absorbed the critique while screaming "Fuck you" in my mind. Some things are better left unsaid, especially during an assessment.

SSG Rose stood away from us writing in a small pad. When we had finished transferring the mannequins into the truck, he called us to him.

"Eat chow, drink water. One-eighty-six, you're dead. Time for somebody else to shine," he said and called another roster number. The weight of responsibility came off my shoulders like Mr. Happy had floated away. Another officer stepped past me, and he and SSG Rose walked from the group as we tore into our rucks and retrieved an MRE. We chewed, drank, and talked about the movement we had just completed, the normal decompression protocol that men follow at the conclusion of a stressful event.

Our new leader came back to the group and told us our next event would not be as hard as the last one. A collective sigh of relief could clearly be heard in response. He explained that we had to move some ammo cases as he began to wolf down a meal. We finished eating, packed our trash into our rucksacks, and began to saunter to where we saw SSG Rose. Just past him were four ammunition crates, each one about three feet long, one foot wide, and eight inches deep. Protruding from each of these rectangles was a rope handle. We surveyed the scene and waited for the catch.

Our leader explained that we had to move these ammo crates to the guerrilla base approximately five miles away. We had three hours to do it. As our squad had nine men, we organized into pairs, with one man getting a break. Together we reached down, and each man firmly grasped the black nylon rope handle on his side. The groans and grunts were similar to our previous event. I knew that at some point we'd have to switch sides. Also, we didn't know if each box was as heavy as the other. After a few minutes of struggling with our loads, we came up with what we thought was a novel approach. We walked for approximately two minutes and then set the box down. The two sides switched and took a step forward, the two men in the lead dropping back to the rear. This approach allowed us to balance the fatigue in both arms. The extra man would get a two-minute break before having to rejoin the dance.

We covered five miles in two and a half hours in this manner. The guerrilla base turned out to be a truck, and we were instructed to load our cases into the back. We received no congratulations for being faster than the allotted time. SSG Rose simply wrote something in his book and said we were done for the day. The sun was low in the sky as we marched, out of step, back into Camp Mackall.

Once we were in the barracks, a member of our team terminated. He simply stated that he didn't want to do this anymore and walked out. Now we were eight.

Following the pattern of day one, each day of team week held two events, one in the morning and one in the afternoon, with an untested member of the team in charge. Most memorable among the Herculean tasks were the jeep, the logs, and the poncho rafts.

When we arrived at the site for the jeep event, we found the vehicle sitting on the ground with no wheels; three wheels were stacked to the side, some lug nuts in the driver's seat and the same steel pipes and ropes from the Mr. Happy event. We were told the guerrillas needed this vehicle for spare parts, and we had to move it to their location using all the supplies provided. Before we were finished, the eight of us had picked the jeep up, put on the three wheels with hand-tightened lug nuts holding them on, and attached steel poles to the chassis so that we could keep the one corner of the vehicle without a tire off the ground while we pushed it down the road.

The log event required a solution that was a combination of Mr. Happy and the ammo cases. We had two logs, and each weighed 450 pounds. We had to carry them six miles. We assigned four men per log, two carrying and two resting. The most any of us could endure under the log was one minute. At the end of one minute, the two resting would come up under the log between the two carrying. The two carrying would scoot out from the ends and begin their one-minute break. Even with this approach, we would have to put the logs down after ten repetitions. We dreaded this, as picking the logs back up and resting them across the tops of our rucksacks was an added but necessary torture. We delivered the logs within the three-hour time limit. I was sure I was an inch shorter after this event.

During team week, there was no gong show at night. After cleaning our gear, the teams sat in the barracks, played cards, read, and talked. Occasionally and without warning, a cadre member would walk into the barracks and announce an inspection in thirty minutes. We would lay out our gear in accordance with the picture on the wall and wait to be inspected. By now we knew the drill well enough that rarely was anyone ever found with a violation.

So it was, with four and a half hours of sleep, we walked out to a pond known as Big Muddy, and there we faced what I found to be the most significant psychological challenge we had yet encountered.

Unlike the other events, all the teams were together this time. We sat in rows in the dark, strung out on the dirt road atop the dam that held Big Muddy in place. All the rubber rifles were leaning against their owners' rucksacks as the candidates stood and chatted under a cloudless sky, wondering what we were supposed to do. From intelligence gathered from the previous classes, we knew this was the last day of team events, or at least so we thought. As we had moved farther into December, the temperatures had fallen commensurately. Without rain, the temperatures were welcomed, as they made movement under the rucksacks bearable. But soon the sun began to peek through the pine trees, and a rumor moved through the ranks: We're making poncho rafts. A thin layer of ice was clearly visible across the entire surface of the pond, which was about two football fields across and extended half a mile back from the dam.

I was incredulous. Without thinking, I vocalized my own concerns by saying it was probably just a mind game. "Surely they wouldn't put us in there." Immediately a member of my team seized upon the comment and made us all smile in the dawn light.

"Yes they would, and quit calling me 'Shirley.'"

We watched as the sun cleared the trees, and the thin crust of ice sublimated into fog. From our perch on the dam, we saw the cadre to our left start what soon became a very large bonfire. A pickup truck with a rubber boat and outboard motor on the back drove past the fire and pulled to the water's edge. Several cadre members hoisted it into the water. Two men climbed in, cranked the outboard, and started speeding around the pond. The ice still in the shadow of the trees broke and began bouncing on the waves of the little boat's wake.

While I was still trying to make sense of what I was seeing, a cadre member called out from the opposite bank to our right and told the first team to come to him. Nine men stood up and made their way to the start point with their rucks and rifles in hand.

For this event, one member of each team would ride across the two hundred meters of water on several poncho rafts, each constructed using two rucksacks and two ponchos, and he had to do so while remaining dry. Those swimming, however, would have to take off their uniforms and boots in order to make the journey. For one, swimming in uniform for that distance would be difficult in the extreme. For another, one would want dry clothes once the other bank with the bonfire was gained.

I watched as the first team stripped, packed their clothes and boots into waterproof bags, and stowed everything in their rucksacks. Naked in the freezing air, they fashioned rucksacks and ponchos into rafts and began putting them in the water. Four of the rafts were pushed together and a canvas stretcher with wooden poles placed on top of them. Fully clothed, the lucky victim climbed onto the stretcher and then four men began pushing him and the conveyance across the pond. The other members of the team pushed the remaining rafts, a man-powered flotilla of olive drab green blobs inching away from us.

The cadre in the safety boat waited until the last raft had cleared the midway point and then sped alongside the team, the wake lifting the green balls like pool toys.

Four teams went ahead of us. We made our way to the bank and began taking off our clothes. While doing so, we listened to the protests of one candidate who was certain we were risking death by getting into water so cold. The exchange went something like this:

"I am a medical professional, Sergeant. You cannot put people in water that cold."

"Do you wish to terminate, candidate?"

"No. Listen to me. I'm telling you, you can't put people in this water."

"Do you wish to terminate, candidate?"

This dialogue continued until every member of the medical professional's team had crossed and was dressing next to the fire. The dialogue ended like this:

"Candidate, either get in the water right now or you're done."

"But, Sergeant—"

"Shut up!" The cadre cut him off. He looked at the far shore and yelled, "Send the truck."

The medical professional was gone by the time we got into the water.

The leader of our team asked who was most junior among us. That is, had we been wearing our rank, who would have been at the bottom of the totem pole? We quickly decided on this person and put him on the stretcher. I and three others powered the raft. The other team members pushed the rest of the rafts. As our bodies became submerged in the water, my stomach muscles went into spasm and began contracting uncontrollably. I clenched my jaw and tried to stop shaking. I watched for the dreaded safety boat, but the cadre had it on the bank and was filling its gas tank.

Our man on the stretcher stayed dry, but at one point he put his hand into the water and held it there for a few seconds.

"Goddamn, that's cold," he said, withdrawing his hand.

One of the other men pushing the raft said through a frosty stutter, "I h-h-h-hope that d-d-d-doesn't count as you g-g-g-g-etting wha-wha-wet." We laughed nervously in response.

Our crossing took twenty minutes. When I reached the far bank, the entire Mormon Tabernacle Choir exploded into the "Hallelujah Chorus" in my head. We dragged ourselves and green masses of dripping-wet gear from the frigid water. The man on the stretcher moved with guilt-ridden urgency to help us get to our clothes, our frozen fingers nearly incapable of bending. Finally, I found my waterproof bag with my dry clothes and a towel and walked up to the fire. Though our feet had been toughened from walking in boots, I was quickly reminded that we did not have the feet of mountain goats. I hobbled over the rocks and roots like a shaking old man, naked with a rubberized canvas bag, to the fire and stood dressing next to other similarly attired men.

We watched the team behind us begin its crossing, and I grimaced as the safety boat and the lone cadre member danced among the candidates, gunning the engine and turning sharply to make the largest possible wake. As the water broke over the rafts, the spectators collectively sucked in air. The rafts were only waterproof on one side, and that portion stayed down in the water. No matter how tightly the hood was tied shut, a hole on top would allow water in. Once water began to soak the equipment, the raft would sink.

As I was bent over, continuing to dress, I heard a shout come from the water, and the engine on the safety boat abruptly stopped. Fully clothed cadre members of cadre next to us started running into the pond.

The scene was surreal. The men swimming the stretcher across were continuing, not knowing that anything had happened. Behind them, two men pushing their own raft watched wide-eyed as one candidate struggled to the bank. Candidates still waiting their turn jumped in to grab him.

Clinging to the sinking green ball, the candidate, whose head had been partly responsible for stopping the outboard, was streaming blood from his wounds. In his zest to see someone sink, the safety boat operator had lost sight of the two men with their green conveyance and plowed right over them, full throttle.

Now using the safety boat as intended, the cadre got both man and tattered raft to the bank. One man had lacerations in his thigh identical to those seen on the backs of hapless manatees in the Florida Intracoastal Waterway. For the man covered in blood, he had a deep gash on the back of his head and one on his foot, as if he had somehow managed to get run over twice while the boat was turning, perfectly spanning a tight arc of churning steel.

We left before the medevac arrived.

Back at the barracks, we spent the rest of the day cleaning gear, playing cards, reading, or talking. That night, the cadre called us into the classroom and explained what we were to do by the next morning. We were to clean the barracks, have our duffel bags packed, and be ready for a road march carrying rucksacks and rifles. Rucksacks would weigh no less than fifty-five pounds without food and water, and they would be weighed at the beginning and the end of the movement. The briefing ended with the obligatory "Any questions?"

One candidate raised his hand and asked the question we were all thinking: How long is the movement? How long do we have to finish? The class erupted in laughter. The cadre on stage just shook his head and smiled.

"Remember, we told you about stupid questions, right?"

That seemed like years ago.

"Does anybody have any questions I can answer?" No hands.

We made short work of the barracks, and everyone was packed well before the lights went out at 2200. Four hours later, they came back on. An hour after that, the buildings we had called home for the last three weeks were dark and empty. We threw our duffels into the back of a truck and made a formation. One cadre marched us from our gated community, and after a few hundred meters he stopped us on a dirt road pointing back toward Fort Bragg.

Another member of the assessment cadre, an officer, explained that this was an individual effort and we were to walk alone. No talking. No sharing water. He wanted us to walk together in isolation.

"Do your best."

In response, we jumped up and down, shaking our gear, checking for potential hot spots with the shoulder straps, relacing boots, drinking water, and eating some MRE.

"You may begin."

Like a great herd of turtles, we launched ourselves into the last event. We became a long line of burdened men, before we thinned to clutches of two or three every few hundred meters. Under a beautiful, cloudless sky that turned gray, then pink, then orange, we marched. The only time we saw cadre was at intersections of dirt roads, where they made sure we turned left or right according to the great mysterious route we were following.

Despite the admonition to march alone, I fell into step with another candidate, and we seemed to have the same speed. His name was Mike, and for the next several hours, Mike and I discussed our families, how glad we were to be finishing, how much our feet hurt, and generally encouraged and cajoled one another through the gut check. Whenever we saw a vehicle coming down the road, we would pretend to be utterly unknown to each other.

The sun was well in the sky when, at the bottom of a hill, we heard the crank of a heavy diesel engine ahead. Mike and I separated. I shuffled to the top of the rise and beheld a sight that nearly brought tears to my eyes: a group of men in black sweatshirts and camouflage trousers standing around old Army trucks. I saw candidates removing rucksacks and passing them to cadre holding scales, the type used to weigh dead deer.

My pace quickened. I had walked continuously for six hours and forty-five minutes, stopping only to piss. My canteens were dry, as I had consumed the gallon and a half of water that we carried. My ruck weighed in at fifty-eight pounds. Someone took my rubber duck, saying I would no longer need it. I was directed into a truck with Mike and sat with my back against the cold steel. I closed my eyes and waited to be transported to any semblance of civilization.

The truck stopped in front of the same barracks we had departed three weeks before. My legs cramped and screamed as I scooted off the back of the truck. With the test over, my rucksack suddenly felt too heavy to carry, but I limped with it over one shoulder and found an empty bunk. I collapsed on the musty canvas mattress, and the springs of the metal rack groaned under my weight.

Eventually, I found the strength to undress, shower, and change into a clean uniform. Word came through the barracks that we could wear running shoes instead of boots, a reward for grinding our bodies to dust. Another candidate with more energy than me shouted from the door of the barracks that the mess hall was open. After three weeks of packaged food, the idea of Army chow was as appealing as anything I could imagine at that moment.

The talk around the table was about the guy who had marched the entire distance of twenty-three miles in five hours and fifteen minutes. None of us could comprehend it. Another candidate at the table provided some background. The guy who had probably set some kind of course record was the same guy who thought we should not move the United Nations to Switzerland because the building was too big and built by Americans. I rolled my eyes and drank chocolate milk until my stomach hurt.

With my stomach distended, I walked back to the barracks and fell asleep. We were woken by a shout, and we all stumbled outside to make something that looked like a military formation. The wrinkled camouflage uniforms, weathered faces, and running shoes did not make for an impressive display of future Green Berets.

A member of cadre, wearing pressed fatigues and a manicured beret set rakishly low over his eyes, explained we were to be back in formation the next day (December 17, 1988) at 0900. We would get the rest of our instructions then. He shouted, "Dismissed!" and the rectangle of men began to dissolve. In a few seconds, he yelled, "Oh yeah, and you're restricted to the barracks," and he laughed. It was a perfunctory effort, as the speaker knew full well that none of us had any intention of staying in the barracks.

I went to a pay phone and called a friend who was already in the SF training pipeline.

"Come get me. Please," I said when he answered.

"Be there in an hour," he replied.

We picked up pizza and beer and went to the place he was sharing with another SF student. Their apartment looked like a sporting goods store. When I was physically incapable of eating more pizza, he drove me back to the barracks. I walked into the darkened sleeping bay with men snoring. Empty food boxes and beer bottles filled the trashcans. I ate a handful of aspirin and fell into the rack.

Breakfast was less an eating competition and more a social event. I sat with guys from my team, and we talked the talk of men decompressing. From formation, we walked into an old theater, now a classroom. The wood floors creaked under us as we took our seats.

The commanding officer, Major Velky, stood at the front of the class. His demeanor was professional and aloof. He explained that as he called a roster number, that individual would report to the NCO at the back of the classroom for further instructions. With those words, the air left the room, and the silence consumed us. Anyone who heard his roster number discovered that he had spent the last three weeks tearing his body down in order to do one of two things. Either he would realize that he had just attended an amazing weight-loss clinic and could return to the regular Army much thinner than he left, or he would be told that his best efforts were deemed less than adequate but he could come back to have all the fun again. Regardless, the people who were about to be called would be publicly humiliated, if only to a small group of fellow soldiers.

The executions began.

Numbers bounced off the wooden ceiling in the silent room. After the first few numbers, I realized he was calling out the failures in numerical sequence, in ascending order. With each number, one man would stand, silently exit his row, and walk to the back of the room. Others, with a number below the one just called, would exhale and display a wave of relief.

The room only buzzed once—when the guy who walked the long march in record time stood and made his way to the back. His face was full of confusion and utter disappointment.

Velky was getting to the high numbers, and my heart pounded.

"One-seventy-six."

I was thinking about the rope failure, the time failure, and failing Ranger school. Failures roared across my mind like a prairie fire.

"One-eighty-three."

Oh, please, God . . .

"One-ninety-one."

My head rocked back on a neck slack like the rope I couldn't climb. I was in. The cadre had sat around and said, "Yeah, let him in."

The survivors, the candidates selected, looked at Velky and followed his gaze out a window. We watched a group of twenty very sad men walk away. The room stayed silent, waiting for Velky to speak. When he thought that those not selected were beyond hearing distance, about a hundred meters, Velky looked back at us and confirmed what we all hoped we knew.

"If you're sitting here, you made it."

Our war-cries could have been heard on the moon. We shook hands and high-fived, grinning like kids with a new bike. The crowd walking to whatever fate awaited them turned to consider the commotion erupting from the dilapidated theater. I have never seen sadder faces on American soldiers.

Velky called out the officers and told us to join him at the side of the room. Twelve of us formed a circle with him. He began to explain what would be expected of us as officers in Special Forces, and that because we had been selected most everyone counted on us to make it to graduation and earn our berets. Early in his discussion with us, he said something, without looking at me, that passed like a small dark cloud over my sun of success.

As I was considering what a big deal I had made of failing the rope climb, Velky said, "Some of you need to work on climbing ropes. You never know when you may have to do that."

I made it my mission to learn to climb a rope like a trained chimp. And I did.

We spent the rest of the day cleaning and turning in our gear. What had started with nearly two hundred men finished with one last formation of around seventy-five.

My friend from the night before collected me and my bags and brought me back to the apartment. After a few beers, we started talking in earnest about what it would mean to wear the hat that said we were different. While neither of us had ever served in SF units, he had begun the training and explained what he had gleaned from the cadre, those entrusted with sharing the secrets to the chosen. The life of a Green Beret was characterized by going to countries that most people in the United States could not find on a map to work with indigenous troops. Nicaragua and El Salvador had begun to calm down by 1988, but the stories coming out of those locations suggested that SF was a big player in the secret war waged under the leadership of the CIA. There were deaths due to combat operations, but no one was receiving combat awards.

But then we weren't going through this life change for medals.

As we talked, I was no longer sure that I wanted to go to Central America or sub-Saharan Africa and disappear as the punctuation mark of a political statement by leftist guerrillas. As the night progressed and the alcohol flowed, the weight of being selected began to weigh on me. My daughter, born after I had volunteered for SF training, was just beginning to walk and was proving to be the mistress of my heart. By the time she was two, I would be a Green Beret on a team and gone for long stretches. I wanted a relationship with my daughter. I wanted her to have a father. I didn't want to be a plaque on a slab of memorial granite for a conflict that no one had even known occurred.

When I got back home, just in time for Christmas, my family members were all smiles and happy that I had made it. But their faces communicated a sense that maybe I had just been diagnosed with an aggressive terminal cancer.

After weeks of trying to tell myself that I wasn't backing out just because I was afraid of dying, I stepped back.

I was a tanker, an armor officer. The chance that there were would be another great tank battle like those during World War II was as remote then as winning the lottery. If I stayed on tanks and didn't pursue a beret, I would be safe, I would see my daughter grow, and maybe even have some more kids. By the time the Christmas season had passed, I convinced myself to stay on tanks.

In January, 1989, the Army sent me to Fort Riley, Kansas, to the First Infantry Division, a unit that had not gone anywhere to kill anybody since it had left Vietnam in 1970. I was given a staff job for most of the year and got home most every night in time to eat dinner with my wife and daughter, who was growing into an amazing little girl. In November 1989, I took command of a tank company, fourteen M1 tanks and around sixty-five men on any given day. I spent most of 1990 drilling with my men and preparing for what was then the pinnacle of any young armor officer's career: a trip to the National Training Center (or NTC) in the high desert of southern California.

At this time in the Army, the NTC was being used as the final exam for commanders. It had a great desert expanse where tanks could scream over the sand in mock battle with an opposing force (OPFOR) that was permanently assigned to the training area. The mission of the OPFOR was to represent the great Soviet horde poised to launch against the north German plains. Many careers were ended in the shadow of the rocky crags of Fort Irwin, home to the NTC. The wars always lasted two weeks, and by the end of the fight, young men knew whether they still had a career in the Amy.

As we were preparing for the big test, in July of 1990, my wife gave birth to my son. While I was on leave and considering all my decisions up to this point, and the fact that I now had a son to bear my name after I was gone, Iraq invaded Kuwait.

Six months later, I was sitting on my tank as part of a vanguard poised to lead the First Infantry Division into Iraq. Yep, I had played it safe. No SF for me. Too dangerous. I'd just ride into the biggest tank battle since World War II.

While we waited to execute, watching planes fly over and then seeing the horizon flash lightning from their bombs, rehearsing how the tanks with mine plows would cave in the Iraqi trenches and bury the inhabitants alive, and eating black flies that swarmed every meal, I got caught up in a little drama that did not register with me at the time as an act of great consequence.

My first sergeant in the Big Red One (the nickname of the First Infantry Division) came to me one day before the ground war kicked off to tell me about a problem. In casual conversation, he had discovered that members of the platoon of crunchies (as tankers refer to infantry for the noise infantrymen make when you run over them) were concocting a conspiracy to kill the platoon leader as we assaulted the minefields. I shook my head in disbelief.

"You sure this isn't just bored soldiers talking trash?" I asked.

"Well, I thought that myself, but they've decided to write off his gunner to get to the lieutenant," First Sergeant Holcomb replied. The gunner and lieutenant sat side-by-side in the Bradley Fighting Vehicle, which was basically a combat taxi designed to move infantrymen rapidly around the battlefield with little protection against serious firepower. "They're more than just thinking about this," he continued.

We called all the players together, I relieved the purported ringleader, a staff sergeant who denied nothing, and I sent him to the rear to be handled however my leadership saw fit. "Case closed," I thought.

While we were still in Iraq, I received word that the Army was sending me to Rutgers University in New Brunswick, New Jersey, to teach ROTC cadets. That assignment gave me the chance to prepare for the rest of my career, whatever it might be. Thinking that I had most likely witnessed the last great tank battle for the remainder of my time in the Army, I began to reconsider my desire to pursue a green beret due largely to something that I didn't expect to find in ROTC: a plethora of SF sergeants.

The SF NCOs cannot stay on teams indefinitely. The body can't take that much punishment, and the mind needs refreshing occasionally. When SF sergeants are not on SF teams, they have to find other jobs in the Army. One of those other jobs did include an assignment to a college campus as an ROTC instructor. For most of 1992, I spent many days training my cadets while in the company of SF guys whose stories enthralled me and whose confidence inspired me. But like thinking of a lost girlfriend from high school, I began to pine for a life behind the veil of secrecy that seemed to enshroud all of SOF. I had also decided to never play it safe again. I started calling the Special Forces assignment officer to see if after five years I would be allowed to return to the SF Q course. I explained that I would attend SFAS again, if necessary. To my surprise, I was told to simply include my certificate proving that I had successfully completed selection. Though there was one administrative hurdle I still had to clear. The commandant of the U.S. Army John F. Kennedy Special Warfare Center and School (known better by its abbreviated acronym, SWC, and pronounced "swick") had to sign a waiver allowing a captain as senior as me to attend.

The commandant at the time was Major General Sidney Shachnow, a Holocaust survivor and a living legend in Special Forces who would not know me if I walked up and asked him for an autograph. But I did, so to speak. Through the various bureaucratic channels my request had to negotiate, and for reasons I'll never know, he signed his name approving my waiver.

But his approval came with a caveat: I only got one shot. In an Army school with a washout rate of up to fifty percent for officers, I had one chance to make it through the six-month course. Injury, academic failure, or anything else that might preclude my graduating once I started in June 1993, and I would be sent back to my tank. Not a bad thing, but not what I wanted.

I was a very senior captain going to a job that placed high demands on one's physical fitness at a time when most officers were beginning to relax. The Special Forces Q course was six months long and was renowned for grinding very good men into dust. If Ranger school is a marathon, then the Q course is a full-length triathlon. Additionally, I would be back on jump status. That is, I would be falling out of airplanes again, having not done so for eight years, not since Ranger school. If I got hurt or otherwise dropped from training for any reason, I would be too senior to go to an SF A-team by the time I got back into the pipeline. I was working in a window of opportunity measured by months, not years. I had to make it in one try.

With these thoughts in mind, I set about preparing myself for the Q course and used my ROTC cadets as training aides, walking with them, carrying my rucksack during weekend training events. As the focus of ROTC training is the same small-unit tactics and doctrine used at Ranger school, I immersed myself in the language of dismounted infantry and administered to myself all the tests required of my charges. After six months, I felt I was as ready as I would ever be.

In May of 1993, and with a green light from the Army to go, I packed up the house and took my wife and two kids to Fort Bragg, North Carolina.

FOUR

IN 1993, the Special Forces detachment officer qualification course was divided into three distinct training phases, each about two months long. The SFDOQC, or Q-course, differed from its enlisted counterpart, the Special Forces qualification course, in that the officers did not receive specialty training. We received an overview of what each specialty course taught. Not so we could perform those tasks associated with being a weapons, communications, engineer, or medical specialist, but to gain an understanding of how to orchestrate the talents of men steeped in their respective crafts. We also trained with our enlisted peers for two of the three phases. Navy SEALs similarly train their officers with their enlisted personnel, and the result is the same: Your reputation in the SOF community begins the moment you enter the training pipeline.

The first phase, experienced by both officers (mostly captains) and enlisted men (mostly young sergeants), focused exclusively on honing skills every soldier should already possess, including light-infantry tactics, patrolling, and land navigation. Before we were allowed to wear green berets, we had to show that we could be soldiers. We had to demonstrate that our knowledge of soldiering allowed us to not only fight well but to be conversant in the required skills so that we could teach others how to fight as infantrymen. When I say others, I mean people from other countries. First and foremost, Special Forces are soldiers who also teach—not teachers who soldier. After SFAS, this phase of training was where most of the washouts take place, and most of the washouts are not technically washouts. They quit.

During phase two, the officers and the enlisted are separated and they are now focused on their designated specialties, which for the officers includes leading, planning, and orchestrating the talents of the eleven men on an SF team.

While the enlisted men learned to make things and heal people as well as to break things and kill people, the officers learned SOF doctrine and how to think in a world without an omnipresent chain of command.

This phase of training combined thought-provoking indoctrination with the most intensely physical events I had ever attempted. These Olympic efforts included the "Trek" exercise, a long-range, multiday land navigation event conducted at that time in the Uwharrie National Forest of western North Carolina. We also went through the survival, evasion, resistance, and escape training course (known as SERE and pronounced "seer"), which is where I discovered what it meant to be slapped in the face repeatedly, physically, and with authority; this was training for what I was supposed to do should I ever be taken prisoner. Nothing in my military career—or adult life for that matter, before or since—has approximated the intensity of the SERE course. That said, I know others who thought of it as a simple exercise in weight loss.

In phase three, the officers and enlisted personnel reunited for the final installment of the Q course, exclusively devoted to what makes Army Special Forces training unique: the unconventional warfare exercise Robin Sage. Conducted in and around Troy, North Carolina, the capstone event of the Q course is named after former Army colonel Jerry Sage, a World War II veteran and Office of Strategic Services (OSS) officer who taught the tactics of unconventional war. During these two months of training we learned rapport-building skills, how to organize clandestine guerrilla groups, and explored the strange nature of unconventional war. I was made to understand the irony of the fact that President Kennedy had established both the Peace Corps and Special Forces, and that the shared political origins of the two groups said something about the unusual place of SF in the military. Kennedy's vision was to have an arsenal of engagement tools, something between an embassy and an aircraft carrier.

Upon arriving at Fort Bragg, I received two surprises. The first was that the cadre had reordered the sequence of the training phases, a change that had never been done in thirty years of the course's existence. That is, my class of thirty officers as well as our enlisted counterparts would undergo our specialty training first (traditionally, phase two), followed by the basics of soldiering and small-unit tactics (phase one), and then straight into UW training (phase three).

The second surprise was my administrative role as the senior captain in the class. I was the class leader and responsible for ensuring that my fellow classmates were informed about the training schedule and any changes that might affect it. As a result, I began to develop a unique rapport with the training cadre and was allowed to occasionally see behind the curtain. This view showed me something that I had not seen in the conventional Army. Namely, the noncommissioned officers of Special Forces really ran the show. I had never seen sergeants, as a group, comport themselves in a manner that made me think "What do the officers do?" Their competence, demeanor, planning, and decision-making skills were easily on a par with what I had observed in the officer corps. And they didn't like the change in the training sequence, but they were trying to make it work, though thirty years of inertia constantly sought to do it the old way.

Bureaucratic machinations notwithstanding, my class of twenty-four officers, ranging from first lieutenants in the National Guard to senior captains in the regular Army, assembled at Fort Bragg for the first time on June 14, 1993, in what felt like a solar oven. The parking lot adjacent to what was then called the New Academic Facility, or NAF, held no shade. Between black asphalt and a cloudless blue sky, we melted in the sun, and in a few minutes our uniforms began to turn black with sweat. As I was ostensibly in charge, I wandered into the building looking for a cadre member and discovered them waiting in an air-conditioned classroom for us. From day one, I began to probe the cadre and look for anything that might give us, the students, a break so that I didn't incinerate my fellow students standing around in a stupid unnecessary formation. What I gleaned was that the cadre

expected us, the officers, to not be stupid enough to stand around waiting to be told to get out of the heat (or the cold) as if we were mindless
sheep.

In the opening days of training, the students got to know each
other as we stood in line and drew equipment, filled out military forms
until our hands cramped, and received introductory classes about what
it meant to become a Special Forces officer. As expected, most of the
class was infantry, though most every other branch was represented—
artillery, armor, military police, ordnance, military intelligence, and
the chemical corps. What I found most significant was that there were
three officers who were already Special Forces qualified.

These men had successfully completed the SF Q course as enlisted
men as well as the Ranger course. They had all attended specialty
schools, like military freefall or the combat divers course, executed
numerous deployments overseas as enlisted members of a Special
Forces A-team, and seemed to know somebody wherever we went all
over Fort Bragg. They had gone to officer candidate school and spent
three years as lieutenants. With all of that behind them, they were now
willing to endure the SF Q course for a second time, all six months of it,
in order to be commissioned officers wearing a green beret.

Unlike SFAS, we had a training schedule for the Q course and knew
where we were supposed to be weeks in advance. The cadre would put
us through several weeks of planning exercises in which, once we were
given a mission like reconnaissance, we would practice and demonstrate our capacity to organize our thoughts into cogent operations
orders and present these ideas in the form of a briefing called the brief
back. While seemingly boring, the brief back is where the officer makes
or breaks his A-team. I learned very quickly that Special Forces was
no different than any other organization when it came to picking who
would succeed and move on. All other things being equal, the team
with the best briefing, who sounded the most confident, would receive
the boss's approval.

For my class, SERE school occurred within the first four weeks of
training. It was my first taste of life without the Army's umbilical cord

for sustainment. No chow lines, no soft-serve ice cream, no burger stands. We were going to learn to live like Daniel Boone.

The last gate we had to pass through before uniting with our enlisted counterparts and beginning the last phase was Trek, the officer-only weeklong land navigation exercise held in western North Carolina. We were all looking forward to Trek—the way a person looks forward to being lowered into a cage with a tiger.

FIVE

SURVIVAL, EVASION, RESISTANCE, and escape training is provided exclusively for personnel with a high chance for capture, but especially pilots and Special Operations Forces. However, it really should be required training for all staff personnel posted to U.S. embassies in the developing world and for parents raising teenagers. The Department of Defense created SERE school after action reports describing U.S. prisoner of war behavior during the Korean War. Stories of U.S. POWs turning on each other and betraying trust started emerging when the truce was signed. Hollywood captured the essence of why we have SERE school in the movie *The Rack,* starring a very young Paul Newman. We were taught that when you're a POW, you're still at war. Never give up. Never betray a fellow POW. And never think that you can't be broken.

Though the SERE course was divided into two distinct components—survival training and resistance training—they were taught together by design. Survival training delved into everything we needed to consider should we find ourselves isolated in an unfriendly country. Resistance training, which incorporated evasion and escape, covered the basics of how to survive emotionally should we find ourselves isolated or, worse, captured. No one can evade capture for very long unless he can sustain himself, and he must understand the basics of first aid without a first aid kit. Likewise, few if any prisoners of war have planned and successfully executed an escape without considering the logistics of eating and drinking while being chased. We learned a phrase that will always raise the eyebrows of any graduate of SERE:

unassisted evasion. When the plan goes to hell and there's nobody to call that can get you, you have to get out as best you can. That's unassisted evasion. First things first: We had to learn to eat the things, like they say in the movie, "that would make a billy goat puke."

In Desert Storm, my tanks could run their engines for no more that twelve hours without being supplied with fuel. Now I might have to go weeks or months without any access to the military supply chain, a supply chain that dwarfs even the largest retail distributor. To put this claim into perspective, the Army is part of the Department of Defense, and the Defense Department feeds up to two million men and women around the world every day, runs the largest air force in the world, and sustains a fleet of floating airports called carriers along with a nuclear arsenal that exists both underground and underwater. With those logistics capabilities in mind, we were going to learn how to gnaw tree bark.

This reality was not a function of operational asceticism. Our mission, UW, required us to sustain operations with resources indigenous to whatever region of the world we found ourselves. Given that most developing nations do not have grocery stores in abundance (and developed nations don't need Green Berets), we needed to acclimate ourselves to a food chain that did not begin with a product wrapped in cellophane. I am reminded of a *Far Side* cartoon where a tyrannosaurus rex is reviewing his daily planner, and every day has the same entry: "Kill something and eat it." That was us.

We loaded into trucks and rode to Camp Mackall, a place I hadn't seen in five years. All the tar paper shacks were gone, but not some of the men who had lived in them. We had a mix of civilian and active-duty military instructors. All the civilians were retired SF, who had served in Vietnam and held the equivalent of a doctorate in living off the land. These guys were Old School, and no one in the class ever showed anything but the utmost respect for them.

Knowing that our chances of being in a survival situation in North Carolina were remote, our instructors taught us principles for assessing what plants were edible and which were not regardless of our location in the world. We learned how to fabricate weapons, how to make rope, and, most important, where to look for water. We learned to make traps for catching things to eat and how to make fire so we could cook the things we caught. Making fire without the convenience of matches or other such fire starters was so difficult that to this day I will not travel anywhere without a lighter. We learned how to fish in the most primitive ways, making our own hooks and fishing line, weaving fish traps, and learning how to emplace them.

The context of our classes was always the same: We learned how to do these things clandestinely so that we could survive and not get caught. We were not just learning to survive. We were learning to survive while we were being hounded in a place where every person, soldier and civilian alike, could be the one who turns us in.

After five days of sitting outside on bleachers, listening to the obligatory opening joke, walking about and examining the plants that could make a "fine tea" or kill us, our survival training required us to move into the woods, make shelters for sleeping from whatever we could find, and kill something to eat. (Up to this point, we had been eating three meals a day and living in the same barracks I had used for SFAS. In order to make us hungry enough to eat something we might not otherwise want to, the cadre restricted us from the mess hall for a day and disallowed any junk food we might have squirreled away.) Each student was given a rabbit or chicken and shown the best way to dispatch it as painlessly as possible. Though there surely was a humane motive for teaching us the painless method, this training also rested on the fact that no one wanted a shrieking animal drawing attention to him while trying to evade detection. I got a chicken.

The most painless and effective way to kill a chicken is to stand on its head with one foot and, using both hands around the body, pull its head off. While tempted to set it down after decapitating it to see if it would run, I felt one death spasm, and then it was still. By the time I was finished preparing it, I was covered in feathers and chicken blood. Those students with rabbits learned to relax the bunny (by petting it) before administering a karate chop to the base of the head.

In addition to rabbits and chickens, a goat was also on the menu. Apparently, this particular goat had been paying attention during previous classes and successfully escaped. Many in the class expressed dismay when we discovered we had lost a big source of protein, and the cadre member responsible for the goat felt compelled to make amends. He disappeared in his pickup truck and returned an hour later with a large dead turkey. Apparently he had driven to a ranch where domesticated turkeys were raised and sniped one with a .22 rifle that he kept for just such emergencies. He dressed and butchered it himself, then passed out large chunks to each of us with a heartfelt apology.

At the end of a week of eating bugs, fish caught in clandestine traps, and most edible plants indigenous to North Carolina growing in the summer, the final exam for the survival phase was to bring a canteen cup of water to a rolling boil in fifteen minutes. We all passed. For anyone who thinks this does not sound difficult, try taking a metal cup, filling it with twelve ounces of water, walking it into the woods with a book of matches, and making boiling water in fifteen minutes, regardless of weather conditions.

The training cadre taught the resistance phase in a classroom setting. The terms Geneva and Hague conventions took on a whole new life in my mind as we learned what could and could not be done to us in the event we were captured, or, more appropriately, what should and should not be done. As we watched film after film of interviews with former POWs, we realized that once we were captured, we were utterly at the mercy of the people we had been trying to kill. Not a great way to start a relationship that could last years. These interviews were all with men who had been captured during Vietnam. Famous among them was John McCain, the senator from Arizona. We also learned that every man has a breaking point, that the "big four and nothing more" (name, rank, date of birth, social security number) could only take us so far. According to the conventions, that is all that a POW is required to divulge. I wondered how long I could hang from the ceiling with my shoulders dislocated before I would beg to tell secrets.

We learned the techniques to resist interrogation. From these classes, it seemed that someone had sat down and codified what every seventh-grader knows intuitively when dealing with adults, specifically parents and teachers. We did role-playing exercises where we practiced the techniques and discovered who among us were good liars and then the eventual danger of being a good liar. Remembering a good lie is difficult after days of sleep deprivation. We learned how to classify information that we might have, what could be given up and what was worth dying for.

While none of the resistance training was highly sophisticated, and much of it was intuitive, the training sought to hammer home the nature of the operating environment in which we would live while resisting. Despite the taped interviews and the assigned readings with stories of POWs from other wars of the twentieth century, I could not wrap my mind around the significance of living as a POW. But I overcame that inability by the time we graduated.

During the last week of SERE school we participated in a field exercise that tested our understanding of the previous weeks. The cadre divided our class into teams of four to six officers and assigned each team an evasion corridor: We had a strip of woods in western North Carolina, defined by paved roads on two sides running north-south. Each lane was maybe three kilometers wide and ten long. We had to stay in our lane while members of the 82nd Airborne Division came looking for us. In order for us to get the full effect of what it means to hide, move, and survive in enemy territory, our training scenario stated we had been operating in a country that had suddenly been taken away from the sphere of U.S. influence due to a coup. One day we were welcomed advisors, and the next we were declared fugitives by the new regime. It could happen. We had to evade capture as we attempted to reach a designated area for recovery. Our evasion plan called for us to find a hide site in a designated location within our respective corridor necessitating a daily move of about six kilometers. A cadre member would meet with each team every day in the designated location and assign certain survival tasks, such as making a fishnet or trap for squirrel, as well as check on the general well-being of the students. At an appointed time, our luck would run out, and we'd be captured.

There were three other officers on my team: Elmo, Stu, and Scott. Together, we were to demonstrate our evasion and survival skills for three days, then get captured and demonstrate what we learned in resistance and escape training for three days. Once all the teams were captured, we would be reassembled as a class in the resistance training laboratory, or RTL, a mock POW camp. And this is where the fun would really start.

One cadre member offered a simple admonition to all of us before we loaded into trucks for transport out to our lanes.

"Don't eat anybody's pets."

That little warning came courtesy of the class ahead of us. In the field and starving, they had apparently gotten hold of a $1,200 collie and turned the poor dog into a campfire meal. The soldiers were made to pay for the dog, as the owner's name was on its collar, and the collar was found hanging around the neck of the student who had lured it into the camp. The meal worked out to $200 per plate. The class laughed at the story (because we're supposed to be barbarians), but most of us understood that eating Lassie was unnecessary. Conversely, another team preceding us by a few months had actually captured a young deer by wounding it. Filled with remorse over hurting Bambi, the team had splinted its leg and was nursing the creature. The cadre found the scene to be a gross misplacement of sympathy. While the collie was somebody's property and probably held a place in a person's heart, the deer was utterly and unequivocally on the menu. A cadre member told the team to eat the deer, or he would take it to a team that would. Cartoons of talking animals could not withstand the reality of such legitimate protein being taken away, and the team ate the deer.

Our truck stopped on the side of a desolate two-lane blacktop, and the four of us walked into the woods to wait for the sun to set and the scenario to begin. From then until graduation, we would be in a tactical scenario, and the only way out of that pipeline was to quit, get hurt, or graduate in approximately seven days.

As the weather was hot, the packing was light. Each of us had canteens, a knife, a compass, a bottle of iodine tablets, and a book of matches in a waterproof bag. The team had a map and was allowed to carry a prescribed length of parachute cord, a couple of ponchos, and a flashlight. Other than uniforms and boots, this was all we had.

Just before the sun set, we made our first mistake in a survival situation. A powerful storm hammered us, and, given the heat, we just accepted the rain and let it soak us. A mass of cooler air came and pushed the front through to drop the temperature twenty degrees. A pleasant breeze accompanied the change in temperature, and what would have made a delightful evening on the front porch now set my teeth chattering. We should have tried to stay dry under the ponchos until it was time to move.

We managed to move without incident to our first hide site just as the sun was turning the dark sky a light gray. We laid the ponchos on the ground and attempted to sleep. Though not carrying rucksacks, we were still exhausted from evading capture all night. The sun was beating straight down on us when we heard someone walking through the woods. We could see that it was an instructor, and we stood up so he could see us.

He asked us how the movement went and if everybody was okay. When we nodded, he prodded further, asking if we had looked for water, made any weapons, or searched for food. We stared back, sensing that his questions were actually indictments. He was an SF NCO, and he began to give us a block of instruction on what he thought of officers trying for a green beret but not acting very motivated. The rebuke was mild by any standard, but that it had come from someone we might lead one day made it especially poignant.

Two of us immediately began making an improvised shelter, while the other two went to look for food. I was on the food-search team. As a team, we discussed what we should build based on what we had to build it with (that is, a knife, some parachute cord, and lots of dead trees), and then split up, my partner and I carrying the empty canteens of the building team in case we happened upon water. The instructor left with a look that said he was pleased we had listened to him. That is, we comported ourselves as if we were taking the scenario seriously. This NCO was pouring himself into our training, knew what we were capable of as commissioned officers, and he wanted to see a return on his personal investment from those he was sending to lead his friends. His face as he left said he was seeing a return.

We found a sad little creek with water about as clear as chocolate milk and only a few inches deep. We filled all the canteens and dropped in iodine tablets. On the way back, we came across a box turtle. I enthusiastically snatched him up and thought: *What a wonderful surprise.* It retracted into its shell, and we carried our find to the others for final adjudication on what to do with it. It was the only creature we had been told that we might come across that carried a disease: leprosy. As our stomachs started to rumble, we decided to make fish bait out of him. We never caught a fish, not for the entire four days we evaded. Maybe the fish knew about the leprosy thing.

Even though blackberry season had just passed its peak, we managed to find some and even ate the overripe ones. We found other edible plants, like ginger and wild scallions, but were quick to discover that we had taken for granted one component of modern eating: salt. We mourned its absence as we munched like cows on grass and onions.

In the heat of a North Carolina summer, we began to stink like farm animals by our second night of evading. After having stumbled down ravines and run from dogs, our bodies were so slashed and bruised that I was beginning to consider getting caught just to avoid another night of beating myself up.

But fatigue-driven, dreamless sleep vanquished such thoughts from my mind as we tried to recover our strength, stretched on a poncho surrounded by fallen trees. We had stumbled into a great place to hide within our designated area. After a few hours of sleep, we attempted to fabricate weapons, mostly throwing sticks or spears. I tried to weave a fishnet from some of the fibers in the parachute cord. I finished with something that looked like an ensemble from Victoria's Secret. It certainly couldn't catch any fish.

While we were sitting in our tree fort trying to make survival craft, we heard a loud, nonhuman grunting sound. The four of us jumped up to see a large deer, a buck with antlers covered in velvet, explaining in deer language that we were squatting in his house.

"Let's get him!" and the chase was on. I had read about aboriginal people doing a team effort called persistence hunting, where they run an animal to death. But we could not have run even a puppy to death. It was over inside the length of one football field. Our exhaustion had manifested itself with leaden legs and heaving chests. I laughed at myself for the weakness I felt and imagined that was what old age would feel like.

Our instructor found us and checked on our status. He seemed genuinely pleased with our survival efforts. I received affirmation close to what I desired, though he was visibly disappointed by my attempt at a fishnet. He nodded knowingly about the deer and our failure to chase it. Before he left, he passed instructions that we were to rendezvous with a white van, at a particular intersection where a dirt road crossed a creek, and he gave us a time to be there the next day.

Initially, I was elated with the anticipation of being captured, of getting it over with.

I would soon realize how stupid that thought was.

After resting for a few hours in the wet sauna of the July woods, I brought myself to a level of wakefulness such that I made some ginger tea. Ginger tea sounds great as a refreshing drink in an air-conditioned environment and prepared with clean water, maybe with some sugar and lemon. Ginger is also one of those plants that are usually consumed in small quantities and not as the sole source of nutrition. Even if consumed alone, ginger would not be expected to make a reasonably healthy person feel ill. Within an hour I was dry heaving. Fatigued, dehydrated, and empty of food as I was, my stomach exploded when the ginger hit it. By nightfall, I could barely stand. After a short debate (Me: "I'll be okay." My team members: "Shut up. You're fucked up, and you're not going to make it unless we get you fixed now."), a member of the team said he was calling for the medevac; he got on the emergency radio and explained my situation. Within a few hours, I was in the back of an Army ambulance with two IVs in me. A medic took my vitals and gave me two and a half liters of Ringer's solution. The IV was followed by a full dose of grief from our instructor.

He came up to the back of the ambulance, doors open, and casually asked me if I knew which SF group I was going to after the course.

"I hope to go to 5th," I croaked in response. The 5th Special Forces Group was based at Fort Campbell, Kentucky, and was responsible for operations in the Middle East.

"I just came from there." He let it float.

"You're not going to call them and tell them I'm a whiner, are you?" I was half-joking.

"I'm going to tell the sergeant major to watch out for Captain Schwalm and make sure he's got plenty of cheese to go with the wine," he replied, laughing, and walked away. The medic treating me grinned at the exchange. Though this banter felt reassuring, as instructors didn't joke with people they didn't like, it was the first time I had considered that everything I was doing in the Q course was being cataloged for future transmission once my assignment after the course became public knowledge.

Yeah, made himself sick on ginger tea. Had to send an ambulance and give him half a gallon of IV solution. Not sure you want him taking the hard jobs. Kind of weak. You know he failed Ranger school because of some "tummy" problem. His little tum-tum just couldn't take it. Hahahaha . . .

Regardless of my fear at what the instructors thought of me, they allowed me to continue. Thankfully, our last movement was the shortest of the three nights, but it also turned out to be the most eventful. Through two nights of evasion, we had never encountered the presence of those that were supposedly looking for us, and we began to question if there was anybody really on the prowl for the SERE students. On our last night, we discovered that most definitely someone was gunning for us.

We were walking in a single file, barely inside the tree line alongside a paved road, and we could see a street light ahead. Too late, we saw the pickup truck parked just outside the main circle of the neon glow. One man in a circle of others standing around the back of the truck snapped his head in our direction as we broke brush in the dark with the stealth of rhinos. They sprinted across the empty road at a dead run, their boots smacking the asphalt. On pure adrenaline, we drove our bodies into the woods while thorny vines shredded our shins and branches smacked our faces. The shouts of "Stop!" and "Halt!" came from people who had been lying in ambush waiting for us, and we blindly ran like horses deeper into the woods. I expected our pursuers to give up the chase after a few dozen meters, but they kept us going for about three hundred. In accordance with our plan, our team scattered, making it more difficult for our pursuers to get us all at once. As I sought to push branches out of my way with outstretched hands, I was glad that I wore glasses because they helped protect my eyes as I ran as fast as I could in the dark. When I could no longer hear anyone behind me, I sat down, drank the gritty iodine water from my canteen, and waited until I thought it was safe to venture out in search of my fellow teammates.

After an hour of panting, sweating, and praying, I began to call out the others' names and eventually heard my own. We reassembled and moved toward our final hide site, arriving at dawn and collapsing onto the ponchos.

At the appropriate time, we moved to the intersection and saw the van just as we had been told. Two men were talking next to it. As we approached, one opened the sliding door to the cargo compartment, and the other climbed into the driver's seat.

"Get in! Hurry! Hurry!" the man behind the wheel yelled through the open door. His urgent tone made the situation seem very realistic. We picked up our pace and crawled onto the floor of the van. The seats had all been removed. The man outside the door covered us in a tarp and slammed the door shut. The driver explained that we were to act like a load of vegetables and that we needed to talk about as much as vegetables would. We got the hint.

We traveled for a few minutes, and then one of the men said, "Coming to a checkpoint. Be quiet." We exchanged glances under the tarp that conveyed the message "This is it; here we go." But we still seemed safe as the driver came to a stop and exchanged some words with a guard of some kind. Our driver explained that he was transporting a load of vegetables, and we made it through the checkpoint without incident. A few more minutes passed, and then we heard: "Another checkpoint; stay quiet." I half expected us to make it through this one as well.

But we did not. The exchange between our driver and whoever was standing at his window became heated. Suddenly, the van accelerated. Shots were fired, and the van skidded to a halt. The door flew open, and unseen hands snatched the tarp off us.

As light poured upon us, we found ourselves staring down the barrels of a dozen AK-47s. Several men wearing the uniform of the fictitious country in which we had been working dragged us from the van. I expected more role-playing, guards trying to act rough, being safe with us, but instead I was violently pulled from the van by my shirt with the strength necessary to throw me. I was facedown, with a rifle barrel stuck in my back and spitting dirt.

"Don't move, pig-dog," came a voice from behind. Hands searched through all of my pockets, and everything except clothing was confiscated. I heard the same being done to the others.

An empty sandbag came down over my head without warning, and the stifling heat was made all the worse. Simultaneously, someone tied my hands behind my back. I listened to hear something out of place—a radio, a polite conversation, someone being addressed by military rank, anything to say that we were in a training environment—but could only hear my own breathing under the hood. Strong hands grabbed my shirt at the shoulders and hauled me to my feet. I tried to look under the edge of the hood but was not so discreet. A hand shoved the bottom of the hood down to my chest.

Hooded and bound, we were placed back in the van, and we rode in silence for several minutes. Then I felt that we were slowing to a stop and could hear shouting through the windows. The sliding door opened, and I was dragged toward what sounded like a mass interrogation, with people shouting questions and receiving answers in muted tones. I felt like I was in a movie, a movie about what most people would consider their worst nightmare. People who hated me now had total control over everything I said and did. I instantly regretted ever wishing to be captured. Someone forced me to the ground and told me to kneel. Everything was being said in accented English, but I couldn't determine what region it was supposed to represent. Our captors would often drop the definite articles as a Russian would while also sounding Hispanic.

I heard other students being interrogated; they were asked basic questions about their names and units. I realized it was my turn when an African-American man lifted my hood, looked me in the eye, and yelled "Name!"

"Schwalm," I replied, trying to sound confident but failing. I saw all my classmates kneeling around me, wearing hoods and with their hands tied behind them. It was a depressing sight.

Standing behind my interrogator, a woman with a clipboard wrote something down.

"What is your unit?" the interrogator demanded.

I faltered. It had never occurred to me to create a cover story for where I was assigned. I couldn't say I was a Green Beret here to train government forces, and I couldn't say I was something other than a Green Beret, as an armor officer would have never been in such a training situation. Then what I thought was brilliant inspiration poured into me.

"I'm not assigned to a unit. I'm an ROTC instructor. I'm just a trainer."

My interrogator looked at me incredulously. My stupidity was so stunning it caused him to drop his accent. "What did you say?" The woman with the clipboard stopped writing and looked at me like something was about to grow out of my head.

I repeated my thoughtful response. He snapped my hood back over my face, and I heard them walk away. I could tell by the look in my interrogator's face that I had done it wrong.

I'm not sure how long we remained kneeling under the blistering sun, but it was long enough for one of us to wilt. I could hear someone behind me moving and then hurried footsteps coming toward him. The ensuing exchange explained all I needed to know about how we were to be treated during this last phase of training.

"What is wrong with you, criminal? Are you weak?" All of it was said in the faux accent.

"I need some water," came the reply. I couldn't tell which one of us was speaking, as his voice was cracking.

"You are indeed very weak and worthless. You deserve nothing, you stupid pig-dog. You come here to kill our people, but we will give you water to show you the compassion of our great revolution." I listened to slurping sounds as whoever it was drank the water, and I became even more resolute in my stand to never be taken alive after this course.

The shouting ceased, and I was left once again with my breathing as the only distraction from the isolation brought by the hood. I tried to imagine how the thirty of us must have looked, kneeling in the sun wearing sandbags on our heads, our dark sweat-soaked uniforms sticking to us like a second skin. The smell of my own breath under the hood almost made me sick. It felt like hours had passed since the ride in the van to our current location, and I shifted my weight from one knee to the other, trying to find some relief on the rocky ground.

Suddenly, I heard footsteps approaching, and someone hauled me to my feet, freed my hands, and guided me into close proximity with the other students, to form a line.

"All criminals listen to me now. Put left-hand on left shoulder of criminal in front of you. When you march, you will say 'boots' when left foot hits ground. You will always march this way."

I could hear someone coming down the line of students, telling each of us what stupid pig-dogs we were and positioning our hands as we had been instructed.

"March," came the command. Still hooded, I tightened my grip on the man in front of me and began to chant "boots, boots, boots" in rhythm with my left foot. We continued like this for several hundred yards along a dirt road. I tried peeking under the hood to see changes in the landscape but to no avail. We came to a halt on a grassy field and were ordered to sit.

I heard people walking by and could sense that we were being taken one at a time away from the group. Someone touched my shoulder and told me to stand. I was guided away from the group and figured, by the leaves that brushed my shoulders and hands, that we were walking along a path in the woods. When we stopped, a voice I hadn't heard before told me to remove my hood. I pulled it off and saw three uniformed men sitting behind tables set up along a well-worn trail.

"Take off your clothes, criminal," one of them said. As I bent to unlace my boots, I saw two armed guards behind me. I noticed the men at the table watching me intently as I pulled off my grimy uniform.

So much for making a run for it.

"Take the laces out of your boots," another one said.

I stood naked in front of my captors and was ordered to spin around slowly. I heard scribbling on the clipboards. One of the men asked me if I had any injuries or pain, and I said no. He handed me a set of what appeared to be light cotton pajamas, a top with no buttons and trousers with a simple drawstring that wasn't long enough to do anything lethal. Told to dress, I was quickly attired in something you might wear in the hospital and jungle boots with no laces. One man behind the table deposited my stinking uniform into a clear plastic bag.

One of the guards put my hood over my eyes and led me back to the group. I could feel the sun high in the sky when we were ordered to stand, make the prisoner train, and start chanting. At some point we must have passed through gates that I had not previously noticed. I sensed that we were near buildings.

"Halt!" came the command. "All criminals removing hoods. Now." The accent was thick.

"I've a feeling we're not in Kansas anymore, Toto," someone whispered. While having the opposite emotional effect, removing my hood was somewhat akin to Dorothy opening the door to the land of Oz. For several seconds we stood around staring and grinning at each other. After only four days without shaving, some of us had pretty healthy beards; others, like me, showed we could never grow a beard. All of our hands were blackened by filth and our eyes were red from lack of sleep. But we grinned at each other nonetheless.

I quickly surveyed the land around us and understood immediately that we were in the resistance training laboratory. This laboratory is a mock POW camp designed for one purpose: to provide the experience necessary to survive with honor if you're ever captured. For me, the RTL was a crucible beyond my imagination.

A part of Camp Mackall and less than three miles from the barracks where I attended SFAS, the RTL sits about two miles from the paved road, on an unmarked dirt lane that runs alongside Drowning Creek, and is a fully functional internment camp surrounded by barbed wire on twelve-foot poles. With towers, spotlights, prison cells, and interrogation rooms, it is a place that successfully transports the students who enter to a nightmare scenario in a fictitious land.

The RTL was designed by Colonel Nick Rowe, a POW during

Vietnam who was held in a tiger cage for five years. His book, *Five Years to Freedom*, details his survival and ultimate escape. Communist agents killed him in the Philippines in 1989 while he was working as an advisor to that country. His legacy lives on at the RTL.

The initial minutes in the RTL set the atmosphere for what was to follow in the next few days. The camp's cadre wore mostly black uniforms or T-shirts, as well as menacing looks they must have perfected over previous classes. Everything they said and did was intended to communicate that they were in charge. Their first order of business was to ensure we understood with crystal clarity that this was not Kansas. Wordlessly, the guards divided us into groups by height and led us to a room with a collection of what appeared to be small plywood closets, each about coffin size but smaller.

With wood touching our shoulders, back, and chest, we breathed in as they locked all of us in hot boxes. Over six feet, I was standing and could feel the inhalations of the men on either side of me. Those under six feet were squatting in boxes that folded them at the waist and knees. Resisting this torture was probably the only time in Special Forces that my life as a tanker paid dividends. I had spent countless hours locked in the turret of a tank while wearing a chemical protective suit with a rubber gas mask. That said, the heat soared in the tiny space, and the wood two inches from my nose started to blur as my mind swam in the stifling confines. I tried to distract myself from my discomfort by thinking of how I taught my son to change the oil in the car, something I had never done with the three-year-old. Before I got to other car repair lessons, the man in front of me made a noise that sounded something between a grunt and a moan.

"I'm feeling sick," he said. "Hey, I'm feeling sick." The sense of urgency in his voice climbed with each syllable. Immediately, the doors opened, and the guards took us to a sawdust pit. In lieu of passing out in the dehydrators, we did pushups and situps until we were covered in sawdust. Again, without a word as to what was going on, the guards reassembled us into four ranks, creating a formation on a yard of smooth gravel. A man with a scar running down his face climbed a railed platform about three feet off the ground. Scarface began explaining our new life to us.

First, he told us that we were no longer soldiers; we were criminals. Second, we were to learn the rules governing the camp: no talking, no singing, no whistling without permission. No eating or drinking or going to the "porcelain facility," as the toilet was called, without permission. He even explained how we were to sit in our cells: modified lotus position (my words, not his), with our legs crossed, hands on knees, forefinger and thumb making a circle. We stood at attention and melted in the sun as he droned on about the compassion we were enjoying as guests of the revolution. He ended by mentioning democracy and the right to vote. With that, he said we could elect a spokesman or senior ranking officer who would be the camp commander's point of contact for addressing prisoner issues.

"Which criminals volunteer to be SRO?" I and another student raised our hands. He told us to prepare remarks, as in a campaign speech, to sell ourselves to the class.

I went first. I felt like this was my opportunity to give the class a morale boost, and after saying that I would do everything to ensure that we were afforded all rights and privileges as POWs according to the Geneva Convention, I concluded with "God bless America." The class repeated the phrase, but I wasn't able to hear all of it.

My hearing was interrupted by an open-handed slap across my face, followed by another, and tears welled in my eyes. I had never known such humiliation as an adult, or how a slap stings differently from how a punch hurts. Scarface had me by the collar, and he pulled my face within an inch of his. I could smell his last cigar.

"You are very stupid, pig-dog," he said quietly. His eyes told me I had made a huge mistake, one that most likely would have cost me my life.

The other student took a completely opposite approach and tried to infuse the class with the sense that this was only training and that we should probably lighten up. He promised beer and pizza for dinner every night, and color TV in our cells. While he did elicit some grins from the class, he never got to the rest of his routine, as Scarface grabbed him, slapped him, and handed him to a man we later learned was an interrogator. He took our fellow prisoner to a sawdust pit where we all could watch and listen as he asked the question: "You think this is funny?" Each question that followed was accompanied by a slap. The grins had been replaced by grimaces and angry scowls.

With both our faces red with handprints, the candidates for SRO stood before the class, and Scarface called for the vote. I "won" in a landslide.

Scarface pulled me aside and explained that I needed to organize the criminals into groups for work parties as well as staff functions. With this done, we were lined up and marched to a low concrete building.

"Boots, boots, boots" came the chant. We stopped at the door. Through the opening, I could see a row of smaller doors, maybe three feet high, disappearing into the gloom that was our cellblock.

Guards led us one at a time to our cells. Mine was the first one on the right. I squatted to walk through the door and found myself in a box four feet long on each side and windowless save for a small opening in the door, big enough to slide a pie pan through and covered by a sliding sheet of metal. I listened as the other students occupied their cells. The guards made a point to slam the door loudly and purposefully behind each of us as we entered. After the last door shut, I listened to boots crunching away in the gravel outside the cellblock and assumed we were alone.

Without a watch, time became a victim of imagination. I listened for sounds coming from the hallway, something that would register a changing of guards or a truck coming or going, anything that might betray a pattern of life, but the area was as silent as a tomb. Sweat poured off my forehead, and my pajamas turned transparent against my wet skin.

I heard gravel crunching as someone approached. The slot in my door opened, and a steel bowl appeared with water. Grains of salt clung to the bottom.

"Drink, stupid one," came the command. I drained the bowl and handed it back through the slot. The process was repeated down the line of cells. I listened as the water boy left the cellblock. I studied my cell, trying to stretch my legs from one corner to the other, imagining spending weeks here. I couldn't wrap my mind around the concept of living in so small a space. I listened to the other students calling out and added my own voice to the simple question-and-answer dialogue.

Even as I spoke, I was truly fearful that someone, a guard, might hear us, and we would all be punished. But I spoke nonetheless. The sound of gravel crunching brought silence.

The slot opened, another steel bowl came through, and I drank the warm salted water. I listened as the water boy made his way down the hall and heard someone say that he needed to go to the bathroom.

"Shut up, criminal." The gravel crunching told us the water boy had left.

Over the next hour, we were given an effective lesson on how much control our captors had over us. I could smell the urine outside my door as my fellow prisoners responded to the bowls of water provided and added my own to what was undoubtedly a stream in the cellblock. Somebody said he was sorry, and soon the smell of excrement mixed with that of the urine. Whoever it was had diarrhea, and the putrid flow ran into the hall. The heat and humidity worked to turn the smells into an aroma that made my eyes water.

While I have no way of knowing how long we stayed in the cells that first day, the sun was just on top of the pine trees when we were brought out into the yard and told to make a formation. It felt good to stand and breathe clean air. I watched as my classmates made four ranks and turned to report to Scarface. He had been replaced by a tall blond man wearing an eye patch. Scarface had told me to bow and say "All criminals are ready." As it was my first time in front of the formation in the context of the RTL, I resorted to old habits.

Ramrod straight and saluting smartly, I exclaimed in my best command voice, "The officers are formed."

His face contorted in rage. He ran at me, grabbed me by the collar, and slapped me. I was not yet accustomed to this level of humiliation, and my eyes clouded in rage and tears.

"You are most stupid SRO I have ever seen," he began in the affected accent of the guards. "You not care about your fellow criminals. You do not think, and they suffer because you are stupid. Watch how stupid you are now." He jerked me around to face the formation. "All criminals pushing up," he yelled.

That command needed no further explanation. Everybody got down and started to do pushups. When I started to join them, One-eye jerked me back up.

"No, you will watch. And you will laugh. You must think this is very funny, so you should laugh. You do not care about your fellow prisoners. Laugh loudly at the pain you have caused them." He released my collar and stepped back.

I tried to summon the most unconvincing laugh I could find and bellowed loudly and, I hoped, stupidly. After the amount of time to do about twenty pushups, he ordered everyone to stand and told me to try again.

I bowed and announced that the criminals were ready. He gave me instructions about work details, such as cleaning in and around the cellblocks and the weeding to be done in the camp garden. He also told us we could now use the porcelain facility, a simple cinderblock hut under a corrugated tin roof with four white porcelain bowls anchored to the concrete floor. Just squat and go. No toilet paper and no bidet, though there was soap and water to wash our hands after we cleaned ourselves.

As we began the tasks assigned, such as hosing our waste out of the cells, guards called certain students by number and escorted them to another building. It was time for the interrogations to begin.

It was dark by the time my turn came, and the guards led me to a room with a metal chair. A single interrogator entered the room and in a friendly tone (though still in the faux accent) he asked how I had been treated and wanted to talk about the nature of our mission in his country. I deflected his questions as I had been trained, and, despite a tone of disappointment in his voice, he seemed accepting of my answers. He called the guards, and they led me back to the rest of the prisoners.

I was beginning to think that this wasn't so bad and that if we just endured the camp and played the game, we'd go home.

Guess again.

One of the most poignant moments in my life occurred in the RTL on that first night. Another student/criminal was accused of a war crime. He was captured with a railroad spike in his pocket (probably trying to make a weapon), and the camp commandant alleged that removing this spike had caused a train to derail, killing dozens of innocent women and children. That the student found it on a road and not in a rail bed was irrelevant. His crime was mass murder, and if convicted the penalty would be death.

As the senior ranking officer, certain unique responsibilities fell to me, such as speaking for the other prisoners. On this night, after having been without sleep for several days, subsisting on blackberries and ginger tea (no sugar), I was supposed to act as defense counsel for my fellow officer who would be shot if I failed. Scarface reemerged in order to preside over the discussion. He ordered the class to sit, and the guards secured the accused prisoner, tying his hands behind his back. A guard handed me a copy of the Geneva Convention, and Scarface said I had five minutes to prepare my case.

I thumbed through the pamphlet, looking for an article that addressed the circumstances in which I found myself. In Article 3, I came across the words expressly prohibiting "the passing of sentences and carrying out of executions without previous judgment pronounced by a regularly constituted court affording all the judicial guarantees which are recognized as indispensable by civilized people." Article 87 prohibits the use of military tribunals to try criminals of war, though many countries that are signatories to the convention exempt themselves from that one. Further, Article 105 explained that I was to have two weeks to prepare a defense. Article 106 gave us the right of appeal "with a view to quashing of the sentence." I figured I had four shots, and one would be the round peg that would fit in the round hole and keep my guy from getting shot.

Not bloody likely.

Clad in my blue pajamas, wearing jungle boots without the laces and with my fellow prisoners assembled behind me, all of us stinking like mildewed rags, I made my opening argument to Scarface.

"Sir, Article 87 prohibits—" I began before he quickly cut me off.

"My country does not recognize Article 87, stupid pig-dog." He lit a cigar with the urgency of waiting for a bus.

I began to argue that my fellow classmate had found the spike already removed from the rail bed. He had no way to know that it was ever part of the railroad; it may have been left over after completion.

"Lie! Criminal is guilty. Shoot him." The guards began leading my brother prisoner to a wall. I could see the class tensing. We were all thinking the same thing: If guards shot him on such trumped-up charges, none of us had a chance. We were not going to wait for them to shoot us one at a time. The majority of the class was getting caught up in the action. We were role-playing as prisoners, but we were taking this make-believe execution seriously.

"Wait," I shouted. "In accordance with Article 106, I wish to appeal." Scarface cracked into a big grin with a cigar sticking out of it.

"So appeal."

"Please reconsider. If you execute him there will be less of us to work." I scrambled for anything I could. I tried to think if there was a magic phrase I was supposed to say.

Scarface let me ramble for about two minutes and then said, "If you will burn a filthy rag, we will spare criminal."

While I was trying to put my mind around what he said, two guards came from behind the building, one with a video camera on a tripod and another with an American flag.

Click. I got it.

The guard carrying the flag treated it like it was diseased, holding it by one corner and dragging it on the ground. The other guards put the camera into operation, its red light burning on the front of it.

"If you burn filthy rag, we will spare stupid pig-dog." Scarface drew hard on the cigar and waited for my response. I watched blue smoke curl in the light shining on the pathetic little drama and felt my legs weaken as the guard with the flag handed me a lighter. I could smell lighter fluid. I hesitated.

All I could think was that this was a real American flag, and I was about to burn it.

With the camera rolling, I struck the flame and touched the flag. It lit up like a torch. The guard dropped it, and I watched it burn in a pile. The tears returned. I was transfixed by the sight of our nation's emblem contracting and turning black. The guard took the lighter back, and I turned to see what was happening with the rest of the class. Scarface pounced.

"You have made very good propaganda, SRO. But, I change my mind," he said. "We shoot criminal anyway."

The role-playing game was long gone. Helpless frustration gave way to rage, and I could tell that the others in the class shared my feelings. While we may have been tired and hungry, we were far from weak and broken. We were all at the top of our physical game, and there were thirty of us. Without a word from me, the class began standing and moving toward the guards holding our brother. The cadre pushed as far as they dared. We were no longer students in a pretend prison sweating it out as students in SERE school. We were commissioned officers in the most powerful Army in the world, and we were about to hand somebody their ass.

BAM-BAM-BAM-BAM-BAM. As if to confirm that my sense of the situation was shared by the training cadre, the machine gun in the watchtower opened up, and we all hit the dirt. The execution didn't happen. Scarface yelled for us to line up; we made the prisoner train and chanted back to our cells. I felt like I couldn't breathe.

I was thankful to crawl into my box. The emotion from burning the flag washed over me as I sat alone, and I was glad no one could see me sitting in my cell looking like a little boy whose new puppy had been flattened by a truck.

As I sat there contemplating my actions of the last thirty minutes, the sliding portal of my cell door opened. A set of eyes looked at me, and someone said in an American accent, "This is an authorized flag disposal facility." The portal slammed shut, and my capacity to breathe returned.

I understood that preserving the sanctity of a symbol was not worth the life of a fellow prisoner. I tried to imagine telling a mother I had let her son die in order not to burn the flag. We could make another flag. We couldn't make her another son.

For the rest of our time in the cells that night, we listened to babies crying, children begging for Daddy to help Mommy, news reports of Green Berets being killed somewhere in the world, music of the great revolution of which we were guests, and anything else the cadre could think of playing over the loudspeakers that might kill our morale.

I slept in fits and assumed the authorized lotus position whenever I heard the gravel crunching. I listened as other members of the class were taken away for interrogation, hoping I wasn't due another turn in the hot seat. After what felt like hours, the guards brought us from our cells and into the yard. I noticed new faces around the camp. The night crew was here. Scarface and One-eye were gone. In their place was a stocky African-American woman. I bowed to her and announced that the criminals were ready.

She pointed at the flagpole and told us to salute the new colors of the great revolution as they were hoisted to the playing of the new national anthem. I contracted all but the middle finger of my right hand and saluted. She backhanded me in the solar plexus and slapped my face while I was doubled over. No tears. I could now handle amazing humiliation.

"Stupid criminal, you will salute flag. You will make propaganda." She glared at me, and her eyes said that if I did anything dumb I was dead. We all saluted in as desultory a fashion as we could muster.

The rest of the evening was a blur, but we did get a meal of rice and fish, which we ate with our fingers. Some of us were taken for interrogation while the others returned to work in the camp garden. I guessed the purpose of being up was simply sleep deprivation. It worked.

Before sunrise, we reassembled and chanted back to our cells. I wanted to be left alone in my cell, to think about what was going on, to try to think of an escape plan. I laughed later at the lunacy of truly effecting an escape, but I really thought at the time that we might try to escape. Thoughts of slipping under the wire evaporated as I dropped into exhaustion-induced sleep.

The sun was up as our second day began. In the gravel yard and surrounded by armed guards, the men and women we came to know as our interrogators led us in classes on the merits of their socialist revolution. We sat on the ground and feigned interest. As the lecture continued, one interrogator explained a special component of the revolution: It was the idea that each of us should seek self-improvement. In order to improve, we needed to identify some shortcoming in our own person, a character flaw perhaps, and share this self-discovery with our fellow prisoners.

The class sat sullenly as the first student stood and said he wished he was taller.

No, no, that wasn't what they were looking for. You can't help your height. Try again.

Each admission brought an immediate insult.

"I wish I read more," someone said.

"Yes, we can see you are very stupid. You will have time to read now," came the retort.

I scrambled for something to admit that couldn't be used against me.

"I need to pray more," I said.

"Yes, yes, we see you are an atheist. You don't need to pray, stupid pig-dog." I sat down.

An African-American officer stood and said, "I wish I wasn't claustrophobic. My brother locked me in a refrigerator when I was five, and ever since then I am very afraid of being confined."

My heart broke. We had two black officers in the class, and the cadre would need nothing to remind them that one man would freak out in the hot box. The class let out a collective groan.

"Very good, very progressive, black one," the cadre said. No retort, no insult from cadre confirmed my fear. If they liked what we had said, we had done it wrong.

The class ended, and we began our daily work details. The sun was

high when the guards began to assemble us for some unknown purpose. Though we were students in training, we crossed a line as soldiers,
now accepting of things that would be unthinkable in the polite society that had created us. We conformed to our circumstances and began
to offer kindness in ways most Americans would find repulsive. For
example, I glanced at the porcelain facility and saw one student with
the water hose shooting a steady stream of water at the butt of another
student whose diarrhea poured like a stream of coffee down his leg. The
cadre saw it too and let the student stop shitting himself before yelling to gather as ordered. Without the hose, the student with diarrhea
would have fouled his trousers and spent the rest of the day breathing
his own putrid aroma.

After I bowed, a member of the cadre I hadn't seen before told us
we could now worship our God who had left us in the prison camp to
rot. I hadn't expected this. Fortunately, an officer who had failed the
previous class due to heat exhaustion and had joined us just for the fun
of the RTL happened to be a Catholic priest. Otherwise, organizing
this effort would have fallen to me.

I was glad to step back and let the padre take the lead.

The cadre addressed our prisoner priest and asked what different
kinds of believers we had. A quick survey showed we fell along a mostly
Protestant and Catholic division. No Jews, no Muslims, no Mormons;
we were all Christians, though divided by denomination. The cadre
told the Catholics to assemble about fifty meters from the Protestants.
The priest asked the Protestants to join the Catholics.

"No," replied the instructor. "You are allowed to worship sepa-
rately." He looked at the Catholics and said, "Your pope does not recognize the legitimacy of their faith. Why should they worship with you?"
The accent was heavy. "They cannot take Communion with you? Yes?"

I was at a loss for what to do. He was right. Unless we were Catholic
and learned the Catholic catechism, we would not be allowed to partake in that sacrament with Catholics, not during a real Mass anyway.
Suddenly, we weren't thinking about escaping. We were thinking about
our differences, which is exactly what the cadre wanted to happen.

While I sat there trying to think of a response, our Catholic priest rose to the occasion. He saw exactly where we were headed and pulled a brilliant move.

"Let's sing a song we all know," he said loudly and started belting out "Amazing Grace." We joined in even as the instructor tried to shout us down.

We made it through the first verse and sang it again, the little victory giving us volume if not great singing voices. Cadre shut us down with guards breaking up our little choir of men in blue pajamas. I remember how light I felt when we sang that song. It was like a light came on inside me for just an instant. We went back to work around the camp and waited for the next show as the interrogations continued. My second one went very differently than the first.

After I had been alone in the room for a few minutes, a male and female interrogator rolled in like a hurricane.

"Who are the members of your team? Who were you training with? Who sent you?"

I started going through all the techniques. Slap. Nope. Not that one. Slap. Huh? That one doesn't work either. Pow. Okay, not that one. By the end of my second interrogation, both of my inquisitors let me know I had failed. I hadn't given up anything, but I was probably also dead.

This failure is not manifestly obvious to the students. A slap simulates a broken jaw. A pop to the solar plexus represents a chest punch. A few minutes in a hot box is intended to imply a fortnight. They can't actually torture us, and they use cues to tell us we are really screwing up. Slapping is not reinforcing the correct behavior.

The sun was low in the sky when I rejoined the class. Students were beginning to come by and pass details of the camp that would be necessary to know if we tried an escape.

"No guards on the back of the porcelain facility."

"Blind spot from the guard tower on the east fence."

I nodded. But how could we plan an escape if we couldn't talk? We had been taught the tap code, where we could communicate by a series of taps in the right sequence while we were in our cells, but without weeks and months of using it (like the guys in Vietnam's Hanoi Hilton), we could only manage to ask each other how it was going.

Scarface was back and he yelled out for us to assemble. I bowed and another cadre member I had not seen told us to sit. We would now seek improvement by pointing out the faults of others. Group critique sessions are not much different than drunken friends getting really candid. The difference between the two efforts is similar to the difference between going down a steep hill on a roller coaster and parachuting from a plane. Both can be fun, but once you leave the plane you're not stopping until you reach the ground. And you will reach the ground. We would not be allowed to pull punches in saying bad things about our fellow prisoners. We were on dangerous ground, and not because the cadre could glean exploitable information about us. We were a class of officers that would go on through the rest of several months of training together, and nothing we did here would be forgotten.

Thankfully, we all used a perverted compliment approach. On cue by the instructor, each of us stood and pointed at another member of the class.

"You work too hard."

"You yell too loud when we salute the flag."

"You rake too fast."

We made it without incident. Each one found something excellent in another to complain about, and the cadre let us go back to work. We were fortunate. There is a legend from one class that a Jewish officer found himself isolated and ridiculed by some of his fellow classmates. The cadre of the RTL had successfully convinced the students that they were no longer in North Carolina, that the Jew was anathema to them, and some students ran with it. Only the efforts of other students kept the event from becoming something utterly toxic to the class.

As the second night approached, many members of the class told me that they did not want to eat the rice and fish ration that night. It had made them sick. With that in mind, I inadvertently set into motion a series of events that got me into serious trouble. As SRO, I was expected to sign for the entire class for some things, but signing our names had been drilled into us as something to question at every turn. We might sign something that would be later used to make propaganda. The prohibition never existed when signing for meals.

Meanwhile, two plastic tubes, placed securely in Styrofoam boxes, had arrived at the University of Pennsylvania, transported in a refrigerator in the back of a FedEx truck; one contained transparent cerebrospinal fluid, as clear as unfiltered water, and another held blood, which started to look like dehydrated urine as, over time, the red blood cells dropped to the bottom. The test tubes were coded 0933, labeled with my initials, SC, and placed in a negative-80 degree freezer waiting for the lab to conduct its tests. They were addressed to the lab run by neuro-oncologist Dr. Josep Dalmau, whom Dr. Najjar had mentioned during his first visit and whom Dr. Russo had since e-mailed to ask if he would take a look at my case.

Four years earlier, in 2005, Dr. Dalmau had been the senior author on a paper in the neuroscience journal *Annals of Neurology* that focused on four young women who had developed prominent psychiatric symptoms and encephalitis. All had white blood cells in their cerebrospinal fluid, confusion, memory problems, hallucinations, delusions, and difficulty breathing, and they all had tumors called teratomas in their ovaries. But the most remarkable finding was that all four patients had similar antibodies that appeared to be reacting against specific areas of the brain, mainly the hippocampus. Something about the combination of the tumor and the antibodies was making these women very sick.

Dr. Dalmau had noticed a pattern in these four women; now he had to learn more about the antibody itself. He and his research team began to work night and day on an elaborate immunohistrochemistry experiment involving frozen sections of rat brains, which had been sliced into paper-thin pieces and then exposed to the cerebrospinal fluid of those four sick women. The hope was that the antibodies from the cerebrospinal fluid would bind directly to some receptors in the rat brain and reveal a characteristic design. It took eight months of tinkering before a pattern finally emerged.

Dr. Dalmau had prepared the rat brain slides all the same, placing a small amount of cerebrospinal fluid from each of the four patients on each. Twenty-four hours later:

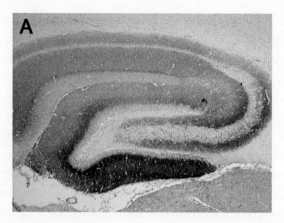

A: Section of rat brain in the hippocampus that shows the reactivity of the cerebrospinal fluid of a patient with anti-NMDAR encephalitis. The brown staining corresponds to the patient's antibodies that have bound to the NMDA receptors.

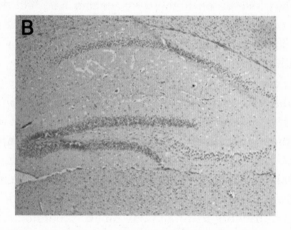

B: A similar section of hippocampus of an individual without NMDA receptor antibodies.

Four beautiful images, like cave drawings or abstract seashell patterns, revealed the antibodies' binding to the naked eye. "It was a moment of great excitement," Dr. Dalmau later recalled. "Everything had been negative. Now we became totally positive that all four not only had the same illness, but the same antibody."

He had clarified that the pattern of reactivity was more intense in the hippocampus of the rat brain, but this was only the beginning. A far more difficult question now arose: Which receptors were these antibodies targeting? Through a combination of trial and error, plus a few educated guesses about which receptors are most common in the hippocampus, Dr. Dalmau and his colleagues eventually identified the target. Using a kidney cell line bought from a commercial lab that came with no receptors on their surfaces at all, a kind of "blank slate," his lab introduced DNA sequences that direct the cells to make certain types of receptors, allowing the lab to control which receptors were available for binding. Dalmau chose to have them express only NMDA receptors, after figuring out that those were the most likely to have been present in high volume in the hippocampus. Sure enough, the antibodies in the cerebrospinal fluid of the four patients bound to the cells. There was his answer: the culprits were NMDA-receptor-seeking antibodies.

NMDA (N-methyl-D-aspartate acid) receptors are vital to learning, memory, and behavior, and they are a main staple of our brain chemistry. If these are incapacitated, mind and body fail. NMDA receptors are located all over the brain, but the majority are concentrated on neurons in the hippocampus, the brain's primary learning and memory center, and in the frontal lobes, the seat of higher functions and personality. These receptors receive instructions from chemicals called neurotransmitters. All neurotransmitters carry only one of two messages: they can either "excite" a cell, encouraging it to fire an electrical impulse, or "inhibit" a cell, which hinders it from firing. These simple conversations between neurons are at the root of everything we do, from sipping a glass of wine to writing a newspaper lead.

In those unfortunate patients with Dr. Dalmau's anti-NMDA-receptor encephalitis, the antibodies, normally a force for good in the body, had become treasonous persona non grata in the brain. These receptor-seeking antibodies planted their death kiss on the surface of a neuron, handicapping the neuron's receptors, making them unable to send and receive those important chemical signals. Though researchers are far from fully understanding how NMDA receptors (and their corresponding neurons) affect and alter behavior, it's clear that when they are compromised the outcome can be disastrous, even deadly.

Still, a few experiments have offered up some clues as to their importance. Decrease NMDA receptors by, say, 40 percent, and you might get psychosis; decrease them by 70 percent, and you have catatonia. In "knockout mice" without NMDA receptors at all, even the most basic life functions are impossible: most die within ten hours of birth due to respiratory failure. Mice with a very small number of NMDA receptors don't learn to suckle, and they simply starve to death within a day or so. Those mice with at least 5 percent of their NMDA receptors intact survive, but exhibit abnormal behavior and strange social and sexual interactions. Mice with half their receptors in working order also live, but they show memory deficits and abnormal social relationships.

As a result of this additional research, in 2007, Dr. Dalmau and his colleagues presented another paper, now introducing his new class of NMDA-receptor-seeking diseases to the world. This second article identified twelve women with the same profile of neurological symptoms, which could now be called a syndrome. They all had teratomas, and almost all of them were young women. Within a year after publication, one hundred more patients had been diagnosed; not all of them had ovarian teratomas and not all of them were young women (some were men and many were children), enabling Dr. Dalmau to do an even more thorough study on the newly discovered, but nameless, disease.

"Why not name it the Dalmau disease?" people often asked him. But he didn't think "Dalmau disease" sounded right, and it was no longer customary to name a disease after its discoverer. "I didn't think that would be wise. It's not very humble." He shrugged.

By the time I was a patient at NYU, Dr. Dalmau had fine-tuned his approach, designing two tests that could swiftly and accurately diagnose the disease. As soon as he received my samples, he could test the spinal fluid. If he found that I had anti-NMDA-receptor autoimmune encephalitis, it would make me the 217th person worldwide to be diagnosed since 2007. It just begged the question: If it took so long for one of the best hospitals in the world to get to this step, how many other people were going untreated, diagnosed with a mental illness or condemned to a life in a nursing home or a psychiatric ward?

CHAPTER 30
RHUBARB

By my twenty-fifth day in the hospital, two days after the biopsy, with a preliminary diagnosis in sight, my doctors thought it was a good time to officially assess my cognitive skills to record a baseline. This test would be a fulcrum, a turning point, that would measure what kind of progress they could expect in the future through the various stages of treatment. Beginning on the afternoon of April 15, a speech pathologist and a neuropsychologist visited me for two days in a row, each for separate assessments.

The speech pathologist, Karen Gendal, did the first assessment, starting with basic questions: "What's your name?" "How old are you?" "Are you a woman?" "Do you live in California?" "Do you live in New York?" "Do you peel a banana before eating it?" and so forth. I was able to answer all of these questions, though I did so slowly. But when she asked the more open-ended question "Why are you in the hospital?" I could not explain. (To be fair, the doctors didn't know either, but I could not provide even the basics.)

After some spotty and tangential answers, I finally said, "I can't get my ideas from my head out." She nodded: this was a typical response for people suffering from aphasia, a language impairment related to brain injury. I also had something called dysarthria, a motor speech impairment caused by a weakness in the muscles of the face, throat, or vocal cords.

Gendal asked me to stick out my tongue, which trembled from the effort. It had a reduced range of motion on both sides, which was contributing to my inability to articulate.

"Would you smile for me?"

I tried, but my facial muscles were so weak that no smile came. She wrote down "hypo-aroused," a medical term for lethargic, and also noted that I was not fully alert. When I did talk, the words came out without any emotional register.

She moved on to cognitive abilities. Holding up her pen, she asked, "What is this?"

"Ken," I answered. This, again, wasn't too unusual for someone at my level of impairment. They call it *phonemic paraphasia,* where you substitute one word for another that sounds similar.

When she asked me to write my name, I painstakingly drew out an "S," tracing the letter multiple times before moving on to the "U," where I did the same. It took several minutes for me to write my name. "Okay, would you write this sentence out for me: 'Today is a nice day.'"

I drew out the letters, retracing each of them several times and misspelling some words. My handwriting was so poor that Gendal could hardly make out the sentence.

She wrote her impression in the chart: "It is difficult to determine at just two days post-operation to what extent communication deficits are language-based versus medication or cognitive. Clearly communication function is dramatically reduced from pre-morbid level when this patient was working as a successful journalist for a local paper." In other words, there seemed to be a dramatic change between the person I had been and the person I was now, but it was difficult at the time to distinguish my problems understanding from my inability to communicate—and whether these would persist in the long or short term.

Later the next morning, neuropsychologist Chris Morrison arrived with her auburn hair piled high on her head and green-flecked hazel eyes flashing. She was there to test me on something called the Wechsler Abbreviated Scale of Intelligence, as well as other tests, that are used to diagnose a number of things, from attention deficit disorder to traumatic brain injuries. But when she entered the room, I was so unresponsive she wasn't even sure that I could see her.

"What is your name?" Dr. Morrison began brightly, walking me through the basic orienting questions that by now I had been conditioned to answer correctly. Her next stage of questions assessed attention, processing speed, and working memory, which she compared to a computer's random access memory (RAM), as in, "How many programs you can have open all at once—how many things you can keep in your head at once and spit back out."

Dr. Morrison provided me with a random assortment of single-digit numbers, 1 through 9, and asked me to repeat them to her. Once we got up to five digits, I had to stop, though seven is the normal limit for people of my age and intelligence.

Next, she tested the word-retrieval process, to see how well I was able to access my "memory bank." "I'd like you to name as many fruits and vegetables as possible," she said, starting a sixty-second timer.

"Apples," I began. Apples are a common fruit to start with, and of course they had been on my mind a lot lately.

"Carrots."

"Pears."

"Bananas."

Pause.

"Rhubarb."

Dr. Morrison chuckled inwardly at this one. The minute was over. I had come up with five fruits and vegetables; a healthy individual could name over twenty. Dr. Morrison believed that I knew plenty more examples; the problem seemed to be retrieving them.

She then showed me a series of cards with everyday objects on them. I could name only five of the ten, missing examples like kite and pliers, though I struggled as if the words were on the tip of my tongue.

Dr. Morrison then tested my ability to view and process the external world. There are many different things that must come together for a person to accurately perceive an object. To see a desk, for example, first we see lines that come together at angles, then color, then contrast, then depth; all of that information goes into the memory bank, which labels it with a word and, depending on the object, an emotion (to a journalist, a desk might elicit guilty feelings about missed deadlines, for example). To track this set of skills, she had me compare the size and shape of various angles. I scored on the low end of average on these, well enough for Dr. Morrison to move on to more difficult tasks. She introduced a set of red and white blocks and placed them on the fold-out tray in front of me. She then showed me a picture of how the blocks should be arranged and asked me to re-create the picture with a timer running.

I stared at the pictures and then back at the blocks, moved them into a pattern that had nothing to do with the picture, and looked back at the picture for reference. I fiddled with the blocks some more, getting nowhere, but refused to give up. Morrison wrote down "tenacious in her attempts." I seemed to realize I wasn't getting it right, which frustrated me deeply. It was clear that, for all my other impairments, I knew that I was not functioning at the level I was used to.

The next step was for me to copy down complex geometric designs on graph paper, but my abilities here were so weak that Dr. Morrison decided to stop altogether. I was flustered, and she worried that moving forward would only make me feel worse. Dr. Morrison was convinced that I was very much aware, despite the cognitive issues, of what I could no longer do. In her review later that day, she marked cognitive therapy as "highly recommended."

CHAPTER 31
THE BIG REVEAL

Later that afternoon, my dad had been trying to interest me in a game of gin rummy when Dr. Russo and the team arrived.

"Mr. Cahalan," she said. "We have some positive test results."

He dropped the playing cards on the floor and grabbed his notebook. Dr. Russo explained that they'd heard back from Dr. Dalmau with a confirmation of the diagnosis. Her words flew at him like shrapnel—bang, bang, bang: *NMDA, antibody, tumor, chemotherapy.* He fought to pay close attention, but there was one key part of the explanation that he could hold on to: my immune system had gone haywire and had begun attacking my brain.

"I'm sorry," he interrupted the barrage. "What is the name again?"

He wrote the letters "NMDA" in his block lettering:

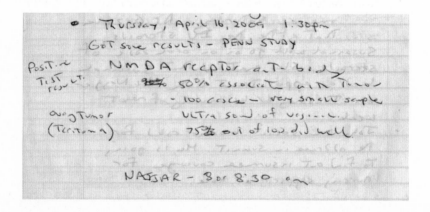

Anti-NMDA-receptor encephalitis, Dr. Russo explained, is a multistage disease that varies wildly in its presentation as it progresses. For 70 percent of patients, the disorder begins innocuously, with normal flulike symptoms: headaches, fever, nausea, and vomiting, though it's unclear if patients initially contract a virus related to the disease or if these symptoms are a result of the disease itself. Typically, about two weeks after the initial flulike symptoms, psychiatric issues, which include anxiety, insomnia, fear, grandiose delusions, hyperreligiosity, mania, and paranoia, take hold. Because the symptoms are psychiatric, most patients seek out mental health professionals first. Seizures crop up in 75 percent of patients, which is fortunate if only because they get the patient out of the psychologist's chair and into a neurologist's office. From there, language and memory deficits arise, but they are often overshadowed by the more dramatic psychiatric symptoms.

My father sighed with relief. He felt comforted by a name, any name, to explain what had happened to me, even if he didn't quite understand what it all meant. Everything she said was matching up perfectly to my case, including abnormal facial tics, lip smacking, and tongue jabbing, along with synchronized and rigid body movements. Patients also often develop autonomic symptoms, she continued: blood pressure and heart rate that vacillate between too high and too low—again, just like my case. She hardly needed to point out that I had now entered the catatonic stage, which marks the height of the disease but also precedes breathing failure, coma, and sometimes death. The doctors seemed to have caught it just in time.

When Dr. Russo began to explain that there are treatments that have been proven to reverse the course of the disease, my father nearly sank to his knees and thanked God right there in the hospital room. Still, Dr. Russo cautioned, even once you have a diagnosis, there are still substantial question marks. Though 75 percent of patients recover fully or maintain only mild side effects, over 20 percent remain permanently disabled and 4 percent die anyway, even despite a swift diagnosis. And those aforementioned "mild" side effects might mean the difference between the old me and a new Susannah, one who might not have the humor, vitality, or drive that I did before. *Mild* is a vague and undefined term.

"About 50 percent of the time, the disease is instigated by an ovarian tumor, called a teratoma, but in the other 50 percent of cases, the cause is never discovered," Dr. Russo continued.

My dad looked at her quizzically. *What the hell is a teratoma?*

It was probably best that he didn't know. When this type of tumor was identified in the late 1800s, a German doctor christened it "teratoma" from the Greek *teraton,* which means monster. These twisted cysts were a source of fascination even when there was no name for them: the first description dates back to a Babylonian text from 600 B.C. These masses of tissue range in size from microscopic to fist sized (or even bigger) and contain hair, teeth, bone, and sometimes even eyes, limbs, and brain tissue. They are often located in the reproductive organs, brain, skull, tongue, and neck and resemble pus-soaked hairballs. They are like those hairy, toothy creatures in the 1980s horror film franchise *Critters*. The only good news is that they are usually—but not always—benign.

"We will need to do a transvaginal exam to see if there are any signs of tumors," said Dr. Russo. "We'll also check her over to see if there's any link with her history of melanoma. If so, we'll have to move on with chemotherapy."

"Chemotherapy." My father repeated the word in the hope that she had gotten it wrong. But she hadn't.

My dad looked over at me. I had been staring off to the side, disassociated from the exchange, not seeming to gauge the magnitude of the moment. Suddenly, though, at the word *chemotherapy,* my chest began heaving, and I let out a deep sigh. Tears streamed down my face. My dad ran from his chair and threw his arms around me. I continued to sob without saying a word, as Dr. Russo waited quietly while he rocked me. He couldn't tell if I understood what was going on or if I was just attuned to the amplified electricity in the room.

"This is killing me," I said, my voice high yet unemotional, despite the sobs. "I'm dying in here."

"I know, I know," he said. With my head in his arms, he could smell the glue on my hair. "We're going to get you out of here."

After a few moments, my sobs stopped, and I lay back on the bed, my head against the pillow, staring straight ahead. Quietly, Dr. Russo continued. "Overall, this is good news, Mr. Cahalan. Dr. Najjar believes that there is a possibility that Susannah could get back as much as 90 percent of her former self."

"We could get her back?"

"There seems to be a strong possibility."

"I want to go home," I said.

"We're working on doing just that," Dr. Russo replied with a smile.

⁓

Over the weeks, I had gone from being a notoriously difficult patient to a favorite, the ward's "interesting consult" for a host of attending doctors, interns, and residents hoping to catch a glimpse of the girl with the unknown disease. Now that we had a diagnosis that had never before been seen at NYU, young MDs, hardly a day older than me, stared at me as if I were a caged animal in a zoo and made muffled assessments, pointing at me and craning their heads as more experienced doctors gave a rundown of the syndrome. The next morning, as my father fed me oatmeal and chopped-up bananas, a group of residents and medical students arrived. The young man leading the group of nascent MDs introduced my case as if I weren't in the room.

"This is a very interesting one," he said, leading a gang of about six others into the room. "She has what is called anti-NMDA-receptor autoimmune encephalitis."

The group ogled me and a few even let out a few quiet "ooohs" and "ahhhs." My father gritted his teeth and tried to ignore them.

"In about 50 percent of the cases, there is a teratoma in the ovaries. If this is the case, this patient may have her ovaries removed as a precaution."

As the spectators nodded their heads, I caught this somehow, and began to cry.

My father bolted from his seat. This was the first time he had heard anything about my ovaries being removed, and he certainly didn't want either of us hearing it from this kid. A born fighter and a strong man for his age (or for any other age), my dad bum-rushed the scrawny young physician and pointed a finger in his face.

"You get the fuck out of here right now!" His voice bounced around the hospital room. "Never come back. Get the fuck out of the room."

The young doctor's confidence deflated. Instead of apologizing, he waved his hand, urging the other interns to follow him toward the door, and made his escape.

"Forget you heard that, Susannah," my dad said. "They have no idea what the hell they're talking about."

CHAPTER 32

90 PERCENT

That same day, a dermatologist arrived and conducted a full-body skin exam to check for melanoma, which took about thirty minutes because my body is covered in moles. But after a thorough search, the dermatologist concluded that, happily, there was no sign of melanoma. That evening, they wheeled me down, yet again, to the second-floor radiology department, where they would conduct an ultrasound of my pelvis in search of a teratoma.

I am awakened, even though I hadn't been asleep. I had imagined this moment: the time when I would find out the gender of my child. Momentarily, I think, "I hope it's a boy." But the feeling passes. I would be happy with either a girl or a boy. I can feel the cool metal of the transducer against my belly. My chest wall leaps up into my throat in reaction to the cold. It was almost exactly how I imagined it to be. But then again not at all.

Distraught by the first ultrasound, I refused a transvaginal one, the more invasive pelvic examination. Still, even from the imperfect first test, there was good news: no sign of a teratoma. The bad news was that, ironically, teratomas were *good* news, because those with them tend to improve faster than people without them, for reasons researchers still don't understand.

Dr. Najjar arrived the next morning alone and greeted my parents as if they were old friends. Now that they had identified the disease, and knew that there was no teratoma, it was time to figure out what treatment could save me. If he miscalculated, I might never recover. He had spent the night deliberating about what to do, waking up in sweats and rambling to his wife. He had finally decided to act with abandon. He didn't want to wait for things to worsen; I was already too close to the edge. He delivered the plan of action while tugging at the corners of his mustache, deep in thought.

"We're going to put her on an aggressive treatment of steroids, IVIG treatment, and plasmapheresis," he said. Although he had a terrific bedside manner, sometimes he expected his patients to follow him as if they were trained neurologists.

"What will these all do?" my mother asked.

"It's a three-pronged attack, no stoned turned," Dr. Najjar said, missing the English idiom. "We're going to reduce the body's inflammation with steroids. Then flush the body of the antibodies with plasmapheresis, and further reduce and neutralize the antibodies with IVIG. It leaves no room for error."

"When will she be able to go home?" my dad asked.

"As far as I'm concerned, she could leave tomorrow," Dr. Najjar replied. "The steroids could be taken orally. She could return to the hospital for plasma exchange, and the IVIG treatment, if the insurance company approved it, could be done with a nurse at home. With all these treatments I believe that it's likely Susannah will get back to 90 percent."

Though I don't remember the diagnosis, my parents tell me that when I heard this my demeanor changed, and I seemed bolstered by the news that I would be returning home soon. Dr. Russo noted in my chart that I appeared "brighter," my speech "improved."

Home. I was going home.

The next morning, Saturday, April 18, I was finally discharged. I had been in the hospital for twenty-eight days. Many of the nurses—some of whom had washed me, others who had injected me with sedatives, and a few of whom had fed me when I could not feed myself—came to say their good-byes. Nurses seldom find out how a patient fares after she leaves the hospital, and I was still in a particularly bad place. A small, hunched-over man entered the room holding papers. He had secured an at-home nurse to tend to me and had recommended a clinic where I could receive full-time rehab. My mother took the papers, but only absentmindedly flipped through them; she would address these later. For now, we were going home, and that was all that mattered.

My mom, my dad, Allen, Stephen, and my college friend Lindsey, who had flown in from St. Louis the day before, all grabbed my possessions—stuffed animals, DVDs, clothes, books, and toiletries—and crammed them in clear plastic NYU "Patient's Belongings" bags; they left behind the flowers and magazines. A transport staff worker helped me into a wheelchair as my mom placed slip-on flats on my feet. It was the first time I had worn shoes in a month.

The night before, my dad had made a sign thanking the nurses for their support. He posted it near the elevators:

THANK YOU

On behalf of our daughter Susannah Cahalan, we would like very much to thank the entire staff of the epilepsy floor at NYU Medical Center. We came to you with a difficult and desperate situation, and you responded with skill and compassion. Susannah is a wonderful young woman who deserved your hard work. Her mother and I will forever be in your debt. I cannot think of more meaningful work than what you do every day.

Rhona Nack
Tom Cahalan

My prognosis was still unclear—the projection was only "fair"—and no one could say with any certainty if I would ever get to that optimistic "90 percent," or if I would ever regain any semblance of my former self. But they had a plan. First, I would continue to see Dr. Najjar every other Wednesday. Second, I would get a full-body positron emission tomography scan (PET scan) that creates a three-dimensional image of the body, which is different from MRIs and CT scans because it shows the body in the process of functioning. Third, I would be enrolled in cognitive and speech rehabilitation, and they would arrange for a twenty-four-hour nurse to care for me. Fourth, I would take oral steroids, receive plasma-exchange treatment, and get several more infusions of IVIG. But the doctors were aware that even months after the disease has run its course and immunosuppressants have been worked into the system, antibodies can still persist, making recovery a painful march of two steps forward, one step back.

They gave my mother a list of the medications I would now be taking: prednisone; Ativan, an antianxiety drug used to treat and prevent signs of catatonia; Geodon for psychosis; Trileptal for seizures; Labetalol for high blood pressure; Nexium to deal with the acid reflux caused by the steroids; and Colace for the constipation caused by the combination of all the drugs. Still, in the back of everyone's mind was that 4 percent mortality figure. Even with all of this, with all the proper intervention, people still died. Sure, they had a name for my illness and actions we could all take, but there was still a long uncertain journey ahead.

Stephen, Lindsey, and I filed into Allen's Subaru. When I had been admitted in early March, it was still winter; now it was springtime in New York. We drove back to Summit in silence. Allen turned on the radio, tuning it to a local lite FM station. Lindsey looked over at me to see if I recognized the song.

"Don't go breaking my heart," a man's voice started.

"I couldn't if I tried," a woman's voice returned.

This had been my go-to karaoke song in college in St. Louis. At this point, Lindsey doubted I would remember it.

I began bopping my head out of rhythm, my arms at rigid right angles. I swung my elbows front to back like I was awkwardly cross-country skiing. Was this one of my weird seizure-like moments, or was I dancing to an old favorite? Lindsey couldn't tell.

CHAPTER 33
HOMECOMING

My mom's house in Summit looked particularly striking that spring day, my homecoming. The front lawn was lush with fresh green grass, white azaleas, and the blooms of pinkish-purple rhododendrons and yellow daffodils. The sun beamed down on the aged oak trees that shaded the maroon door at the entrance-way to the stone-front colonial. It was gorgeous, but no one could tell if I even noticed. I certainly don't remember it. I just stared ahead, making that constant chewing motion with my mouth as Allen swerved into the driveway of the place I had called home most of my young adult life.

The first thing that I wanted to do was take a real shower. There were still clumps of glue in my scalp that looked like pebble-sized pieces of dandruff, and I still had the metal staples from the surgery, so I could not be too vigorous with my washing. My mother offered to help, but I refused, determined to do this small thing on my own, at last.

After a half hour, Lindsey headed upstairs to check on me. Through the opening in my bedroom door, she could see me sitting on the bed, freshly showered, with my legs flexed rigidly off the side, fidgeting with the zipper on my black hoodie. I was struggling to connect the zipper with the pull. Lindsey watched for a moment, unsure of what to do; she didn't want to embarrass me by knocking on the door and offering aid, because she knew I didn't like to be babied. But when she saw me go limp, drop the zipper, and begin to sob out of frustration, she headed into the room. She sat down beside me and said, "Here, let me help," zipping up my hoodie in one fluid motion.

. . .

Later that evening, Stephen cooked a pasta dinner as a quiet celebration for my return. Allen and my mom left the house so that
the three of us could have some alone time. My mother was so
relieved that they finally had a name for what ailed me that she
had truly convinced herself the worst was behind us.

After dinner, we sat outside on the back patio. Lindsey and
Stephen made small talk while I stared ahead, as if I didn't hear
them. But when they lit cigarettes, I got up without a word and
walked inside.

"Is she okay?" Lindsey asked.

"Yes, I think she's just adjusting. We should give her a moment
alone."

*They are smoking together. Who knows what else they'll do
together.*

*I grab the home phone. For some reason, I can't remember
my mother's number, so I look it up in my cell phone. Ring, ring,
ring, ring.*

*"You've reached Rhona Nack. Please leave a message after the
beep." BEEP.*

*"Mom," I whisper. "He's going to leave me for her. Please
come home. Please come home and stop them."*

*I pace around and watch him from the kitchen window that
looks out on the patio. He catches my eye and waves. Why does
he want to be with a sick girl? What is he doing here with me? I
look at him waving, certain that I have lost him forever.*

When my mom listened to the voice mail, she panicked: I was
becoming psychotic again. Because Dr. Najjar was often difficult
to reach, she dialed Dr. Arslan's private number, which he had
given her the day before we left the hospital. She was worried that
NYU had let me go home too soon.

"She's acting paranoid," she said. "She believes that her boy-friend is going to run off with her best friend."

This concerned Dr. Arslan. "I'm worried that she may be reen-tering a psychotic state. I would give her an extra dose of Ativan to calm her for the night and then check in with me tomorrow." In my case, though, the return to psychotic behavior was actually a sign of improvement, because the stages of recovery often occur in reverse order: I had passed through psychosis before I got to cata-tonia, and now I had to pass through it again on my road back to normality. Dr. Arslan didn't forewarn us about the progression of the disease, because no one yet knew that people often slid back to psychosis. It would be only two years later, in 2011, when Dr. Dalmau released a paper with a section on that very subject, that the stages of the disease would become widely known.

Lindsey's weekend with me had come to a close. She and our friend Jeff (my karaoke partner in St. Louis), who happened to be in New York for an unrelated trip, were planning to drive the six-teen hours back to St. Louis together. When she called to give him directions, he said he'd like to see me. She warned him I wouldn't be the same.

Jeff rang the doorbell, and my mom invited him inside. He spotted me hovering beneath the staircase, slowly approaching the doorway. He first noticed my smile, a frozen, vacant, idiotic grin that frightened him. I held my arms out, slightly bent, as if pushing my body against a door. Nervously, he smiled and asked, "How are you feeling?"

"Goooooood," I said, drawing out the syllables so much that the one word took several seconds. My lips hardly moved, but I maintained piercingly direct eye contact. He wondered if I was trying to communicate through my stare. It reminded him of a zombie movie.

"Are you happy to be home?"

"Yesssssssss," I said, drawing out the "s" like a strained hiss.

Jeff didn't know what to do next, so he leaned forward and embraced me, whispering in my ear, "Susannah, I want you to know that we're all here for you and thinking of you." I couldn't bend my arms to return the hug.

Lindsey, who stood behind us watching the scene, readied herself for the good-bye. She was not prone to histrionics and hardly ever cried. She had been so stoic throughout the visit, never once letting on how agonizing the stay had been for her, but she couldn't contain herself anymore.

She dropped her luggage on the floor and embraced me. Suddenly I was crying, too.

Lindsey left that morning not knowing if she would ever get her best friend back.

CHAPTER 34

CALIFORNIA DREAMIN'

On April 29, less than two weeks after leaving the hospital, I returned to New York University Medical Center for another week of plasma-exchange treatment. Because my symptoms were no longer considered epileptic but related to autoimmune encephalitis, I was placed on the seventeenth floor: neurology. Unlike the epilepsy unit, this floor in the old Tisch Hospital had not been redone. There were no flat screen televisions, everything seemed dingier, and the patients here seemed older, frailer, and somehow closer to death. A senile woman in a private room at the end of the hall spent her afternoons screaming "PIZZA!" over and over. When my dad asked why, the nurses explained that she loved Fridays, which were pizza days.

I shared a room with an obese black woman named Debra Robinson. Though she suffered from diabetes, the doctors believed that her underlying issues actually stemmed from colon cancer, but they still hadn't confirmed the theory. Debra was so overweight that she was unable to leave her bed and go to the bathroom. Instead, she did her business in a bedpan, periodically filling the room with all sorts of putrid smells. But she apologized every time, and it was impossible to dislike her. Even the nursing staff adored her.

The plasma exchange was done through a catheter inserted directly into my neck. "Oh my god," Stephen said, as he watched the nurse insert the needle. It made a "pop" where it pierced my jugular vein. Holding the catheter in place, the nurse spread heavy tape, the consistency of masking tape, around the catheter to keep it upright, jutting out perpendicularly from the right side of my neck. The tape was so harsh that it left red welts on my skin. Though the catheter was hideously uncomfortable, it had to stay in place for the whole week, over the course of my treatment.

The plasma-exchange process originated with a Swedish dairy cream separator created in the late 1800s that sets apart curds from whey. Scientists were so inspired by this simple machinery that they attempted to use it to separate plasma (the yellow-colored liquid that suspends cells and contains antibodies) from blood (which contains the red and white blood cells). The blood streams into the cell separator, which, like a spin dryer, shakes up the blood, cleaving it into those two components—the plasma and the cells of the blood. Then the machine returns the blood to the body and replaces the original plasma—which is full of the harmful autoantibodies—with a new, protein-rich fluid that does not contain antibodies. Each process takes about three hours. The doctors had prescribed five sessions.

My friends were allowed to come and go as they pleased during this second stay, and they all received specific requests from me: Hannah brought more magazines; my high school friend Jen brought a pumpernickel bagel with butter and tomatoes; and Katie brought Diet Cokes.

On my fourth day in the hospital, Angela arrived for a visit, but she was still startled by how terrible I looked. She later e-mailed Paul that I was "pale, thin, out of it . . . Pretty scary." I still had a long way to go.

It is my last night in the hospital. My roommate Debra just got news: she does have colon cancer, but they caught it early. Debra is celebrating with the nursing staff. They came by to pray with her. I understand her relief, how important it is for your illness to have a name. Not knowing is so much worse. As she prays with the nurses, Debra repeats over and over again, "God is good, God is good."

As I reach to turn out the lights, I feel compelled to say something to her.
"Debra?"
"Yes, dear?"
"God is good, Debra. God is good."

The next morning I was released again, and Stephen took me out on a drive in my mom and Allen's car around Summit. We drove past an old mental institution called Fair Oaks, now a drug rehab center; the high-school lacrosse field where I once played goalie; and Area 51, a house on the outskirts of Summit where our mutual friends lived and partied years ago. When we reached a red light, Stephen turned on the CD player. The tinkling of Spanish flamenco guitars drifted through the speakers.

"All the leaves are brown and the sky is gray. I've been for a walk on a winter's day." He recognized the song; it was one of his favorites, a song that brought him back to his childhood, when his mother used to listen to the Mamas and the Papas with him on the way to run errands. "Stopped into a church, I passed along the way. I got down on my knees and I began to pray."

As if on cue, Stephen and I together belted out the chorus, "California dreamin' on such a winter's day!" For a moment, Stephen took his eyes off the road and glanced at me in astonishment and joy. Finally, here was the confirmation he had been waiting for all these weeks: I was still in there.

PART THREE

IN SEARCH OF LOST TIME

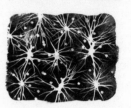

*I had only the most rudimentary sense of existence,
such as may lurk and flicker in the depths of an
animal's consciousness; I was more destitute of human
qualities than the cave-dweller; but then the memory,
not yet of the place in which I was, but of various other
places where I had lived, and might now very possibly
be, would come like a rope let down from heaven to
draw me up out of the abyss of not-being, from which
I could never have escaped by myself.*

MARCEL PROUST, *Swann's Way: In Search of Lost Time*

CHAPTER 35

THE VIDEOTAPE

I insert a silver DVD marked "Cahalan, Susannah" into my DVD player. The video begins. I see myself at the center of the screen, peering into the camera's lens. The hospital gown slips off my left shoulder and my hair is stringy and dirty.

"Please," I mouth.

On the screen, I stare straight ahead, lying on my back as rigid as a statue, my eyes the only feature betraying the manic fear inside. Then those eyes turn and concentrate on the camera, on me now.

Fear of this sort is not something we typically capture in photographs or videos of ourselves. But there I am, staring into the camera as if I'm looking death in the face. I have never seen myself so unhinged and unguarded before, and it frightens me. The raw panic makes me uncomfortable, but the thing that truly unsettles me is the realization that emotions I once felt so profoundly, so viscerally, have now completely vanished. That petrified person is as foreign to me as a stranger, and it's impossible for me to imagine what it must have been like to *be her*. Without this electronic evidence, I could never have imagined myself capable of such madness and misery.

The video self hides her face under the covers, clutching the blanket so hard her knuckles turn white.

"Please," I see myself plead on video again.

Maybe I can help her.

CHAPTER 36

STUFFED ANIMALS

"What did it feel like to be a different person?" people ask.

It's a question that's impossible to answer with conviction, because, of course, during that dark period, I didn't have any real self-awareness that allowed me the luxury of contemplation, the ability to say, "This is who I am. And this is who I was." Still, my memory does retain a few moments from those weeks right after the hospital. It's the closest I can get to recapturing what it was like to feel so utterly divorced from myself.

A few days after my first hospital stay, Stephen drove me to his sister Rachael's house in Chatham, New Jersey.

I remember the view from the car's passenger seat window, driving past the familiar tree-lined suburban streets. I stared out the window as Stephen's free hand held mine. I think he was as nervous as I was about my reintroduction to the real world.

"Good turkey," I said, out of the blue as we turned into the driveway. It was a simple reference to the night in the hospital when Stephen had brought roasted turkey leftovers for me from his family's Easter dinner. He couldn't help but laugh, and I smiled too, though I'm not certain that I was even in on the joke.

Stephen parked the car next to a woodshed under a basketball hoop. I reached for the door handle, but my fine motor skills were still so weak I couldn't open the car door, so Stephen ran to the passenger side and helped me out safely.

Stephen's sisters, Rachael and Bridget, and their young children, Aiden, Grace, and Audrey, were waiting in the yard. They had heard snippets of what had happened, but most of it had been too painful for Stephen to recount, so they were largely unprepared.

Bridget, for one, was shocked by my state. My hair was unkempt, and the angry red bald spot from the biopsy was exposed, complete with metal staples still suturing my skin together. Yellow crust covered my eyelids. I walked unsteadily, like a sleepwalker with my arms outstretched and stiff and my eyes open but unfocused. At the time, I knew that I was not quite myself, but I had no clue how jolting my altered appearance must have been to those who had known me before. Recalling moments like these, which occurred frequently during this tentative stage in my recovery, I wish I could, like a guardian angel, swoop down and help protect this sad, lost echo of myself.

Bridget told herself not to gawk and tried to hide her nervousness, concerned that I would sense it, but it only made her feel more flustered. Rachael and I had met at her daughter's first birthday party back in October, when I had been outgoing and talkative and, unlike many of Stephen's previous girlfriends, not at all intimidated by the closely knit nature of their family. The transformation was extreme, as though a hummingbird had turned into a sloth.

Because they were toddlers, Audrey and Grace didn't notice that anything was wrong. But Aiden, an outgoing six-year-old, kept his distance from me, clearly unnerved by this strange new Susannah, so unlike the one who had played and joked with him only a few months earlier. (He later told his mom that I reminded him of the mentally handicapped man whom he often saw at their public library. Even in that half state, I could sense his apprehension, though I was bewildered by why he seemed so frightened.)

We all stood in the driveway as Stephen handed out the presents. As soon as I'd gotten out of the hospital, I felt compelled to give away the stuffed animals that had accumulated while I was sick. Grateful as I was for them, they served as plaguing reminders of my childlike state, so I wanted to purge myself of them by handing them off as gifts to the kids. Aiden said a quick thank-you and stood behind his mother as the two girls hugged my leg, each with their own high-pitched "Thank you!"

This initial memory, my first of many interactions with the outside world to come, lasted a mere five minutes. After Stephen handed out the presents, the conversation lulled, as everyone around me struggled internally to keep the superficial flow of words going while also concentrating on ignoring the obvious pink elephant in the room: my shocking state. Would I always be like this? Normally I would have attempted to cover up the silences with my own banter, but today I couldn't. Instead I stood mute and unemotional, internally desperate to escape from this painful reunion.

Stephen was highly attuned to my growing unease, so he put his hand on the small of my back and guided me to the security of the car that would return us to the inner sanctum of our little protected world at home. Though the scene was brief and largely undramatic, and may seem insignificant in the overall scheme of things, it is branded into my mind as a key moment in the initial stage of recovery, viciously pointing out how painful and long the road to full recovery would be.

Another homecoming stands out for me during that same hazy posthospital period: the first time I saw my brother after the hospital. While my life had changed forever, James had been completing his freshman year at the University of Pittsburgh. Though he had begged to visit me, my parents had remained adamant that he complete the year. When school finally ended, my father traveled to Pittsburgh to help bring my brother home, and over the course of the six-hour drive, Dad shared what he could about the past few months.

"Be ready for this, James," my father warned him. "It's shocking, but we need to focus on the positive."

I was out of the house with Stephen when they arrived. My father let James off in the driveway, because my parents, though on far better terms than before, were still not friendly enough for home visits. James watched a Yankees game while he anxiously

evaporated, fear turned to rage, and I resolved to go through these creatures with a mindlessness I wish I could have found more often in my
life. I had no intention of overthinking my circumstances and trying to
reason with a pack of dogs.

They were losing their little fuzzy minds. Behind them, directly
along my line of travel, were two rows of three or four mobile homes,
and I was going to have to walk right between them, well within the
two-hundred-meter limit.

I grabbed my toy rifle by the barrel and started swinging the butt
like a baseball bat as I walked slowly in my own little valley of death. I
knew if I ran they would be on me like stink on shit. And I'd go back
to Ranger school before I walked back down the cliff I had just scaled.
Swinging in a wide arc, I plodded my way into the trailer park. I never
got a good look at any of the dogs, but the occasional yelp as my rifle
butt connected with one confirmed that they were getting close enough
to bite me.

I was sure that all the commotion we made—my cussing the dogs
and their howling, barking, and crying—would certainly bring someone to a window or make a door open. Every trailer was lit from within,
and the satellite dishes told me they had televisions.

Apparently, the entertainment inside was pretty good. Not one
person ever appeared. My passage took several minutes, and then it
seemed I had crossed a magical line. Inexplicably, the dogs left me,
and I continued on until I was sure I was out of their range. I entered
woods, took a knee, and pulled hard from a canteen. I was mad at the
dog attack, and I drew focus from the anger. I replaced the bulb in my
flashlight, checked the map, and stumbled in the dark for a couple of
hours. I decided I was not going to sleep until I collapsed. I had to make
back the time.

I came out of the woods into a large open field. I checked my compass and discovered it'd be at least a mile before I hit forest again. Climbing a barbed-wire fence, I felt dizzy. I noticed the trees, dark shadows
in the night. They joined me as I walked past, looking as if they were
walking along.

The hallucination lasted for only a few moments, but I knew my fun meter had exploded. I pulled my sleeping bag out and threw it open on the ground. I took off my boots, crawled in, and looked at the gray clouds passing through a break in the canopy.

I blinked, and when I came to, the sun was shining brightly on me. I climbed out of my bag, stretched, changed socks, put instant coffee in my mouth, and washed it down. With breakfast behind me, I made my way to what I hoped was my last point. Straight-line distance, I had covered fifty kilometers over the last two days. Add 20 percent for changes in elevation, and it was closer to sixty clicks.

I walked up to the point sitter, who regarded me with what might be described as depraved disregard if he had known what I had just done to get to that point. We repeated the ritual of the previous days. I waited with dread for the part of the liturgy where he says, "Your next point is . . ."

"Ready to copy?"

"Yes."

"Your next point is . . ."

I wanted to weep as I wrote down the letters and numbers that defined a spot on my map seven kilometers away. I refilled my canteens, added fresh rations, changed my socks by his fire, and headed out. My legs felt like lead and my feet were cannonballs welded to the end of them.

I did two miles on black asphalt with the sun straight overhead.

When I left the pavement, I crossed open fields until I ran into hills with gated gravel roads. With the gates closed, the roads barred the cadre from patrolling. I climbed the fence and flew down the rocky way, bouncing with a bunny-hop stride. The road turned, and I continued into the trees with a mile to go. In an hour of breaking brush, I could smell smoke and knew I was close. I had a sense based on the distance I had covered over the last three days that I should be at my last point.

I looked at the empty knife sheath on my web belt, the only proof that I had lost anything other than my glasses. No one would remember if I wore glasses or not at the start. They weren't an issue. The knife sheath was different. While the knife was personal property, its absence was manifestly obvious in a culture that treated big knives with near phallic respect. I threw the leather carrier on the ground and kept moving. No one would know whether I had started with a knife or not.

I approached the man who I prayed was my last point sitter.

"Name," he said.

"Schwalm," I replied. His eyebrows arched, and he reached for his radio. I dropped my ruck and sat on it, my dog club across my knees.

"He's here," he said into the handset.

I wondered if I had been spotted on the road and failed *in absentia*.

I couldn't hear the other end of the conversation, but it was brief.

"Roger. I'll tell him." He put the handset back on the radio and looked at me. "You're done, sir, but they were expecting you here a lot sooner. The commander wanted to know when you got in."

"Did he say why?"

"No. I think he just wanted to know you had made it."

That day, I learned that utter disregard for professional well-being as characterized by ignoring the rules can bring professional success. That was not what the Army had taught me up to that point.

I finished Trek with twelve hours to spare. I spent the night at my last point and awoke to the point sitter's radio announcing the end of the exercise. Four others had come in during the night and made a circle around the fire. The trucks came for us, and we headed back to Fort Bragg.

Triumphantly, I came home from the land nav. I was going to my last phase of training after a long weekend. My achievements would not diminish. I was not going to be a loser, not now, not yet, anyway. I threw my ruck into the garage and headed for the shower.

Later, pulling hard on an ice-cold beer, noshing fried chicken and aspirin, I settled in front of the television. I turned to CNN and watched slack-jawed as dead American Special Operations personnel were dragged through the streets of a city I could not find on a map. My friends, other students aspiring to be Special Operations personnel, called me and asked if I was watching. Yes, I replied. Thank God they didn't ask me if I understood what I was watching.

Friendly dead, eighteen. A Ranger company of over 120 men had taken 80 percent casualties. That had never happened, not since World War II.

Soldiers with the weight of the most powerful war machine history had known behind them, with technology the likes of which warfare had never seen, faced a dark, mostly uneducated sea of men, women, and children who only knew that something terrible was unfolding.

For one period of darkness, fighting men, bona fide commandos, the best America could muster, struggled in a maelstrom of violence that tested them to their cores. They all passed. They didn't all live.

Watching the news, I grimaced as I recalled my pity party in the creek.

Of the thirty or so officers who went out, we lost one officer to Trek. He was found standing too close to a house. Not walking on a road, not catching a ride, not doing anything but coming out of a tree line near a house and being seen by a cadre member. If I'd been caught on the road, you wouldn't be reading this book.

The British SAS have a good motto: Who dares, wins.

Sometimes.

EIGHT

AFTER A FEW DAYS' RECOVERY from Trek through classroom instruction, we headed back to Camp Mackall to join our enlisted counterparts who were now steeped in their specialty crafts—weapons, engineering, communications, or medicine. Here we were formed into teams that would stay together for the remainder of the course.

My student team was composed of four officers (one of whom had been recycled from the previous class as a leadership failure) and eight enlisted personnel. Some guys went by last names, some by first, but the informality of our meeting set the tone for the rest of my time on active duty. Bottom line: We were all students, no one closer to being an SF soldier than another. Yes, there was rank, but I quickly realized while talking to the enlisted students that their time in training had made them specialists in their focus areas: weapons, demolition, communications, and medicine. As we moved into the metal huts that had housed me five years before during the selection phase and sat around getting to know each other, I heard them discuss the seriousness of their decision to go SF—what they knew they would have to do to endure the last phases of training and what they thought they brought to the team. No one mentioned rank. Everyone talked of newly acquired skills born of the tough enforcement of standards. What was on our collars didn't matter as much as what was in our heads. In SF, it doesn't matter who you are, the only thing that matters is what you can do.

We were a mixed-bag team. Dave and Mike (two other officers) were field artillery and infantry, respectively. Gus, also an officer and from the previous rotation, was distinctive on several counts. One, he was African-American. Two, he was built like a college linebacker, which is what he had been. (He had a Greek omega letter branded into his left arm that was the size of a horseshoe.) Three, he was coming from Signal Corps, not the bastion of maneuver warfare, but you can't do without them. Four, he had a brother who was already in SF as an enlisted guy. Five—and this distinction didn't surface until days later—as a function of his deeply held religious beliefs, if he told you something, it was true. If he told you that he was going to jump on a hand grenade as it came through the door, you could be certain that should one roll in he would be in the air headed for it. So, on the one hand, he was physically imposing enough to make most people on the planet think twice before starting an altercation with him. On the other, he wasn't a Ranger; and worse, he was Signal Corps, known in the pejorative as a signal weenie, less manly than, say, a bratwurst. I didn't discover the racism he was facing until later in our training. One thing to note: If you see a group picture of Special Operations Forces, of any ilk, the demographics are usually about as diverse as an Amish picnic.

As a recycle (the term we used for guys on the second try), Gus was both guide and target. He could tell us where the mines were and who to trust. But we all knew that as a recycle he had a big red dot with black concentric circles on his back. Once the cadre had declared him unfit for graduation, the rest of them watched for confirmation of the indictment during his next attempt. Recycles were marked men.

Our enlisted personnel—comprised of two medics, two commo sergeants, two engineers, and two weapons specialists—had been everything from mechanics to infantrymen before passing SFAS. Ramos (built like the martial arts expert and movie star Bruce Lee) was the most senior, already a staff sergeant. I noticed our cadre would eye him intensely. Officers were not expected to be experts in anything except mission planning on an SF team. NCOs, on the other hand, were all about expertise. By the time Ramos had been on a team for two years, he would be eligible for promotion to sergeant first class. If NCOs are the backbone of the Army, an SFC is considered the spinal cord of an A-team. Usually, an SFC has many years on a team and several deployments. Ramos would be relatively junior in experience but he would hold a position of authority due his rank. The cadre didn't like it.

Ironically, what should have been considered a strength for Ramos was his reserved nature. Special Forces likes to tout itself as the quiet professionals. Ramos was very quiet—sniper quiet. When he said something, it was important. Otherwise he just sat and listened. Throughout our training, the cadre misconstrued his silence as lack of leadership potential. I saw him as a man who knew what he was and didn't need to impress anyone with his powers of rhetoric. I was thankful that we became friends during this phase of our military careers because he saved me from being bounced from the course for a dumb mistake, one that could not be forgiven. I will describe that later.

We spent several days rehearsing small-unit tactics so that we could learn to function well as a team. The ranks we wore lost their conventional power as we learned to act as one, each bringing his special skills, not his pay grade. None of us ever tried to pull rank, and I never saw it in any of the other teams either.

We demonstrated mastery of basic infantry skills: moving through the woods at night, setting ambushes, conducting raids on targets, establishing patrol bases in the swamps around Mackall, and basically reliving Ranger school but with one major difference. Where Ranger school sought to teach and evaluate leadership using small-unit tactics as a medium for analysis, the SF Q course taught small-unit tactics with the intent that we master them by the end. Our leadership skills were under the microscope as well, but the actual technique, tactics, and procedures of planning and executing combat operations were the focus. As a result, guys with Ranger tabs were being told that they were not patrolling well. Such criticism is like telling a priest he's praying incorrectly.

In Ranger school, as long as everything was done in accordance with the Ranger handbook (the Bible of small-unit tactics), it didn't matter how well it was done. The Ranger course was intended to train soldiers in leadership, the finer points of small-unit tactics coming as a consequence of the medium used to do such leader training.

The SF qualification course sought to make us experts in guerrilla warfare, and we were expected to be masters of small-unit tactics upon graduation and for one very simple reason. SF teams do not normally conduct combat operations with other SF teams except in a support role. Rangers usually deploy in a battalion-size organization—a thousand, roughly—and usually fight in groups of thirty-five or more. At this phase in our career, the SF officer students had the leadership piece well developed. We needed to learn the tactics that would keep us alive if we had to lead indigenous troops who may have little in the way of technology. Tactics and tricks of the trade were our focus.

While our engineers showed the team how to increase the lethality of explosives, our medics explained how to rig an IV bag to administer it to another teammate quickly. Our weapons sergeants gave us classes in field maintenance of weapons, and the commo guys showed us how to make antennas out of wire, plastic spoons, and old D-cell batteries. Our training cadre offered pointers along the way, and while we were constantly under observation, I could tell when the instructor crossed over from being an objective evaluator to an earnest SF guy who wanted to share what he had learned.

I drank it in. This was the soldiering I wanted to master.

I loved my tank, the big heater with the exhaust that could boil a cup of water in five minutes. I will always thrill to the memory of my men preparing their vehicles in the dark before we launched in Desert Storm, the turrets spinning in the dark as the gunners bled the hydraulic lines of any air bubbles, the *ka-chink* of machine guns being loaded and charged, the deafening roar of the cannon spitting a red tracer thousands of yards across the sand, the camaraderie of sitting on the back deck cleaning weapons and listening to stories.

But I wanted to know if I could make it without being connected to the Army's umbilical cord and with the latitude of being deployed into a situation where my boss may not even be on the same continent.

As fall approached, we enjoyed crisp, dry weather as we spent a few nights freezing in foxholes where we demonstrated that we knew the basics of infantry tactics. We took turns being in charge of missions, taking patrols from the planning phase to execution and then conducting an after-action review. Also, we were back on jump status. Some of our training missions began with falling from a plane at night while wearing about 150 pounds of tactical equipment and parachute. But each mission was always couched in the context of working with people who did not speak English and did not have logistics like we thought normal in our own Army. The idea of leading guerrillas or the troops of another country's army was still abstract to me. But this concept would soon seem less far removed.

Over the course of several weeks, our feet continued to toughen to the point that no one got a blister, even after walking in wet boots for days. Once I quickly turned around and surprised myself when something on my back banged into a tree. I had forgotten I was wearing a seventy-pound rucksack. We sat for hours drinking sodas and cleaning weapons after a patrol and would eat together in the Camp Mackall mess hall, chowing like condemned men. Here we would tell our stories: about girls, parties, cars, life before the Army, where we wanted to go after the Q course. By the time Thanksgiving came, we were a team.

The last week was instruction in the art of unconventional warfare. We talked about the seven phases of an American-sponsored insurgency, which is politically the core of UW. We would displace a government or whatever is running the country by training, advising, and equipping fighters whose goal of changing the status quo through force of arms aligns with U.S. national interests. The phases—preparation, initial contact, infiltration, organization, buildup, employment, and transition—are intuitive. The president signs a finding or declares war, allowing U.S. forces to go someplace outside the country and partake in violence to achieve a national goal. The secretary of Defense (SECDEF) with a staff numbering in the tens of thousands, basically the whole Pentagon and the other commands scattered around the world, conclude that the best way to do this involves UW. There are only two groups of folks that do UW: the CIA and the Army Green Berets. Since the president told DOD to do it, CIA is in a supporting role. (To be clear, this supporting role is tantamount to the safe cracker's role among other thieves in a bank heist. Nobody's getting in without him. More on that later.)

From there, one of the five SF groups is alerted. Each group is regionally oriented. That is, if you go to 7th SF Group at Bragg, you're going to hear people speaking Spanish in the halls of the headquarters, as their focus is Central and South America. 5th SF Group has responsibility for the Middle East, 1st Group the Pacific, 10th Group Europe, and 3rd Group had Africa and the Caribbean. Some of this orientation has changed since the September 11 attacks, but that's how it stood in 1993.

Once alerted, the group staff would allocate teams to the mission, and then intelligence from the target area would begin to flow in. This is where the CIA's role is the linchpin in the creation of the machine for the mission. The CIA has the standing authority to be everywhere all the time. Not so DOD. If the CIA chooses not to share something with us, oh well.

With whatever intelligence is provided, when the SECDEF says "Go," a bunch of Green Berets put all their stuff on metal pallets and fly to a staging base and then flow into the target area. After they link up with the guerrillas, they assess their needs, meet their needs, train them, and then get them to the right fight at the right time in order to achieve the most effect with the indigenous forces available. Once we win, we transition these battle-hardened fighters to functioning members of society—say, dairy farmers—do some high-fives on the tarmac, and then head for home.

Now imagine Santa Claus and the Easter Bunny riding double on a unicorn and that's about how close the doctrine of UW relates to reality. We didn't know that. Yet.

The most outdoor fun we had during the UW instruction was the hands-on training that showed us how to establish clandestine bases for covert aircraft. We learned how long each plane that might support us required for landing and takeoff and how to mark drop zones for bundles of supplies. A plane that could do short takeoff and landing (STOL) spent the day dropping supplies and landing on our primitive efforts at making a secret airport. The pinnacle of excitement came during the message pickup (MPU) class.

I would never have believed we would be expected to do this if we hadn't been trained in it. In order to get the names of the guerrillas to other agencies in the U.S. government, we had to make a roster and place it in a container about the size of a small coffee can. The can is connected to several meters of white rope, maybe a half inch thick. This rope is suspended between two twenty-one-foot poles, making a loop big enough to drive a Greyhound bus through. The plane lines up an approach between the poles and deploys a small boat anchor on twenty feet of similar white rope from an open door. The plane approaches with the boat anchor trailing and, with students holding the poles and looking down as if in prayer, snatches the loop from the poles. A man in the back of the plane hauls in the rope with the anchor now connected to the loop with the can. We were advised that there had only been one fatality during all the years of training in this technique—a captain who had been nailed by a wheel when the pilot flew too close to the ground.

One thing during the UW class instruction that we danced around was the importance of an agent network. We talked about the need for assets throughout the area of operations, but we never discussed where these agents would come from. Did we recruit them? Would they be turned over to us from the CIA? (After experiences later in my SF career, I have to laugh at the thought of a CIA officer turning an agent over to an SF guy, but I guess it could happen. I would imagine such an officer would either be reassigned to custodial duties at Langley or just discover that his access badge didn't work anymore.) The logistics of an agent network was never explained as we completed our classroom instruction.

This omission was necessary, as it would have touched upon tradecraft, those techniques specific to handling paid agents and the necessary clandestine communication skills, and we had personnel from other countries in our course. Still, I imagined the cadre sitting around after the students left discussing how they had just given us classes on parenting but neglected to explain the act of copulation.

"Boy, are they in for a big surprise."

We loaded the trucks that would take us back to Bragg for a four-day Thanksgiving break. Shaking hands, we wished the best to each other. We knew that when we came back, it would be for the last phase, the unconventional warfare practical exercise, the application of the classes we had just finished. Our green berets were within reach; graduation was only thirty days away: December 18, 1993.

The only thing I can remember about the holiday is that I ate everything that wasn't nailed down.

NINE

WE GATHERED at the appointed place and time, stomachs somewhat bloated from a four-day weekend of eating, and waited for the buses to take us back to Mackall. Each man shared news of his holiday. As most Americans headed to the mall for the official Christmas shopping season of 1993, we headed for the woods. Two officers received ultimatums from their wives: Either their husbands voluntarily terminate the course or they were filing for divorce. One terminated. The other one was getting on the bus with us. I considered how awful this horrible frame of mind such a crisis created must have been combined with the last phase of training.

The last phase had a name, Robin Sage, and had existed in one guise or another since 1964. We had heard the stories throughout our entire time training. Named after former Army colonel Jerry Sage, a World War II veteran and Office of Strategic Services officer who taught unconventional war tactics, Robin Sage was and is the only UW training event in the Department of Defense and has a cast of hundreds supporting it. The entire city of Troy, North Carolina, and its surrounding area becomes "Pineland." In Pineland, we would test our unconventional warfare skills that we had yet to learn. The scenario made Pineland a contested front between a government hostile to U.S. national interests and a network of guerrilla fighters that we would be sent to lead. This capacity to train, advise, and equip foreign forces is what makes a Green Beret a Green Beret.

We discussed and speculated this last phase that faced us. One thing that cropped up was our role in the exercise. During this training, while we were all trying to convince the cadre we were competent enough to be sent as an SF group, we were also role-players in this exercise fulfilling the requirements of our specialty (that is, weapons, demolition, communications, and medical). Role-players may seem an inappropriate title, as each man was operating within the purview of his specialty, but the reality was that none of us had ever performed his specialty in an unconventional warfare environment. We were learning and practicing something that had been done by only a handful of SF soldiers in real-world situations, almost all of them in clandestine or covert settings in Southeast Asia and Central America and usually while working for the CIA. Unlike a real SF team, where close association over years allowed for cross-training in the different specialties, our student team had nothing as a frame of reference except the UW training we would receive and the individual specialty training each had acquired in the preceding months. If the engineer recommended something stupid, like leaving behind a particular piece of kit, the rest of us would go blithely along.

But we figured since we weren't the first to go into the training and certainly not the worst to ever try, we should just get into it as deeply and intimately as we could.

The cadre ensured that just such a focus filled our minds. We got off the bus, walked into our little steel house, and disappeared into the world of Pineland.

TEN

AN SF TEAM preparing for any mission goes into a strictly enforced isolation. None of us had undergone such a protocol. This type of separation is different from what I experienced in SERE. During most training events, students cannot get to a phone (or, now, the Internet). SF takes this one step further. SF teams in isolation can only speak to other members on the team. Period. There's no contact with other teams; forget calls home.

Escorts, minders of sorts—known as the area specialist team, or AST—become your portal to the outside world. Need to go work out? The SF team would change clothes and along came the AST. Time to eat? Get the AST. The term AST carried over from the 1969 SF manual. The AST was, indeed, supposed to be part of a team that was utterly immersed in the cultural dimensions of the target country and could answer questions about the indigenous people we were about to visit, the ones we would need to have as friends. If the AST didn't have the answer, it knew how to get it. For Robin Sage, the AST guys were just minders when we left our hooch and carried our written questions to the intelligence section played by the cadre.

The no talking to other teams in isolation came from the idea that what we were doing was compartmentalized and there was a need to prevent one team from compromising all the others. Isolation was enforced with draconian seriousness. Legend holds that a member of one student team broke the vow of confidentiality by talking to a cook in the mess hall. The cook asked the student how he wanted his eggs, and the question apparently disarmed the student. After getting the order, the cook smiled behind the glass of the serving line and asked if they were getting ready to head out. The SF candidate, within three weeks of earning a green beret, replied yes. *Compromise.* He didn't get to eat breakfast. The AST escorted him out of the mess hall. He was dropped from the course but allowed to try again with the next class three months later.

The cadre briefed us on the current situation as we began to plan. Pineland had been invaded by a neighboring country, and the indigenous population waged a guerrilla war in response. The similarity between Free French partisan forces during the Nazi invasion during World War II was intentional and represented the best-case political scenario for a UW campaign. A foreign power has invaded a country friendly to the United States, and our measured response was to send advisors and equipment to help the people set themselves free. The cadre provided exhaustive descriptions of the history, belief systems, and culture of Pineland. The goal was to craft an experience that forced students to believe that they were no longer in North Carolina or even in the United States. The people of Pineland were, of course, from the southern United States, and they brought the real-world belief system from that region, including an intense devotion to the tenets of Christian Protestantism. But the scenario imposed an alien cast on to this aspect of the culture. The truck drivers we were to meet weren't deacons at the Forks of Little River Baptist Church; they were shamans, according to the staff, and powerful leaders among our guerrillas. The Pineland culture had been virtually untouched since its creation for the Q course, and it mixed real-world experiences from southeast, southwest, and central Asia, Panama, the Middle East, and west Africa with the NASCAR culture of western North Carolina.

While in isolation, the team divided along military specialties. The engineer studied maps of bridges; the weapons specialist began scouting for clandestine training sites so the guerrillas could practice marksmanship in secret; the communications sergeant cut wire for field antennas; the medic studied the diseases we might face. The officers, meanwhile, began putting everything together into a coherent plan. This plan addressed infiltration (sneaking in, which is in itself an act of war), rendezvous with guerrillas, training and equipping them, fighting alongside them, the overthrow of the occupying power, and then demobilizing the fighters.

In Robin Sage, the cadre engineered a scenario that managed to compress these complex social and operational processes into the timeline of a two-week training cycle. For instance, each day of real time was a month within the exercise. In accelerating the clock in this manner, the training cadre simulates the process by which a real-world A-team would build rapport with a guerrilla force, take it through all the phases of a U.S.-sponsored insurgency, and then go home, all in two weeks.

Under this kind of pressure, we had to become open to many sudden realizations. One followed the adage that amateurs talk of tactics while professionals study logistics. We would not be getting our food from Mother Army. What do the guerrillas eat? Our intelligence indicated that they ate wild game and livestock donated by sympathetic members of the local population. However detestable an MRE might be, each meal had enough calories to allow the fuel-devouring American GI to keep going for a day. After three days, our supply that we had brought would be gone. What if the guerrillas we link up with are hungry? Do we share our chow? What happens if we all run out of food? We could hunt, but that would mean shooting our weapons. Do we need to bring a suppressor for at least one gun so we can shoot with some assurance that we won't be heard?

These thoughts brought home a literal gut-level appreciation of our safe havens. We had to count on the people to let us operate around them; we had to be safe to train, perform medical procedures, teach classes, and take part in other actions necessary to establish and employ a guerrilla army. We had to be able to hide in the wilderness surrounded by people who knew the ground intimately. Our boot prints in the mud would scream that somebody new had shown up. Our expended cartridges (should they be left behind after a fight) had to match those of the guerrillas, and not many people carried the M16A2 automatic rifle with M855 green tip ammunition. The report of our rifles could not be different. The locals could easily hand over evidence of "furriners" if ever we gave them cause—say, by accidentally shooting one of their sons we mistook for a member of the Pineland army. If the people turned against us, we were dead, no matter how good a shot we might be. No safe haven, no active insurgency.

The term "catastrophic loss of rapport" kept popping up. Up to this point, all of us had been raised as members of an Army that didn't care if anybody but the people that sent us liked us. In UW, the concept of rapport compelled us to acknowledge we were entering into a popularity contest with the existing government of Pineland, and the local population was the target audience. Gaining rapport with the guerrillas would be paramount before we could even start training and equipping them. And then rapport with the local population had to follow; this would be our only measure of what we were really fighting for: legitimacy.

How the local population supported the insurgency, actively or passively, would be the "legitimacy meter." The locals probably wouldn't like it if our guerrillas kidnapped young boys to fight, and we wouldn't last too long—probably less than a week. But if we provided medical aid through a clandestine hospital that alleviated the suffering of the locals, they might end up liking us and wanting to help us, by warning us if government troops were patrolling a certain area. The more we talked about it, the more the healing arts began to emerge as the best icebreaker when we contemplated how we would build rapport, and our medics emerged as the essential personnel in our mission. Not the demolition expert, not the weapons specialist; the medic would be the most effective weapon in initiating the process of overthrowing the Pineland forces.

In a way, we would start the campaign with the medics.

Catastrophic loss of rapport could be applied to many relationships. In the context of a UW scenario, it's like a bad divorce, only both sides are armed and dangerous. Rapport is pure art. "Please like me." But, like most relationships that are sure to be subjected to life-and-death crises, the rapport must be sincere, legitimate. Living with our indig made every day a test of our sincerity. One callous remark, an accidental death, hitting the wrong target, or any kind of collateral damage could put us at odds with the very people we had come to liberate. If we lost legitimacy with them, we lost it all. The people need do very little to destroy our efforts; actually they had but to do nothing: stop feeding us, not warn us of checkpoints, fail to provide early warning. Not helping us was actually safer for the people of Pineland, given that the fictional forces chasing us had complete freedom of movement to enforce their will. We were hiding in the woods like a bunch of criminals.

Rapport became the focus of much of our mission planning. Little things I had never thought about rose up as potentially undermining rapport. Normally, when our intelligence told us that nerve gas had been used in a theater of operations, we would carry protective masks. The cadre told us that Pineland had used gas to flush out the guerrillas from their bases in the wilderness. But the fact that we could not bring enough gas masks for everyone required us to leave rubber face saunas behind. You can't very well build rapport with someone, or swear a blood oath with him, only for him to ask why you have protection that he doesn't have.

I tried to imagine a conversation with the guerrilla leader if nerve agents were introduced. "Hey, chief, based on my observation, that last artillery barrage left some of your guys stepping and jerking like they're being electrocuted. I'm going to guess that we just got gassed. Excuse me while I don my pro mask and believe me when I say I'm really sorry."

That didn't brief well. The question we came to ask ourselves was: "Is their cause worth dying for?" We hoped the answer was yes, and therein lay our hope that the indig would see our commitment, and, thus, we would gain legitimacy.

We were given five days to plan a mission that would last at least a year and required us to employ critical thinking in an operational environment that we had only begun to understand. One planning consideration that had never cropped up before was money.

As soldiers in the conventional Army, we touched money that was our own. Period. The U.S. government did not give combat soldiers a bag of money to do with as they pleased, or at least without someone providing oversight. In the world of UW, as in any insurgency, after ideology, money was the lifeblood of the enterprise. We were given 10,000 don, a don being the currency of Pineland, in the form of paper money, not unlike what you might find in a Monopoly game. Our guerrillas and others helping the fight would require payment. We were taught that we may have to buy weapons on the black market, buy gas for a truck ride, or provide payroll for our guerrillas. We divided the don into bundles among us to hide in our rucksacks, the same place where we hid our socks, rations, and everything else we carried.

One event that really stuck with me during isolation was a brief but poignant exchange between Captain Gus and an SF sergeant, a member of the cadre assigned to us for Robin Sage. It was in the middle of the week, and we were in the teeth of mission planning. The walls of our hooch were covered with maps and lists of things to do. The heat was on inside, and we were in T-shirts, busy planning a U.S.-sponsored insurgency, when I heard the sergeant first class say something to Gus. They were standing behind me, and Gus asked him to repeat himself.

"I said, don't feel bad if you don't make it this time either. Most black guys don't."

I turned to see Gus's eyes getting large, and the good sergeant demonstrating clearly that he didn't realize his life was in danger.

"What do you mean?" Gus asked. The Omega brand on his arm seemed to grow.

"I mean, look around SF, sir. A lot of black guys don't make it," the sergeant continued. "You just don't see many black guys."

"Why do you think that is?" Gus's nose flared across his face, cheekbone to cheekbone. It was easy to imagine him reading the actions of a quarterback, and then skewering the guy, maybe putting him in the hospital. Sergeant Clueless, athletic but not even close to Gus's size or demeanor, continued along a path of self-destruction.

"I don't know," he replied thoughtfully, like a guest on a talk show, oblivious to the sword of Damocles about to drop. "I've heard it's because you guys don't swim good. Or just don't swim."

Gus was livid. I hazarded an ass-whipping and stepped in.

"Gus, please step outside with me. I need to talk to you," I tried.

"No," he said emphatically, never taking his eyes off the NCO.

"I want him to explain his theory as to why a lot of black guys don't make it."

I thought I saw the lights come on inside this instructor's head. "Hey, sir, don't get mad. I'm just calling it like I see it." False alarm—he still didn't get it.

Realizing that Gus might just beat everybody's ass if further provoked, I changed my focus to the sergeant generating all the bad feelings.

"Sergeant," I said, "I think we need to change the topic. I don't think this conversation is going to help anybody."

"Whatever," he replied, and he walked out of the hooch, still clueless.

Before Gus could speak, I said, "I'm taking this up the chain. I will talk to the commander out here if I have to, but you will get an apology. That was utterly disrespectful."

Gus calmed down, and we kept planning. Another NCO came into the hooch to check on us, and I took a chance that maybe he was not a Klan sympathizer and pulled him aside. When I explained what happened, he whistled and said he would be right back. The team knew the topic, and we waited to see what would happen. Eventually, the NCOIC (noncommissioned officer in charge) came to our hooch and asked me to step outside. He outranked everybody in the cadre except the commander, who was a major. When I recounted the events in question, he asked for me to send Gus out.

Later, Gus told me that a sincere apology had been made and that he was good to go. Thanks to our amateur anthropologist in the guise of a training cadre, we lost more than a few man hours of planning time for the most important training exercise of our careers up to that point. We continued planning and rehearsing, and even with the lost time we felt we were ready for game day. But I never forgot how nonchalant the sergeant's racism had been. He really believed black people couldn't swim.

On the first day of December, 1993, the team assembled to brief our UW plan. Upon entering our hooch, the SF major responsible for this phase of training asked me my social security number.

When I told him, he smiled and congratulated me for being picked up early for major. He said I could break isolation to call my wife and tell her the good news. On the way to a phone, I had only one thought: *I'm screwed.* Now I would go to an SF unit as a promotable captain, a status only conferred on SF officers who had already successfully commanded an A-team. I thought: *Who is going to want me? I'm not even Ranger qualified, and if I graduate this course, I will be a promotable SF captain with not one day on a team.*

We presented our plan to cadre who role-played as senior officers. They asked questions and provided insights into considerations we had overlooked before approving it. Dazed, I went through the motions while my mind tried to understand what my new status would mean to my career in Special Forces. At the conclusion of our marketing pitch begging the boss to send us, the cadre explained I would be the officer in charge for infiltration. The others would get their turn after we linked up with the guerrillas.

We spent the afternoon preparing for our night jump into Pineland. We rigged our rucks and weapons for static-line parachute drop, rehearsed actions in the drop zone, and waited for dark. Once our feet hit the ground, we would be armed Alices in our own Wonderland.

ELEVEN

THE PLANES WARMED UP on the runway at Camp Mackall airfield, sitting like giant gray ghosts, screaming in the dark. We shuffled up the ramp of the C-130 and drank in the exhaust of jet fuel. As my team was scheduled to be the first to jump, we were last to load into the plane. I looked into the aircraft and saw that every seat had been taken. Cadre ordered us to sit down on the lowered ramp. Like turtles, we rocked back on our chutes, rucks between our legs, while a wide yellow cargo strap was passed across us. So, strapped to the partially opened tailgate as human duffel bags, we would fly into Pineland like riding in the back of a pickup truck, only faster and higher. On signal, we would have to take off the strap, climb to the door of the plane, and jump into the night, floating into the fields and farms below. During prejump, the cadre let us know that the local electric company had cut the power from the high-tension lines to prevent students from landing in the wires and being incinerated. The locals might be without lights while the jump was made.

Before takeoff, somewhere in the dark, someone—I never found out who—spotted my team secured like dead deer to the plane's ramp and ordered us off. We waddled back into the shed where we had rigged our gear, sat down, and listened as the planes left us behind.

After midnight, our cadre arrived in a truck, told us to derig (military parlance for "take the chute off"), and get in the truck. We had mixed emotions about not jumping and driving by truck to the link-up point instead. Some of us wanted the bragging rights of jumping in; others were just happy not to risk injury after months of training. What would have been a ten-minute plane ride became a two-hour journey in the back of an old Army truck wearing all our hot gear as we fought the wind chill.

Upon disembarking, we moved past signs that indicated we were entering Uwharrie National Forest. We walked a mile or so from the road, established a perimeter, and took turns trying to sleep. I watched the sky start to lighten and checked the map. We were about two miles from the link-up point, where we were to meet guides who would take us to the clandestine guerrilla base. I asked Gus if this was how it had played out during his earlier rotation, and he said yes.

Robert Jordan, a member of cadre who had been with us during previous weeks, would stay with us throughout the exercise. Staff Sergeant Jordan had become the most important person in my life at that point. If he said Captain (on the promotion list to Major) Schwalm was fit to command an SF A-team, in three weeks I would have a green beret on my head and a long tab on my left shoulder announcing that I was qualified for the Special Forces. If not, I was done. It was that simple.

I expected this link-up stage to be something of a formality. "Hi, I'm Tony Schwalm. We're from the United States, and we're here to help." Then we'd walk a couple of miles to a base camp, play the rapport game, and then get into the serious business of showing off how adept we had gotten with our training.

Guess again.

Jordan told me to proceed to the link-up point, somewhat artificially, as the time was off, but I spread the word to the team and moved us down a trail. I spotted two guys in civilian clothes carrying rifles ahead of us. I stopped the team, and we made a loose perimeter in the woods. As I cautiously approached the pair, they eyed me like I was a black man seeking admission to a KKK rally.

I opened with the innocuous sentence intended as the exchange of bona fides, the sign and countersign that we are all who we say we are. To the outsider, the ritual may seem contrived, as we were twelve American soldiers, each with an assault rifle or a machine gun and a ruck on his back that was at least seventy pounds (the medics hauled close to eighty pounds apiece), and these two guys just happened to be in the middle of nowhere waiting for something. It didn't matter if they were double agents. We were there and had been seen. If they didn't answer correctly, I would have to kill them and make lots of noise. Unless something else indicated otherwise—like Jordan telling me not to—we would then go immediately into unassisted evasion, sending blind radio messages along the way, which for us meant walking south to the next country, represented on the map as South Carolina.

The year before, a student team had done just that and ended up evading detection by everybody, including the cadre, for seventy miles. They called the exercise headquarters where the cadre orchestrates Robin Sage after three days of evading and called for extraction exactly in accordance with their plan. They were heroes for pulling it off.

Even if the guys on the trail did answer correctly, they could still lead us into a trap. We were at their mercy and had no one but the twelve of us to rely on. One of the guerrillas responded to the challenge ("Do you have a match?") with the appropriate response ("I don't smoke."). Like the puppetmaster dressed in black, Jordan stood off to the side, observing me while writing something in a little green book.

"Get your people up here. You don't have to guard nothing here. You're surrounded anyway," one of them said as I approached. I looked at Gus. His face said this wasn't what had happened last time. If we really were surrounded, I could get my whole team killed by acting like Custer at Little Bighorn. I called the team forward.

"Give us all your ammo and maps."

I was dumbfounded. The man playing the role of our guide read my face and began to immerse himself in the part.

"We're not going anywhere until we have all your ammo and maps," he yelled. "We don't know who you, we don't trust you, and we're not letting you anywhere near our camp until we know you can't hurt anybody or find your way back."

I looked at Gus and the other officers. Shrugs, arched eyebrows, and headshakes told me nobody had any better idea. I looked at Jordan, who returned my stare as blankly as a statue.

"Okay, men, dump the ammo." We made a pile of loaded magazines and belts of machine-gun ammo. Our guides put all of it into a heavy-gauge bag. We passed our maps to them, and the maps went in the bag as well.

"Now, if we find out that anybody held out on us, whoever it is, that guy is getting shot."

We looked at each other and made noises to indicate that we weren't holding out on them.

"You better not be," he warned. "Let's go."

We walked in single file along well-marked trails, whispering to each other, seeking affirmation. Our guides carried canteens and the stuff they'd taken from us. We were under heavy rucks and had to step quickly to keep the pace. After four hours, we were drenched with sweat, and some on the team were beginning to fade back. Our guides yelled at us, accused us of being weak, and openly questioned whether we were fit enough to be fighting with them.

My temper rose. Something was wrong. According to the scenario, we had been invited by the leadership of the insurgency to come. We complied with the guerrillas' strict sense of security. Now we were just being walked into the ground. I called for a rest halt.

Our guides made faces while explaining that we were holding them up and that we needed to get to the base camp. I asked how much farther.

"When we get there," came the acid response.

I choked back the "Fuck you too, pal" and kept going.

Jordan stood to the side and watched with a face of detached apathy.

"Let's go, c'mon. We ain't got all day," the nameless guides hurled at us.

We struggled to our feet, helped those with the heavier loads up, and continued. The sun was disappearing behind a ridge when we were instructed to stop. We knew we were close. One of the guides stayed and one left, presumably to announce us to the guerrilla chief. We took a knee, thankful the gut check was finished.

The guide came back after a few minutes, wearing an angry face.

"You guys got us compromised. We're having to relocate to another site. Get your guys in there and grab any equipment you see lying around. We have to go now! Understand?" he said, and he looked at me like I was a small child.

I couldn't let the opportunity pass, as only he was close enough for a comment that I didn't want others to hear.

I put on what I hoped was my best "Listen to me" face and said, "What goes around, comes around."

His role-playing countenance of evil guide instantly evaporated, replaced with one of contrition. "Sir, I'm just doing what they tell me." He was genuinely concerned that when this charade was over he may have made a real enemy. I regretted my comment.

"Forget it. You're doing great."

The shadows were long as we entered what had been the camp. There were boxes of rations, five-gallon water cans, and a tripod for a machine gun. We each grabbed something and moved on quickly. I put the tripod across the top of my ruck. It added about twenty pounds to the load.

We walked and staggered for three more hours, always encouraging one another. What infuriated me was that I knew most of the cadre I had encountered could not have done this. And then I came to the realization that Jordan wanted somebody to quit. I believed we all knew we were too close to quit, but this gut check was harder than anything we had done in selection, more difficult than any single movement at Ranger school. Was it some sort of test to see if we were stupid enough to walk all night, or to see if I was too weak to challenge the wisdom of marching to the point of exhaustion on the first day, with two weeks of training ahead of us?

I queried the other officers. We all agreed that Jordan just wanted somebody to quit, and we had to gut it out.

It was dark when one of the guides instructed me to stop the team. We had arrived at the new base. The guerrilla chief would see me in the morning. I saw a small fire about two hundred meters away and could make out the silhouettes of those we had come to help. The fire grew to a blaze.

Even without maps, I knew we had walked over undulating terrain for at least sixteen miles. I carried on my back five pounds more than the weight of both of my children, then ages three and five. The team collapsed outside the new base and formed a circle, each man facing out. Our guards rotated between watching us and standing around a roaring fire. Our uniforms were soaked with sweat, and the chill of a winter night bit into our salt-stained legs and arms. We shook like dogs shitting razor blades as we ate our cold rations. We took turns sleeping and pulling security until the sun came up.

Link-up complete.

TWELVE

DAY TWO OF ROBIN SAGE started cold, with the sun offering little in the way of warmth as the light filtered through the leafless trees. My legs cramped from the slightest contraction. Ramos was the acting team sergeant, and he went from man to man, checking with each one. If the intent of the monster rucksack movement had been to make one of us quit, it had the opposite effect. The team was now as tight as any group of students could possibly get. With camaraderie established, we had one mission and one mission only until we achieved success: build rapport.

From link-up to the first combat operation, everything we did with the guerrillas was about building rapport. "I'm from the U.S. government, and I'm here to help." With that said, expecting big smiles and spontaneous celebration from the indigenous population was not part of this training scenario. Any student preoccupied with thinking about how much fun and adventure could be had, as a barrel-chested freedom fighter running around the world with a license to kill, now understood how reality falls short of fantasy. Trigger-pulling skills were now secondary. Our objective as a team was to win friends and influence combat operations as we trained and equipped our guerrillas to bleed resources from the occupiers. Like armed Dale Carnegies, not James Bonds, we had to persuade the Pineland guerrillas that their fight was our fight. They had to accept us, and they would only accept us if our words and deeds resonated true, legitimate. The game Jordan had devised to test us in this effort was diabolical.

Sometime that morning, a guerrilla came to me and said the G chief needed to see our medics. The pair grabbed their empty rifles and aid bags, about twenty pounds apiece, and headed to the blazing fire. A few hours after their departure, a guerrilla brought us the bag with the ammo and maps, but he offered no explanation as to why the items had been returned.

I guessed our medics were doing something right.

While the rest of us sat in our perimeter, we discussed everything that had passed over the last twenty-four hours and looked for meaning in our rejection by the guerrillas like jilted lovers.

"What was that about?" was the general question on our minds. None of us had ever heard of a day-long infiltration on foot over a distance that long. I kept asking myself if I had done the right thing. What was the right response to surrendering our ammo? Should I have said, "No, we're not walking any farther until we've rested"? While my legs and feet would have gladly greeted such a pronouncement, I remembered the team that had refused to do the telephone-pole drill in SFAS only to be told that they were out of the course if they didn't get their asses in gear and start hauling logs.

Every hour or so, one of the medics would come to our circle and give us an update on what was happening. This usually meant a report on how many guerrillas there were, how healthy they were, status on their logistics, and other necessary but mundane information. Later that day, one of the medics came to me and said the G chief wanted to speak to me.

One important factoid requires attention at this point. Two sets of cadre conduct Robin Sage. One set is composed of the SF sergeants who had been training us during the last few weeks of the Q course, like SSG Jordan. The other set is guest cadre, and they perform "in role." That is, they are part of the scenario but are drawn from the active-duty SF groups on a rotational basis. Usually, the guest cadre plays the role of guerrilla chief. The nuance of having guest instructors was lost on me at first, but the significance soon manifested itself.

Right then, however, I was the leader of a student team trying to win a green beret. When the medic brought me the message to report to the chief, I lit up. My legs quit hurting, I wasn't cold anymore, and my adrenaline started pumping.

I thought, *All right, now we can start training them and get this show on the road.*

I could smell the smoke from the fire as I approached and saw what appeared to be a throne made of plywood. It had a high back and rested on a wooden base. When I got into the center of the guerrilla base, I saw this powerfully built bald man sitting on the makeshift throne and holding a staff adorned with chicken feet. To his left was a thin but athletic bearded guy with a ponytail hanging out of his baseball cap.

The man on the throne identified himself as the chief. I addressed him by his name (memorized during isolation) and began my introduction, which I had rehearsed ad nauseam. The spiritual advisor (think shaman or medicine man) cut me off.

He explained that they had found a thief among their guerrillas and were going to execute him. He wanted to know what I thought about it. I could feel my face flush as my brain began trying to change directions.

I stammered that we needed everybody for the liberation of Pineland and perhaps we could rehabilitate the thief. The spiritual advisor asked if that's how we treated thieves in our army. I replied that we would have a trial first. He seized upon that and announced we would have a trial that night. He sent me back to the team and kept my medics.

It didn't occur to me that the chief hadn't done any talking.

I explained to the team what had happened. We didn't have a clue how to proceed. The fact we were still outside the base put us on guard. We devised a plan in case of an emergency situation resulting from a catastrophic loss of rapport. We decided that, if the guerrillas looked like they were going to kill me or did kill me, then this loss of rapport had been realized. On the signal (me yelling "Yogi Bear"—I'm not kidding—as loudly I could) or, if I was already dead, the sound of gunshots, they would either come to rescue me (not likely) or avenge me (very likely, as we had our ammo back) and then walk to South Carolina.

Huddled in a circle on the side of a frozen hill, waiting for a mock trial that resembled the one in SERE school, I found our reasoning to be flawless and our plan viable. My reasoning stemmed from the presumption that no matter the outcome, I would be role-playing a dead guy and wouldn't have to walk to South Carolina.

When it was completely dark, a guerrilla came to escort me to an audience with the chief. Again, he was silent. Again, I missed that. The spiritual leader convened the court. The charges were simple larceny. The accused, a kid of maybe nineteen years, had stolen food. He had been caught red handed. The penalty was death. The spiritual leader turned his gaze on me.

I explained that we needed all our men. Perhaps the thief could be punished another way and rehabilitated, I offered.

Was the Green Beret from America going to be responsible for rehabilitating the thief, came the question. Would I stand in his place for execution if he stole again?

"Ah, no," I replied. Wrong answer.

The medicine man reasoned that I obviously didn't care if someone stole from the guerrillas, thereby demonstrating a gross breach of trust. Therefore, I was no better than the thief, a worthless addition to the headaches of the brave guerrilla fighters. I was grabbed by several guerrillas and tied to a tree. Later, I reflected on the movie *The Green Berets,* which had a scene where a Green Beret valiantly slays several Viet Cong in hand-to-hand combat. I must have missed that block of instruction. I had to remind myself that we were role-playing and to get over myself.

Tied to the tree, I implored the chief and his medicine man to reconsider. I tried to explain how we did it in the United States, but those comments only infuriated the audience. After what seemed like a half hour of yelling and attempting to get myself untied, the medicine man decided to spare me but shoot the accused thief. If his intent was to show me the hypocrisy in my loss of concern for the hapless lad once my own skin was at risk, he had succeeded.

When they released me, SSG Jordan called a timeout and led me to a log, where we sat in the dark and talked about what had just happened. I watched his mustachioed face glow red in the dark as he lit a cigarette. I had no idea what was coming.

"How do you think that went?" he asked.

"Not too good."

He asked me what had motivated me to try to save the thief. I answered that I thought his execution would cross the line into human rights abuses, and such accusations, proven or otherwise, could undermine the insurgency. He pointed out that we have capital punishment in the United States. But there are courts, I retorted. He came back with the idea that because we have people in black robes, and it takes several years to see an execution, killing a guy our way is better than killing a guy the Pineland way.

"Have not innocent men been executed under our system?" he asked.

I grew up Macon, Georgia, in the 1970s, where if you were black and got arrested you were already guilty. Courtroom trials often, but not always, were perfunctory exercises that, at least in my mind, extended all the way to death-penalty cases. "Got it," I replied.

That chat left me with an idea that has stayed with me all my life. Two right answers could be argued. I could have said the issue of punishment among guerrillas was of no concern to the SF. They have their system; we have ours. The other answer was, yes, I would indeed stand in his place for execution if he stole again. The second answer would have resonated with the guerrillas in that I saw their cause and my contribution as an all-encompassing mission, one worth my life. That said, I should have never put my life in their hands in such a manner. But the option was viable, if ill advised.

They were my clients. I had volunteered to help them in their cause. Dying next to one of them was most definitely on the table.

I got back to my team and discovered they were all awake, and for good reason. Unbeknownst to all of us during the trial around the fire, my fellow students had crept up to the perimeter of the base, waiting to see if the time had come to kill all the guerrillas in order to rescue me. They did not hear me yell "Yogi Bear" and they returned to our little perimeter when they saw me untied.

Thankful not to be walking to Bennettsville (in South Carolina), we put one man on watch, and the rest of us bagged out. We didn't make a fire because we thought it communicated weakness. But we did use our sleeping bags, as another night of shivering crossed the line into stupidity. I disassembled myself—boots and uniform—and gleefully crawled into my sleeping bag. My eyes had barely closed when I was shaken awake.

"You need to come with me, Captain," a voice in the dark said. It was the spiritual leader, come out of role.

We walked in the dark, using no lights, to a fallen log.

"We need to talk," he began. "You're fucking this up."

My fatigue evaporated, and I hung on to his every word. "What am I doing wrong?"

"For one, you're not reading these people. You're trying to show us what you know, not that you care what we need."

"I'm not following you," I replied. "We can't even get in the G base. How are we supposed to begin assessing?"

"Have your medics asked us any questions? You guys are going through the motions. That's not what we need."

I groped for words to fill the silence but was glad I had opted to shut up.

"We need leadership, we need guys that can come in, rapidly assess, and start gaining rapport." I realized I had the wrong antecedent for "we." He had switched from the role of guerrilla leader in a Robin Sage exercise to master sergeant from 10th Special Forces Group.

"I can lead," I said, though the words sounded feeble as they left my lips.

"Maybe in whatever branch you came from, but I'm not getting that here, not now," he said. The ensuing silence added weight to his words.

I breathed deeply and waited for the rest. I didn't have to wait long.

"Do you know where Kurdistan is?" he asked. I shifted my weight on the log.

"I've heard of it," I tried in response.

"That's good, since it doesn't exist."

I realized I should shut up.

"I just got back from northern Iraq. The Kurds call the area Kurdistan. The Iraqis call it Iraq. The Turks bomb the shit out of the Kurds whenever they feel like it. My team was running food and blankets to thousands of Kurds. We didn't go there trying to show them what we knew. We went there trying to find out what they needed. Am I getting through to you?" he asked dispassionately.

I began to believe that either the guy really liked me or really hated me, but either way he was trying to save me from failing the course.

"Yeah, you're getting through." I felt like I'd been kicked in the stomach. I gleaned from his revelation that he was from 10th Special Forces Group, then at Fort Devens, Massachusetts, and, at the end of 1993, he was just back from an extended stay in northern Iraq with the Kurds. His view of how Robin Sage should play out was colored mightily by his experiences in "Kurdistan." While his status as guest cadre was known to our instructors, he was just another role-player to us students.

At this stage, I didn't know anything about guest cadres or 10th SF Group in Kurdistan. I was just afraid of leaving the course a failure.

He stood up. Lecture over. "I hope you're trainable," he said as he walked back to his fire.

We were all awake before dawn, our gear secured, cold rations and colder water for breakfast. I relayed to the team my impromptu encounter with the spiritual leader. We agreed to spend the rest of the morning asking questions of any guerrillas we could talk to and trying to find out what they needed. Seemed like a fairly simple task to me, but now I felt like I had made the whole effort too hard. We needed to get into receive mode. I didn't know how else to do that, and none of the rest of the team did, either.

A guerrilla came from the fire and summoned the medics. They knew what to do, and I hoped to see results from this new approach. Technically, we were three days into an exercise that lasted only fourteen, and nothing was happening except that a bunch of soldiers were playing mind games with each other while camping in a national park. I noticed SSG Jordan talking to my mentor from the night before. The body language was combative between them. As students, we soon learned something that the instructors hadn't realized when this SF master sergeant came to help make Green Berets out of us: His experiences in Operation Provide Comfort (the name of the mission in northern Iraq post–Desert Storm) had made his thinking as different from our training staff as if he had just gotten back from Mars.

The medics, as they had the day before, would bring tidbits of information: for instance, that the G chief wanted his men vaccinated or that one of the guerrillas had a sick wife. The team would digest these factoids, like stockbrokers analyzing the market, and forward a theory of how we were to proceed. On one occasion I hazarded an unsolicited walk to the G base. The G chief sent a runner to tell me he didn't need me. So we simply waited and watched our medics come and go.

The cold day stretched into a colder night, when, for no reason that I could determine, the chief sent for all of us.

By that point, I really didn't care about the scenario, none of us did. We had tried to play the game, and everything we did was wrong. We just wanted to warm up by the fire. We dragged our gear into the warm glow and settled into an uneasy circle. Our welcome felt artificial, like a kind word from a playground bully. Whether contrived to move us along in the exercise or the result of successful rapport building, the G chief made the change in our disposition manifestly apparent.

He sat with us around the fire and said more in ten minutes than I had heard in three days. He explained that we had earned his trust and that of his men, enough at least to let us help them with an important operation. This operation would be our test, to see if we could live up to our reputation as Special Forces guys. He had information from the "Underground," the network of spies that had infiltrated the Pineland security apparatus, that a commander of the occupation force would be crossing a bridge about ten kilometers from our current location in two days at 1800 and would be in a white pickup truck. The area commander, the G chief's boss and as yet unknown to us except by his name memorized during isolation, had directed that this guy was not to make it across the bridge.

This part felt like any infantry school, but without the yelling. The team physically began to fill spaces among the guerrillas on the perimeter away from the fire. We hoped these spaces would be filled operationally and socially—that is, as part of a team, U.S. and indig.

In the morning, the SF guys started the process of formalizing the guerrilla organization, getting the names of all seven and other pertinent information like boot and uniform sizes, with the notion that we would send this information up to our headquarters via message pickup (we had rope to make the apparatus necessary for the plane to swoop down with the boat anchor and take it). In return, a plane should fly over at a designated time and place and kick a bundle via parachute that contained all the war-making material our guerrillas would need, including guns and ammo.

The last bureaucratic detail was an oath of allegiance to the free Pineland forces. We tried to make the ceremony somewhat solemn, but the ritual rang hollow to me. These guys, according to the scenario, had already shed much blood, theirs and that of their enemies, and now we had to have them swear they would keep doing it.

We then set about the task of training our guerrillas to fight. In accordance with our doctrine, a reconnaissance team headed for the bridge to make sure the place wasn't a trap for our main force the next day. While some of us guided the guerrillas in rehearsals of the actual operation, others made a sand table, a little model of the area where the ambush was to occur, based on the topography shown on the map and the personal recollections of the guerrillas who were from the area. As the sun set and the temperatures dropped, I felt buoyed by the level of rapport we seemed to have established and the amount of training we had done.

Day Five started clear and dry. While I was still the team leader, SSG Jordan said Mike was to lead the mission. Mike was an infantryman, Ranger qualified, part of the invasion package that had gone into Panama in 1989, and he was utterly at ease as he gave his mission brief to the other members of the team. In order to make the hit time, we figured he had to leave with the assault force no later than ten hours prior. All but one guerrilla went on the mission.

They departed on time, with a cadre member sent from Mackall to evaluate how the ambush went. The medicine man and the G chief disappeared. I guessed they went someplace to grab a shower. They were, after all, role-players. I pulled out a brown towel and wiped myself down with baby wipes in the warmth of the fire. Jordan came over, and we chatted.

He mentioned that he had to overrule our guest cadre or we would still have been outside the base. I nodded. I realized he was confiding in me.

He explained that the medicine man wanted us to explore the realities of UW, such as he had experienced in northern Iraq, but that he—Jordan—had a schedule for assessing each of us. We each had to take a patrol of SF and guerrillas and hit targets, a la Ranger school. I was still in the hot seat as team leader until further notice.

I spent the rest of the day with other members of the stay-behind crew to check our defenses around the base, looking at fields of fire, positioning our machine gun, and other normal infantry tasks, like cleaning my weapon. I made coffee on the fire and chatted with whoever was around. The sun disappeared behind a ridgeline before six o'clock, and we waited in the growing darkness for news via radio about the ambush.

What I didn't realize was that from our base on the top of the hill, we could see down the valley to the ambush site. At exactly six o'clock, we saw flashes of light on the horizon, and a red star cluster, like several Roman candles, arched into the purple sky.

I was ecstatic. The G chief and his medicine man had returned, and I pointed out that our guys had hit the target right on time. They nodded and smiled. I wanted someone to say "Good job."

Nothing. Zilch.

The patrol was supposed to stay out of the base that night and return along a different, longer route the following day. Mike sent us a signal saying all was well, and they were heading for a hide site to spend the night.

I slept like a dog, with a big smile and contented warmth in my sleeping bag.

Day Six began with breakfast alongside the medicine man, who informed me our valiant warriors had killed a friend of the resistance, a vaunted member of the underground who had risked everything to help us. The guy in the truck was not a commander of the occupation forces, but a Pineland patriot who had the misfortune of being in a white pickup truck on a particular bridge about six miles away at 1800 last night. A member of his family was coming to see me, the leader of the American soldiers come to help, and wanted to pass on some information directly to me. Our victim's family apparently did not know yet that we committed fratricide. I was to stand by for a visit from the kinsman, named Cliotis. His role in my little drama will become apparent in a moment.

"How do you know who you're supposed to kill?" The question from training rang in my head.

I went immediately to other members on the team. Gus and Dave had the same thought I did: Jordan was trying to trick us into an unassisted evasion scenario. We couldn't imagine a better reason for catastrophic loss of rapport than killing a member of the Free Pineland Forces we had come to assist. Our gear stayed packed. We just had to pick it up and go, go south for seventy miles.

Cliotis arrived later in the morning. I could tell by the haircut and mustache the guy was active duty, but he was older, probably another senior SF sergeant or warrant officer. He was all smiles and big handshakes, happy to meet us Green Berets, just over-the-top enthusiasm. Then he slipped in heartfelt thanks for the operation from the previous night.

"Heard you guys had a mission on the bridge last night. I bet that went well, huh?" He looked at me like a cat waiting for the mouse to run.

"No," I replied, in my most dispassionate tone. "We apparently had bad intelligence. We killed . . ." and I said the name I had been given, the name of he who was to the resistance what Father Flanagan had been to Boys Town.

Whoever was playing Cliotis showed great consternation. "Bad intelligence?" he began. "What do you mean? Didn't you vet the source of this information?"

"It came from the medicine man. We thought . . ." I tried, and he cut me off.

"You took intelligence from someone you call the medicine man and launched an attack?" The incredulity contorted his face such that his mustache was an arch of hair over bared teeth. If he'd been a dog, I would have shot him out of fear.

"How do you know who to kill?"

I realized that Jordan played me. The rapport issue was never resolved. The people were the prize. Everything was about gaining and maintaining rapport without forgetting why we were there. Right then, whatever we thought we had for rapport was gone.

I tried to envision how we looked to the cadre.

"Let's kill some dude on a bridge tomorrow night."

"Sounds good to me. Everybody saddle up. Yeee-haw!"

I and my team had demonstrated the analytical prowess of young children turned loose in a toy store. We deserved to walk to South Carolina.

"Yeah," I replied, dropping all pretense, "we fucked up. I fucked up." I looked him in the eye because to do otherwise may have brought a slap, the way he was looking at me.

"I agree," he said. "Who's going to take care of his family? Who's going to be a father to his children?" He kept the questions coming like artillery rounds, and they hit me hard enough to make me feel like whale shit.

"We'll provide what funds we can to the widow," I said, trying not to sound feeble.

"See that you do," he said, and he walked away in disgust.

Later that afternoon, the assault team returned, and I could tell by their faces they knew something had gone wrong. I pulled Mike aside with the other team members in a tight huddle away from the fire. The fatigue of the past few days creased Mike's face like a mask. He looked twenty years older as he explained what happened.

When he had linked up with our recon team, they pointed out an outpost of enemy forces, maybe four guys, near the bridge and on the far side of the river. This was good. The outpost could not interfere with the mission, as they were cut off by the river. He put an element in place to engage them and remained focused on the operation to execute an ambush at the appointed time. On cue, a white pickup had crossed the bridge, where the good guys opened up like it was a day on a machine-gun range and killed the enemy soldiers on the outpost and the man in the truck. When his guys ran onto the bridge to collect anything that could be used for intelligence purposes, Mike discovered that they had not killed an enemy commander. He didn't know who they had killed other than the soldiers guarding the bridge. His call on the radio had been only to tell us that the operation had proceeded as planned, and that none of our guys were lost. (Minimizing radio traffic was a given in guerrilla warfare and precluded a full report of all that had happened.)

When I briefed Mike on the political significance of who we had taken out, his face went blank. Without saying a word, we looked at each other with the understanding that we might be walking for days.

Neither the medicine man nor the G chief had mentioned our mistake, and I was certainly not going to broach it. But that night, the G chief summoned me to his throne and explained that there would be a meeting of the area command. I was to choose one other officer, leaving our weapons at the G base, and travel via truck to the meeting site. I would meet the area commander, the guerrilla leader responsible for several bands of fighters throughout occupied Pineland.

From the training calendar perspective, I now knew we would not be executing an unassisted evasion. We needed to get through the scenario, and there were certain training objectives that had to be achieved. This night was the area command meeting training objective. After this, if we followed the phases of a U.S.-sponsored insurgency, we would be in full-blown guerrilla warfare against the occupation forces. Meeting the area commander was the last necessary step, in order to get his guidance on the conduct of the campaign, before letting our guerrillas loose.

I imagined somebody like Scarface from the SERE school would play the area commander, someone built like truck with a big Fu Manchu.

The G chief and medicine man accompanied Dave and me to the rendezvous point to meet our ride. At the appropriate time, we walked from the base to a dirt road, and in less than a mile, we met a man with a pickup truck. The hood was raised, a signal meaning he was there for us. We walked to the back, and the G chief stopped us before we could climb under the tarp.

"You brought your map, right?" asked the medicine man. I nodded. "Got some don to pay the driver?" I did. I gave the gray-haired gentleman at the front of the truck a hundred don and shoved the wad of a few thousand back into my cargo pocket.

"Put your hands behind your back," the G chief said, removing a length of parachute cord from his pocket. He tied our hands and hooded us with sandbags. We sat on the tailgate, and someone dragged us in. I heard the tarp pulled over us, the hood slammed shut, and off we went.

Facedown on the steel bed of the truck, we bounced for thirty minutes. The truck came to a stop, and I heard the tarp pulled away. A new voice told us to scoot out.

"Damn, Dai Uy [pronounced die wee], your hands are blue. Who the hell tied this?" the voice said. Whoever spoke tried to tell me several things in this sentence. First, he was Vietnam vintage—*dai uy* was Vietnamese for "captain." He had the bona fides of being a Green Beret in Vietnam when I was a kid. Only people who had been in-country as a combatant and had worked with South Vietnamese forces would use the indigenous term. Anybody else, regardless of other distinctions, would be a pretender to the throne in saying *dai uy*. Second, he was trying to reassure me that, as bad as things might seem, it was, after all, training. "This too shall pass." Third, he wanted to demonstrate compassion by commenting that my hands had been tied tight enough to cut off the circulation, and this, in his highly esteemed opinion, was unacceptable.

I didn't hear the nuance then. I was mad. I remained silent and sullen under my hood. The hand tying, the truck ride, bad intelligence, sixteen miles of walking, constant mind games, Yogi Bear, giving up our ammo and maps, and now being led blindly into a building to meet the area commander put me in the frame of mind to tell this training cadre and the generals running this show to fuck themselves and keep your green beret. Give me my seventy-ton Winnebago with the cannon and machine guns as the standard trim package, and you guys can liberate the oppressed without me.

"You got a step in front of you," my guide said, and he held me by the shoulder as my foot found it. Looking down through the bottom of the sandbag, I could see the wood slats of a porch, a threshold, and then oak flooring, worn and scarred. The light coming through the mesh of the bag was dim and orange. The bag came off, and the scene looked like a Hollywood set for the Spanish Inquisition.

Dave and I stood side by side, and confusion replaced my anger for a moment.

The room had a desk, and behind the desk was a woman. She had very dark, close-cropped hair framing a pale face, and her eyes lanced me through black-framed glasses. She wore an old fatigue shirt. Seated next to her was my G chief's witch doctor. He considered me as one might a shank of meat hanging in a butcher shop. The space around us was entirely illuminated by candles on every flat surface. When I turned to see the rest of the room, a gun barrel was put into my back and someone yelled, "Face the commander at all times." My anger returned.

The woman asked me if I knew the man seated next to her. I said yes, he's the medicine man. She exploded, explaining how stupid I was, and how America did not care about the Pineland struggle by sending idiots like me. She explained the witch doctor was the G chief, and only an emotionally dysfunctional bona fide moron would not have realized this fact after several days of living with her brave and ingenious freedom fighters.

I clenched my jaw. I tried to explain that we would continue to improve, that we would be helpful, and that were utterly committed to the free Pineland forces.

"You killed one of our best agents. It will take months to replace him, if we can. What am I supposed to tell his wife? Huh? What about his kids?" She laid into me like a dog on a steak bone.

I looked at the medicine man. His face said "Go ahead, try to blame me."

I pushed back with discretion, or at least I thought so. "The intelligence said the enemy commander would be driving a white truck and would be at the bridge . . ."

"The intelligence? Do you know how many white pickup trucks cross that bridge every day? What time do you think people get off work? You know, even during the occupation, people go to work. That is a concept you understand, right?"

"Yes," I replied through gritted teeth. I have never touched a woman in anger, but I wanted to kill her right then.

I began moving closer to the desk. My body language clearly communicated that I wanted to get in her face. I wanted to yell that we were doing the best we could with what we knew. I had thousands of don in my pocket. This was money to give to the widow, a death benefit of sorts, but I didn't want to give her the chance to throw that gift in my face.

I saw her eyes look behind me. She took a cue from someone and then said to another unseen person, presumably the guy with the gun in my back, "Check his pockets."

I looked down and instantly got "Eyes forward!" yelled at me. I felt a hand grab my map, return it, and then remove the money.

"We'll give this to his family," she said. Our gift was now a fine, taken at gunpoint.

She looked at the G chief, the *real* G chief.

"Good luck," she said to him in a grave tone. Then to me, "Get out of here. Try not to kill any more of my people." She wasn't shrieking, but it was closer to that than a warm, friendly farewell.

Whoever was behind us put our hoods on and led us back to the truck. Our hands weren't tied this time. The G chief ordered us into the truck with the admonition not to speak. The tarp was replaced, and as soon as we were on the road, Dave and I started commiserating.

"Fuck him," I yelled over the roar of the truck. In the dark, we pulled our hoods above our faces. The streetlights dimly lit the space between the tarp and truck bed, before eventually disappearing as we left whatever town we had been in, leaving us in complete blackness. We stormed over the lack of respect, the incomprehensibility of the scenario, the mind games, and a lack of understanding of what we were supposed to do. Nothing we had encountered so far had been even close to what the intelligence had suggested back at Mackall. We called the G chief everything we could think of, made sophomoric sex jokes about the area commander, and in general did not follow the instruction to remain quiet during the return trip to the G base.

Without warning, not much slowing, the truck came to an abrupt stop in the middle of the road. I knew we had to be on a state highway because of the speed we had and the smoothness of the ride. The tarp flew up, but from the front of the truck.

There was the G chief, ball cap and ponytail, sitting on the edge of the truck bed, back to the cab. He had listened to everything we said. He grinned demonically.

"Get out!" he yelled. "It's too dangerous to transport you. You can't shut up! Get out!"

We threw our hoods off and clambered over the side. The truck drove away, and we stood there like discarded dogs, watching the taillights get smaller.

Now I understood why they wanted to make sure we had our maps.

A single streetlight shown in the distance along the road, and we headed toward it. As we walked, like players in a bad Shakespearean production of an unpublished tragedy, storm clouds rumbled over the mountain, headed straight at us.

"I'm not walking in the rain. Unless that's a bank up there, or somebody's house, we're staying there," Dave said. I was ready to relinquish decision-making to Zip the Chimp at this point, and I agreed that was a great idea.

We were completely on our own. Nobody knew where we were, we had no radio or weapons, and we still didn't know where we were in relationship to the G base.

The light marked the entrance to a church. Most churches are depicted on military maps (as we try not to bomb them), and this one was. We quickly discerned we were six miles from the G base.

"I think we're being taught another lesson," I offered.

Dave agreed, and we started trying to break into the church. Rain began to fall. I spotted a concrete outbuilding, like a tool shed, in the dark and thought we might have better luck there. Dave found a small door at ground level with only a simple latch. We slid into the crawl space under the building and closed the door behind us.

"What's today?" I asked. "If it's Saturday, we have to be out of here before church tomorrow."

Dave checked his watch. "No, we're good."

The rain came down in buckets. I fell asleep on the dank dirt of a church shed, wrapped in an Army-issue rain jacket with a black watch cap pulled over my ears.

I fell asleep with the simple question: "What am I doing here?"

The next morning, we crawled out into a gorgeous early winter day, the sky scrubbed blue and clear, and began making our way to the base. We walked up to our little band of fighters, and everybody—students, guerrillas, cadre—seemed genuinely glad to see us. Apparently they thought we had become lost in the teeth of a cold winter storm.

SSG Jordan pulled Dave and me to the side of the base and gave us a quick read-out on how things had gone the night before with the area commander. I didn't do well.

Jordan explained that about ten feet behind me, watching and listening to the exchange, was a gallery of training officers and NCOs, representing collectively well over a hundred years of SF experience, including time in Vietnam. By losing my temper, by trying to intimidate the area commander, I had demonstrated a gross lack of political acumen necessary to function on my own in the ambiguous world of unconventional warfare. I had failed miserably and was punished.

Had the meeting gone well, we would have been driven back to our base. Lesson learned.

Jordan also relieved me as team leader. Not because of my screwup, but because it was time for another officer to have his time in the barrel. I gleefully accepted my reduced responsibility and became the junior weapons guy on the team.

THIRTEEN

THE REST OF OUR TIME in Robin Sage was very similar to Ranger school, without all the yelling. Everyone had to have a turn as patrol leader, taking a mix of SF and indig from our base to do a mission, normally raiding a fixed site manned by the "enemy." The days ran together: send out reconnaissance, plan the mission, brief it over a sand table, rehearse, go, hit, recover, and repeat. But the differences between what we did at Ranger school and the SF Q course were obvious as we went deeper into the scenario.

We were liberating Pineland. Our patrols, while necessary for evaluating the students, were part of a greater campaign. There was no campaign at Ranger school, only patrol after patrol until graduation. In the SF Q course, each mission presumably built upon the other. Yes, our successes were contrived, but such a construct was necessary because no one knew if we had really killed the enemy since we were shooting blanks. Within the context of a campaign, of being a team among other unseen teams, on one particular day toward what we knew had to be close to the end, an operation from a nearby team had an impact in our area of operations. That is, they did something, like killed the wrong guy, and supposedly upset our local population. At least, that's what our G chief told us. In retrospect, I think it was an excellent injection into the scenario. Things that were being done by other Americans in the area would obviously affect our rapport with the locals. Still, we were planning a mission, and a student who needed to show his mettle was anxious to lead his patrol and get this part of the evaluation behind him. The chief let it be known that we should probably rethink this op due to this new information, and didn't we think it would be better to just chill for the rest of the day. In other words, the G chief didn't want us going out. Maybe he was mad at Jordan and was using us kids as a weapon, or maybe he was sincerely trying to make us play the game. Whatever his motivation, we were open to his assessment and sage advice.

His suggestion was tantamount to recommending a nap to someone who hadn't slept in three days. We rubbed our faces thoughtfully as if considering the efficacy of his approach, nodded at his wisdom, and headed to the fire to make some coffee. SSG Jordan walked over and asked how the planning was going.

"G chief thinks it's a bad idea to go," I replied, grinning. Turnabout was fair play, right?

"What?" He looked around for our chief. "No, that's bullshit. You have to go. The battalion commander is coming to see this mission. Shit," he said and walked away, presumably looking for the guy who was screwing up the training plan.

We did the mission, and the battalion commander, the real one in charge of all our training, was pleased at our performance.

The following day, Dave was the team leader, and I was his assistant. He was directed to meet with an arms dealer, and I was to go along as both security and a sounding board. I had a few hundred of the fake dollars on me, and with two guerrillas as backup, we all went to a rendezvous point to meet "Paddy."

Paddy wore a black ski mask, a turtleneck, jeans, and hiking boots. With about as much body fat as the machine gun slung across his back, he looked like a professional bodybuilder and spoke with a heavy Irish accent. We understood that we were going to buy weapons for our guerrillas from the black market, and Paddy was our arms broker. This event stuck with me and surfaced prominently in my mind in the days after the September 11 attacks. I will explain later.

We made our deal and shook hands. We were going to buy several Russian-made AK-47s (no cheap Czech knock-offs for us, and we didn't want the new AK-74, as ammo would be hard to find)—paying half up front and the rest on delivery. After the deal, Paddy took his mask off, and we discovered our Irish arms dealer was a Marine officer,

Major Powers. He complimented Dave on the great negotiating skill demonstrated and generally said we had done a good job. I discovered in 2001 that there was only one problem with the scenario.

It was illegal. In 1993, the Department of Defense was precluded by law from providing "lethal aid" to anybody but its own soldiers. Only the State Department and the CIA had the legal authority to provide weapons and ammunition to actors in other countries. In the case of the State Department, the United States could provide anything desired to another country, state to state. As for the CIA, under the authority of U.S. Code Title 50, the United States could provide lethal aid to nonstate actors: for example, insurgents or guerrillas attempting to overthrow an oppressive regime. Based on the fact that buying weapons was still part of the Q course in 1993, I can only surmise that all of us in the world of Army Special Forces were very surprised when in October of 2001 the A-teams that went into Afghanistan to train, advise, and equip the Northern Alliance were not allowed to provide anything but blankets and food until a workaround could be devised.

During Dave's mission and acting as assistant patrol leader, I found myself preparing frenetically as Jordan threw another curveball at us. We were to move our guerrilla base; we had been compromised and forced to relocate. I was running from man to man, ensuring that everybody had everything we needed to move; nothing would be left behind to support the fact that Americans were operating in the area. I knelt to talk with Ramos and, after a brief exchange, bolted to go to another position. Fatigue, adrenaline, and stupidity combined in me to produce a near-fatal result.

When I felt that everything was ready, I approached the fire and joined others waiting for the word from the G chief to make our move. I stood talking with SSG Jordan and other members of our team for about fifteen minutes and noticed them looking at me and then exchanging glances. I wondered if my fly was open.

Ramos professionally and deliberately walked up to me with my rifle and, in full view of all those assembled, handed it to me and said, "Here you go, sir. It should chamber now."

"Thank you, Sergeant Ramos." I played along. "Was it just dirty?" I smiled at my self-deprecating humor.

He grinned back. "No, sir. Your buffer spring is worn out. It should work now, though."

Jordan nodded approvingly. Instead of being bounced from the course for losing control of my weapon, I made another student look good in the eyes of cadre while saving my own ass. By the end of Robin Sage, I was able to pay him back.

Throughout Robin Sage, I could see that Jordan was watching Ramos, as were other members of cadre who would occasionally come to see us perform actions on the objective. Like me, Ramos was very senior to be coming to the course. He would arrive on the team as the most junior guy for SF experience, yet carried the seniority of his rank. The cadre didn't like anyone jumping in line based on rank. Among SF NCOs, time on a team is similar to Navy fighter pilots counting the number of landings on a carrier: the more, the better. Other members of the team noticed the special attention shown him as well. As a final test, Jordan made Ramos the patrol leader for what we learned later was our final mission. The team and our guerrillas rallied around Ramos. Everybody worked to make him look good.

Two members of the team and me were responsible for building his sand table, the scale model he would use to brief how he planned to employ us. We made as exact a replica as possible of the terrain in which we would operate. We opened our blank ammunition rounds and made lines of gunpowder depicting the route we would walk from the base to our objective, which for the purposes of the scenario was an antiaircraft cannon.

At the appropriate time, we all assembled around the sand table to receive our instructions from Ramos. Beside him stood Jordan, clipboard in hand, wearing an expression of anticipation, like a cat watching a mouse hole. The solemnity of the moment was comparable to the mission brief we had received prior to the ground war for Desert Storm. As Ramos began to describe how we would move to our target, a member of the team struck a match to the gunpowder, and everybody watched as a flame raced from where we were to where we wanted to go.

Ramos said, "And that's just how fast we're going to move, too." The showmanship and ensuing laughter had the desired effect. The tension evaporated, and Jordan's face relaxed. He shook his head as if to say, "You guys just kill me."

Ramos, his Asian features usually inscrutable, smiled broadly and finished his presentation flawlessly, glowing with confidence.

As we moved to get our equipment, Jordan said something that told us the end was near.

"All SF students, don't leave anything in the base. Take all your shit."

Twelve days had passed since we walked sixteen miles in order to get started. My rucksack, still easily sixty-five pounds, felt remarkably light as we moved to our final objective.

The enemy gun and its crew of five men was positioned toward the front of a single-room log cabin. The owner of the cabin had been one of our most staunch supporters through the years as the battle of Pineland had raged around him. He had been there when Pineland was first invaded, as it was four times every year since 1964. He had seen the invading forces change uniforms through the years. As he undoubtedly had done with countless other classes when they came through to liberate Pineland, he was sitting on his front porch, rocking patiently, waiting for us to attack. When we came by, low-crawling through his front yard, he did not seem to see us until several of us were in his view. He smiled broadly and became motionless as he watched us sneak into position. His wizened face glowed like a child's at the circus when we launched the attack. His admiration for us has stayed with me ever since.

A member of the team looked at him and politely offered the universal signal for "Quiet," index finger to mouth. The old man nodded. Our enemy, less than fifty feet from us in front of the house, was not expecting a daylight attack, and they were visibly shaken when our guerrillas opened up with the machine gun. I caught a glimpse of the old man in the corner of my eye. He sat in motionless amazement as we flowed over the target, "killing" everyone on it.

Jordan watched the action from a white van parked discreetly at the top of a hill. He drove down to us as we were finishing our actions on the objective and told us not to leave the area. A few minutes later, one of our communications specialists related to us that the radio was alive with traffic indicating that the free Pineland forces, in collaboration with a coalition of conventional ground units, had succeeded in displacing the occupation forces. Pineland was again free.

Our guerrillas came out of role and shook our hands, telling us they really enjoyed the experience and wished us luck. I discovered that the guy I originally thought was the G chief was actually a buck sergeant in the military police. I complimented him on his command presence and told him he should really consider becoming an officer. He thanked me and said he had enough problems as an NCO. All of our guerrillas were military policemen from the 18th Airborne Corps at Fort Bragg. One of them said he looked forward to seeing us around base. A member of the team, referencing that these guys were Army cops, replied, "I hope not."

We spent the last two days of Robin Sage conducting civil-military operations and demobilizing our guerrilla force, which meant telling our guerrillas they were now free to return to their normal lives. I had to laugh. Had we actually done this U.S.-sponsored insurgency as we had planned it, we could have several dozen, if not hundreds, of armed and trained insurgents, men who would have spent the last year learning the craft of guerrilla warfare, turned loose back on the society we had just liberated. Add to our merry band our sister team's fighters, and the number easily climbed into the thousands.

Demobilization, as we say in the Army, was a pencil drill. Even in training, we acknowledge that we, Special Forces and the Department of Defense, don't have the resources to stand up an economy capable of absorbing the numbers of fighters we could create. As I stood there with my fellow students, grinning and hoping that we had finally finished, I realized that as a cancer-causing agent I was much easier to introduce than I was to cure. Once the UW strain is released into the body, if it takes hold, the reversal of arming hordes of men and women and teaching them to kill is tantamount to weaning a crack addict from cocaine. Demobilizing a guerrilla force is so hard the instructors at the SF schoolhouse don't even pretend to be able to do it. We talked about it and moved on.

All the student teams, ten in total, assembled along a creek, made ten circles of gear around stacks of firewood, and camped as a class for the next two nights. The war stories of the other teams' experiences flowed into the early morning. The smell of wood smoke, weapons oil, and snuff will always remind me of those two nights. During daylight, we did civil-military operations, or CMO.

Civil-military operations turned out to be chopping firewood for select members of the local community who were too weak to do so for themselves. This hearts-and-minds campaign was a legitimate and competent effort to keep us—the U.S. Army, that is—in the good graces of the fine citizens of Troy, North Carolina, and the surrounding area. Robin Sage doesn't work without role-players, and all the role-players are volunteers. In the mornings, student officers and enlisted alike would draw double-headed axes from the back of a truck and begin whacking on trees the Forestry Service had cleared from various parts of the national park. In the afternoon, we filled trucks with split firewood and delivered it *gratis* to more than a handful of little old ladies and one old man, the one who watched our last mission. Scenes of Jordan being hugged by platoons of elderly women are forever burned into my memory. Most poignant was the sight at our elderly admirer's house.

Outside his small cabin, he had a wall of split wood at least fifty feet long and six feet high. We had used it to hide our assault force and were successful in doing so. With what we delivered, several feet were added to his wall. A few of us carried many loads inside and stacked them near his wood-burning stove. His house was composed of two rooms, a kitchen and a living area, of maybe five hundred square feet. No TV, no microwave, no air-conditioning unit; his stove dominated the house. He obviously lived alone and, by all observations, quite contentedly. If we had not delivered to him the equivalent of several hundred dollars of hardwood, split into easily handled staves, and stacked no higher than he could reach, I have no idea what he would have done for heat in the winter. We left him with enough wood to hide a battalion behind.

Nearly in tears, he thanked us profusely, shook our hands, and waved us goodbye as we rode away in the back of a truck. The lesson was that what we had done for him would carry over for the next class, and in a real-world scenario, his gratitude may result in helping one of our teams who otherwise might have to fight their way out of a situation he could have prevented.

Our last night at Robin Sage, Robert Jordan called each member of the team individually to him for what was, I discovered, our final assessment. Each of us would leave the glow of the fire and after a few minutes return to send the next man.

My turn came, and, though I thought I had made it, my stomach knotted.

"Good job, sir," he said. "You made it. Any questions for me?"

"No, Sergeant," I replied. "I learned a lot."

"That's what I like to hear. Good luck at group."

I'm sure that as I walked back to the fire, my grin was reflected visibly in the light. All of us were relieved when Gus and Ramos returned saying they had also made it. Everybody on the team passed. Other members of the class were not so fortunate, officers and enlisted alike. Their reasons varied, but it usually came back to not treating other members of the team or the guerrilla force with respect. Sometimes the cadre perceived a lack of leadership skill that can only be tested in Robin Sage. What works in an infantry unit does not always fly in a UW scenario. Soldiering skills were rarely the issue. To fail the course at Robin Sage was particularly painful. It's like running a marathon and a referee pulling you from the course about hundred feet from the finish line.

The truck ride back to Bragg was over in forty-five minutes, and in a blink, we reappeared from the isolation of the little metal sheds and the world of Pineland. Armed Alices back from Wonderland.

In the few days preceding our graduation, the battalion commander, Lieutenant Colonel Wilderman, summoned me to his office more than once. He saw that I had two big problems, resulting from early selection for promotion to major. First, most Army units, SF included, would treat me as a major. That is, I would be carried on the manning roster as a major even though I wouldn't pin on the rank for another year and a half. SF team leaders were captains, not majors. According to regulations, any SF unit that accepted me could put me on a B-team (the headquarters elements responsible for six A-teams). B-teams were intended to be commanded by seasoned Special Forces officers, not a former armor guy with twelve parachute jumps to his credit. It had happened that these guys made it through the filters and rarely ended well. Second, with only a year and a half remaining to wear my captain rank, I could no longer afford to spend six months in language school, and I had to take a language test in order to get a rating before I could go to an SF unit. The language issue was nonnegotiable. I told him I thought I could get a basic rating in Spanish. He said he hoped so and gave me the building number on Fort Bragg where I would go to take the test. Until I brought him my test scores, he could not recommend me to any of his friends at 3rd or 7th Group, where Spanish was spoken. I was to take the test the Monday following our graduation.

On graduation day, I was first across the stage to shake hands with retired Major General Joe Lutz, who had been a tanker and an SF officer, serving with distinction in Vietnam and Thailand. His stature in the SF community could be measured by many tangible successes, and, most significant, he had been the driving force in getting the Army staff to approve a Special Forces tab, like the Ranger tab, for wear on the left sleeve above the unit patch. The length of the tab, bearing the words "Special Forces," spawned another euphemism for a Special Forces soldier: long tabber. "He's a long tabber" was how one Green Beret could tell another that a third person, usually not present, was one of us.

As he handed me my diploma and we shook hands, General Lutz glanced at my ribbons and noticed the Bronze Stars. "Where were you in combat?" he asked, not letting go of my hand.

Before I could answer, a colonel standing behind him, assisting in the graduation ceremony and someone I had never met before, responded, "Captain Schwalm was a tank company commander in Desert Storm, General."

With that, he released my hand and sent me on my way with one word ringing in my ears: "Outstanding." If the ghost of John Wayne had materialized in front of me and offered great words of encouragement,

I could not have felt any more pleased than I did shaking hands with Joe Lutz.

My children were still young and not sure what to make of all the pomp and circumstance. My parents came for the ceremony and beamed at their boy. My wife gave me a fearful grin, not really sure what this change in headgear would mean for us. I know many SF officers who have been married for decades to the same woman. I know many more who are divorced. Ultimately, I ended in the latter group.

But on that day in December of 1993, my childhood dream became my reality. I was a Green Beret, and joy coursed through me like a river.

FOURTEEN

IN A RENTED HOUSE in Fayetteville, North Carolina, I spent the weekend glancing at a Spanish-language dictionary, trying to recall vocabulary from high school and college courses. Ready or not, Monday morning arrived, and I went out the door wearing my brand-new green beret and the long tab that announced to everyone that I was in fact Special Forces. Within two hours of leaving the house, I had taken the test and received a minimum passing score (1+/1+, a rating indicating that I could read and understand spoken Spanish well enough to order beans and rice with a beer in most restaurants south of El Paso, Texas). After the exam, I visited Colonel Wilderman's office for an assignment.

Standing outside Wilderman's office, I considered my options. I was either going to 7th or 3rd Group, both at Fort Bragg. The 7th Group had been around for a long time and had performed multiple covert and clandestine assignments throughout Central and South America in the 1970s and 80s. Every member of the training cadre in the office that day who saw me waiting to find out where I was going encouraged me to go to 7th. The 3rd Special Forces Group had just been activated. That is, the Army was trying to establish the new group almost from scratch, and in buildings across the street from 7th Group. The group's operational area was to be Africa and the Caribbean, and, despite the absence of a full complement of men and equipment, the Army was sending training teams to countries in those parts of the world. The word in the community was that things were not going well.

I had no idea what that meant.

Colonel Wilderman walked out of his office and gave me a grim look. "Tony, I'm sorry. I couldn't get you into the Seventh. They say you're promotable, and if you go there, they're going to slot you in a major's billet. No A-team time." He searched my face for a response. He seemed relieved I didn't start crying and continued.

"Third Group, on the other hand, said they'll take you right now, and they will put you on a team until you pin on major. You okay with that?" Again, he searched my face.

"Yes, sir," I replied, beaming. "That's why I just did all this shit."

"That's what I thought. Take some leave, we'll get you orders, and you can sign in down there after New Year's." We shook hands, he wished me a Merry Christmas, and I floated with a gigantic grin out of the building to my car.

Christmas and New Year's Day were celebrated. My children opened many presents. My wife cooked many meals; I'm sure I ate them. That's about all I remember. I was going to 3rd Special Forces Group (Airborne), and I was going to be a team leader. My clarity of purpose was absolute, my focus laser-like. The world faded to background noise as I saw the crest of a mountain I had climbed my whole life come into view.

I was standing on the beach, having considered the sand and trees.
Thank you, Mr. Crane, I'll finish this scene my own way.

On January 10, 1994, I walked into group headquarters and found my way to the personnel office. I handed a copy of my orders to a major, who identified himself as the adjutant, the officer in charge of personnel. He looked at the orders and then at me. He made a face to indicate that he was about to ask me a very important question, like where was my spaceship.

"When did you get these?" he asked.

"Right before Christmas, sir," I replied. My stomach began to knot.

He shook his head and exhaled audibly through his teeth. "Wait here," he said, and he walked away. A few minutes later he returned and told me to report to the command group across the hall. There I was to meet the deputy commander and the chief of staff, both of whom were lieutenant colonels and the right and left arm of the group commander.

I followed in the direction the major pointed and found Lieutenant Colonels Roy Dunn and Dave Schroer waiting for me. Their faces said I was trespassing. After a few minutes of dialogue, I discerned that no one had known I was coming, and the more I talked the more suspicious the two gatekeepers became. Later, after the meeting, I discovered the reason for their concern.

Some officers were coming to SF in order to rehabilitate their careers. That is, they had done something really bad and were trying to find a new life under a green beret. Problem was, most of these people should never have been allowed into the Army, much less the Special Operations community. Additionally, 3rd Group had started with a mix of people from the other groups. In order to create it, the Army staff had authorized the transfer of SF qualified officers and NCOs to be a base for the new group. The men assigned were fine, but the group was still in an ad hoc status. In order to flesh out the junior ranks, easily half of the newly minted Green Berets coming out of the Q course went straight to 3rd Group. There were no standard operating procedures, no institutional memory—only the way everybody had done it at other places. There was a sense of making it up as we went. The result of all these circumstances occurring simultaneously was that if a bad leader did make it through the filters, which did sometimes happen, he could not only cause damage to the organization but create an international incident, like the president of the United States getting a call in the middle of the night.

You didn't have to be psychologist to figure out these guys did not like how I appeared. The interrogation continued, punctuated by short lectures explaining the expectations of my being a team leader.

I wondered if they were expecting to scare me off, to have me just walk out and say, "Gosh, this is really too hard."

Finally, one of them asked a question that allowed me to redeem myself.

"What year group are you?" Translated: How long have you been in the Army?

"I'm year group eighty-four, sir." Translated: I've been in ten years. That got a response: Either I was really a dirtbag or something so different as to not be useful. Most everyone else in my Q course was year group 1988 or '89.

"You're up for major this year."

"I'm already promotable, sir. I got picked up below the zone in the Q course." Translated: The Army thinks I'm pretty good and picked me for early promotion to major. But they did that while I was still a tanker. Rest of the story: I have trashed everything in order to be a Green Beret.

"Certainly not the normal career path." Translated: Let me know how that works out for you.

"I'm supposed to be taking a team in second battalion," I said, then decided it was time to shut up. The worst thing anyone can do when entering a hierarchal organization is to appear to know more than people who have been there for a while and are in leadership positions. Rather than tell me I didn't know my ass from a hole in the ground and explain that it was impossible for me to know if I would get a team (the normal course of action), they both gave me knowing nods, shook my hand, and told me where I could find second battalion.

Satisfying them that I would not end up as the basis for a phone call to the president in the middle of the night, I walked to the headquarters for second battalion. Again I found the personnel office, handed a set of orders to someone who looked like he knew what was going on, and waited for the second round of interrogation. It never came. The battalion adjutant, a young captain, shook my hand, welcomed me to the battalion, and said the battalion commander would like to meet me.

"Right now?" I asked.

"Yeah, he's got nothing for the next few hours, so this is a good time."

I decided that he was probably Old School. Thus it was best to report in using the Old School protocol: knock, enter, come to attention, salute, and say "Captain Schwalm reports, sir."

Lieutenant Colonel Gary Michael Jones, my new battalion commander, told me to come in and intercepted me halfway to his desk, his right hand extended. At 6'1" and weighing around 205, I never thought of myself as a small guy, but when we shook, my hand disappeared inside his dinner platter–sized paws. He had played football at

LSU, and there was a rumor he had played professionally. No one knew where. He was big enough to turn heads, but no one would stare.

The second thing I noticed was that he didn't have a Ranger tab.

We talked for about thirty minutes. Inside the first ten, he obliterated any prejudice I may have had that he was a dumb jock. He explained that I was going to command Special Forces Operational Detachment Alpha 364, and in just a few sentences, he gave me an adrenaline rush like I hadn't experienced since being alerted for Desert Storm in November 1990.

First, we were on tap to do something in Haiti, something real, with bullets. I was taking notes, like I was taught in the conventional Army, and as I wrote the word *Haiti,* he stopped me.

With hooded eyes and a cautionary wag of his index finger, he said, "You don't want to write that down."

Second, I was taking a HALO team. High-altitude, low-opening, HALO parachuting was very similar to skydiving, and not at all like the static-line parachuting I had done. In a HALO rig, the jumper tried to get out of the plane as high as possible in order to avoid detection, and he usually had to bring his own oxygen. The course was five weeks long, starting at Bragg and finishing in Yuma, Arizona. Third, within the next sixty days, my team and I were going to Trinidad and Tobago to conduct exchange training with their military.

The lieutenant colonel paid equal attention to my personal life— asking me about myself, my career, my family, and my goals as an Army officer. I was struck by his confidence, his easy manner. He knew who he was, what he wanted to do, and how he was going to get there. I decided right then that I would follow him into a burning building.

The half hour went by in a blink, and he yelled out his office to the adjutant, telling him to call my new company commander, Major James Sawyer. I was to be escorted, not sent like a delivery boy. We continued talking until Sawyer arrived, and I left with the feeling that I had a boss who would cover my back.

Sawyer, too, came off as a straight shooter. He reiterated many of the points that Jones had made and began giving me specifics about the team I was to lead. ODA 364 did not have a captain in it, and no one seemed to remember him. The acting team leader was Chief Warrant Officer Ozzie Soto. The team sergeant was SFC Roy Spivey. My first thought was: *Oh no, I'm busting up a happy marriage.* As if reading my mind, Sawyer informed me that Ozzie was probably going away for an extended temporary duty. When I asked where to, he said very matter-of-factly that nobody knew and probably nobody was ever going to, except Ozzie and whomever he would be working for.

———

Walking through glass doors, we stopped by his office, where he introduced me to his sergeant major, Lou Palm, and the other members of his staff who composed the B-team. The mood was cordial and collegial. I was made to feel at home. Eventually Sawyer said it was time to meet my team, and he walked me down the hall, a long corridor about six feet wide, with four double wooden doors on each side. Behind two doors were supply rooms. Behind each of the other six was a Special Forces detachment, an A-team.

Sawyer knocked and tried the doorknob. It was locked. Checking his watch, he said we should meet him in his office after one o'clock to try again.

At 12:50 I was sniffing around the B-team. At one, there was still no Sawyer. At 1:10, I was sure the good major had been involved in a fatal or near-fatal car accident, and I decided to introduce myself without him. I knocked, turned the knob, and finally finished my journey down the rabbit hole.

The room had a twelve-foot ceiling and was maybe thirty feet square. Wall lockers ringed a group of men sitting at a large table. All eyes were on me.

"I'm Tony Schwalm. I'm your new team leader." I tried to sound eager but not too eager.

Spivey stood, smiled, and said, "Welcome to 364, sir. We heard you were coming." I spent the rest of the afternoon talking to the team and getting to know names.

Spivey and Soto were old hands from 7th Group. Brent Miles, our only medic, had come from 1st Group and had served in a Ranger battalion. Jim Robinette, Ron Sable, Darin Barber, and Dave Takaki had all come straight to the team from the Q course. Spivey told me we were due another man, Gus Duran, who was coming from 7th Group and should be reporting soon. One member of the team, Fred McCoy, was at a leadership school and would be gone until after we got back from Trinidad. Sable was under orders to go to HALO school while we were gone as well. We talked about the upcoming trip to Trinidad, and I could tell the team was stoked to be going outside the United States for a real training opportunity. Outside of a war zone, these exchange training events helped keep our cross-cultural communication skills honed.

Soto ended the day by reminding me that I needed to sign for everything, meaning that we would inventory the team's equipment. Once completed, I would sign as the responsible party and take that burden from Soto. The timing was perfect for him, as he was about to leave for an extended period. While I dreaded the administrative headache, I knew it was one of the best ways to gauge the health of the team. Lost equipment? Dirty equipment? At the end of three days, I concluded my team had no problems. But I was surprised by the pieces I inventoried.

Except for a few items of communications gear, their equipment would have been readily recognizable to any Green Beret from the Vietnam era. The team camera to be used for reconnaissance purposes was a Canon F-1, circa 1972, and it appeared to have never been out of the box. We had lots of radios, several state-of-the-art, and could talk across most of the spectrum, from HF to satellite systems. What we didn't have were small, lightweight radios that we could use to talk among members of the team, like the kind policemen and firefighters used. We could talk from anywhere in the world to any other place but not to each other in a tactical environment. But what I found most troublesome was the medical gear.

Devouring one corner of our team room were three metal boxes, each about the size of a small refrigerator and weighing about forty pounds. The contents of those boxes would provide the tools and materials to make a clandestine guerrilla hospital circa 1952. Bone saws, scalpels, and an autoclave were just a few of the items.

"Have we ever used any of this stuff?" I asked.

"I think we cooked lobsters in the autoclave once," came the response.

Coming straight from the Q course, all of this equipment made perfect sense to me. We would have to be self-sufficient, self-contained within our area in a UW campaign. Depending on what country we were operating in, our SF medic may be the best doctor any of our guerrillas or their families had ever seen. What I found troubling was that none of the gear had been exercised. That is, we had not gone out to the woods with one of these medical kits and tried to establish a hospital. Consequently, other than the occasional lobster bake, all of this equipment, surely worth hundreds of dollars, sat locked up in boxes. Every SF team had the same kit. There were approximately 270 SF teams on active duty at this time, and each one had three boxes of medical gear sitting locked up in a team room. Nobody wanted to drag the boxes around for fear of losing something, because whatever was lost would have to be paid for.

Other than the satellite radios, we had nothing special for equipment. Standard Army issue seemed to be good enough for Army Special Forces. The more I inventoried, the more I realized that what made us special was how we were employed: our UW mission set, the latitude we were given due to the lack of access to the chain of command, and the time horizons within which we operated—months and years, not minutes and hours. While guerrilla warfare is only a component of unconventional warfare, the nature of those operations drives the time train, and it is this train, unfortunately, that drives the political decision-making informing the military decision-making. You cannot go to another country, establish rapport with the rebels, train and equip them, to include building and sustaining a clandestine hospital, win the war, and then (this is the hard part) sustain the peace all in a two-year election cycle, not without an amazing amount of political will the likes of which was not seen in the last half of the twentieth century.

Just as this was occurring to me, I put it aside and continued happily along as a newly minted detachment commander. Our mornings began with physical training as tough as I had ever done. I was the new guy, and the team put me through the paces. Where I had always been one

Normally, whenever a member of the Department of Defense—or y member of a U.S. government agency, for that matter—travels on ficial business, he or she is entitled to funds above the normal comnsation for expenses incurred as a result of said travel. But this was t the case in 3rd Group. The leadership team of the group was makg a statement about frugality. Whatever the motivation, the guys on e team suffered for effort.

Whenever an officer or an enlisted soldier travels for temporary ty, he or she is entitled (not mandated to receive, but *entitled* if thorized by the commander) to what is known as incidentals: funds tended to defer the cost of, say, laundry or deodorant.

Not in 3rd Group.

Whenever an enlisted soldier travels for temporary duty, the comander can allow him to keep drawing an allotment known as separate ations. Separate rats, as they are known, are intended to buy food for a oldier living off post with his family. Usually, separate rats become an visible part of a soldier's paycheck (but very visible when they disapear).

Not in 3rd Group.

The result of such penny-pinching had several adverse effects on morale, most manifested in a T-shirt that began to appear. The front howed a 3rd Group logo. The lettering on the back read: "DIRTY DEEDS DONE DIRT CHEAP." This T-shirt was not popular with the roup staff. No one dared wear it in the group area, but the shirt was ot uncommonly seen across the back of a guy on a Harley going down Yadkin Road in Fayetteville. No one had to see the front to know the guy was in 3rd Group.

When I had been on the team about a month, I learned that we had to certify before we could deploy outside the United States. Certification was a team gut check intended to make sure that we had not become lazy and complacent under our green berets. The battalion staff gave each team a briefing that described the training scenario. We were to jump into Camp Mackall, move to a target, put "eyes on" for twenty-four hours, and then conduct a raid. Pretty straightforward. Jones set aside an entire week to conduct the certification and, in addition to the

of the fastest runners among my men as a tanker, I wa
the pack. Soto ran like a gazelle. Despite abdominal s
school, I thought I had pretty good abs. But Robinet
sion to rest. He could do the flutter kick, feet six inche
and on his back, until the rest of the team quit. One da
we were trying hard enough, so he called us all pussies a
disgusted.

Whenever we could find the time, we went to th
one of the large wrestling mats, and practiced jujits
would usually lead the sessions, and it was a great way to
While we would practice submission moves (make the
out, thus surrendering), Dave would always stress the
understanding that we were not learning to fight. We
fight the guy; we wanted to kill him as quickly as pos
reminded each other that if we were fighting hand-to-ha
to be really, really bad.

The operational focus was preparing for Trinidad
weeks to develop a program of instruction, prepare our
tify our equipment needs, and, most important, prepar
for approval by the group staff. This is where I came in.
were to run a commando course, a modified Ranger scho
include land navigation, shooting, small-boat operation
swimming, and concluding with small-unit operations.
Soto and other members of the team on what my role wa
would usually say the same thing: "You just have to get us
briefing."

Major Sawyer provided me the template for the Pow
sentation I was to produce, and I set about filling in all t
data: training calendar, training objectives, logistics (whe
stay, what we would eat, how much ammo we needed, et c
most important, the cost of it all. How much of the tax
lars were we going to spend training these Trinidadian co
As I began to compile cost data, I rapidly and regularly en
deeply rooted bitterness by the guys on all the teams agains
staff three levels of command above us.

tactical scenario, required each team to do two days of land navigation as a group. That is, we navigated from point to point while practicing our tactical movement techniques as a unit. Seeing my team maneuver in the woods that I had just left several weeks before as a student drove home a few learning points.

First, a Special Forces team is not a rifle squad led by a captain. We were designed and equipped to operate as a team, alone. While we look like any infantrymen, Army or Marines, we have the skills but not the numbers. There is no doctrine, no plan, for A-teams to fight alongside the other A-teams. We fight shoulder to shoulder with soldiers from other countries. That's what makes us special. We do that by design while everyone else does it by exception.

Second, most of the men in our team were in their late twenties to early thirties. While we were very much in our prime, we were coming to the end of it. We didn't bounce back as fast from long rucksack movements. That said, our years gave us an emotional maturity that prevented us from making stupid mistakes that affected our physical fitness. Translation: We had outgrown drinking ourselves into a coma and then trying to come to work; we didn't carry gear we didn't need just for the sake of having it; and we made judicious use of terrain to avoid what happened to me during Trek and my great map adventure.

I complained with the rest of the members of the team that it was bullshit to continue to make us prove we could do our jobs, but, secretly, I relished the opportunity to live with my team in the woods and hear what they considered important about being a Green Beret. I kept thinking to myself that now I would be let into the dark secrets of being a Green Beret. Alas, there were no surprises from those moments around a fire, boots off, socks drying, the training day done, and the stories told. The common theme was the same: What was essential was working with people from other countries. The Q course had prepared me for life on an A-team. The week passed, the team did well, and we trucked back to Bragg tired, dirty, and certified. Our focus returned to preparations for the upcoming trip.

Soto and Spivey traveled to Trinidad the month before I arrived and secured a school that would be empty during our time there. The school was used to teach commercial fishing right on the water; it had rooms enough so that each of us would have our own, held plenty of storage, and, most wonderfully, included a kitchen. We would be given a bag of money to buy our food and feed ourselves.

I composed my briefing and consulted with other team leaders in the battalion. Most were envious of my team's feeding arrangement, as it provided us great latitude in not having to live on the host nation food. There were three issues with trying to live on host nation food for six weeks. First, we have a high calorie requirement compared to those of soldiers in other countries. Second, we are spoiled for the food that suits our taste. Third, new food that we're not used to has the potential to make us sick. The other option that we did not have to explore was taking prepackaged food (like MREs, tray rations, and cartons of milk that don't require refrigeration) brought from Bragg. I saw teams load small mountains of shrink-wrapped food and long-shelf-life chocolate milk in order to feed themselves while deployed.

Soto and Spivey had done very well in finding us a place with a kitchen. Of the seven teams going into the Caribbean during this time, each team to run its own commando course for its own group of indigenous troops on its own island, we were the only ones with this arrangement, and the team appreciated what they had.

While my guys rehearsed their classes, I practiced my briefing. I gave it to the team first. They made suggestions and corrections, which I incorporated. Then I (with Soto and Spivey at my side) made my presentation to Sawyer and his sergeant major. One part that kept getting everybody's attention was the slide depicting how much ammunition we were taking. We were planning to do a lot of live-fire training and were taking thousands of rounds of rifle and machine-gun ammo. Throwing that much lead downrange caused Sawyer to worry that we only had one medic. He then directed the medic from another team, SSG Tony Aydellot, to accompany us for the trip. SF medics were in such short supply that they were commonly assigned to teams other than their own in order to create some redundancy in medical support, especially when the mission was going to take place in a country were medical support included chanting.

Other than the concern about medics, they raised no issues. The few questions asked were fielded by my experts. We had been taught this approach in the Q course. The team leader has no opportunity to know the subjects of weapons, demolition, medicine, and communications as well as his NCOs assigned to these specialties. We were warned—and rightfully so—to be the Maestro, the conductor, the guy with the baton leading and organizing the orchestra, and to not try to be first chair violin and master of every other instrument as well. Sawyer gave me a thumbs-up and sent me to Jones.

Lieutenant Colonel Jones immediately began asking questions, probing me to see what level of familiarity and expertise I possessed. One of our requirements while deployed was to make a daily communication back to Bragg via radio, either HF or satellite. Jones pressed me on which radios we would be using for that. I hesitated and then said I would defer to Spivey, whose mouth I could see opening as he tried to save me. Jones cut us both off.

"Tony, I'm trying to set you up for success, buddy," he said, and a look of fatigue washed over his face for a moment. "The group commander expects you to know everything."

I'm sure my face took on the look of a hog staring up at a ceiling fan.

He turned to Soto and said, "Ozzie, get him up to speed. Or you guys won't go."

I started to protest, and he stopped me with two big hands in the air. "I know. That's not how it's supposed to be. But it is. You don't have to know everything. Just everything on the slides." Then he hit me with his most famous line. "That's the bottom line." We understood that a "That's the bottom line" comment from Jones meant "Now shut up and do what I said."

We were scheduled to try again in two days. The team spent the time pouring everything they could think of into my head, and I tried to memorize it. When I finished briefing Jones the second time, he smiled and told me to say it just like that for the group commander. The next day, all the team leaders scheduled to deploy for training lined up outside the group commander's office. I was allowed to bring Spivey but was made to understand that he could not speak.

It didn't appear to me to be a special way of doing things; it just seemed strange.

About twenty of us trooped into the group commander's conference room carrying notebooks, maps, and diagrams all describing how we were going to train soldiers on different islands in the Caribbean. Thanks to Jones, there was very little one-upmanship. We weren't exactly homogenized, but someone wasn't going to look good at someone else's expense. We each had twenty minutes. Fortunately, I was last. After two hours of the same briefing with different names, even the most punctilious staff will begin to wane. As long as I didn't say something really, really stupid, their faces said they wanted me to finish quickly. I took a chance and ran quickly over things I heard the other briefers get stopped for. They were all waiting for the most important slide: cost. But this one passed the sniff test, and we were done. Thanks to Jones, we all survived. He correctly anticipated every question we were asked.

As we left the group headquarters, the team leaders were high-fiving. Spivey was beaming at me.

"You done good, sir," he said. I beamed back.

We spent the next several days loading our gear onto Air Force pallets and doing final rehearsals for the classes that we would give the Trinidadians, or Trinis, as I discovered they called themselves.

I would be taking my team to Trinidad. My boss would be 1500 miles away. If I screwed up, it would be the U.S. ambassador who notified my chain of command.

Spivey and I flew ahead to make sure everything was ready for the team when they arrived with all our equipment. They came down on military transport, and we flew commercial. While the normal time for promotion was over a year after the announcement, I felt I could be promoted to major and off the team at any time. Consequently, I knew this might be my only trip with the team. I drank in every experience and packed them as tightly as I could into my memory.

FIFTEEN

ON MARCH 13, 1994, we arrived in Port-of-Spain, Trinidad and Tobago. Two of the three bags I checked were lost. The customs officials were very cooperative but required proof of military service due to all the camouflage gear I said would be in the bags. Apparently, most of Central and South America as well as the Caribbean treat camouflage as an item for war use only. My bags arrived at the hotel later that night.

The following day, Spivey and I met with the TTDF (Trinidad and Tobago Defense Forces) leaders to finalize the training schedule. The operations officer for the regiment, Major Jacobson, appeared to be a very likable man with a professional air. We also met with Captain Garcia, our liaison with the training regiment for any materials we would need. We learned from that first meeting that the TTDF didn't think much of their American trainers: The proposed training schedule was not hard enough. The TTDF wanted a Ranger school with a pass-or-fail criteria for graduation. After reviewing the proposed training schedule, Captain Garcia commented that TTDF could have trained this POI, or program of instruction. Realizing that to disagree with him would be further insult, I agreed and said I would take any input under advisement.

When the rest of the team arrived, Spivey and I planned to address the training regimen to satisfy the leaders in the TTDF that it was strenuous enough. I feared that we would destroy some of their soldiers' careers by creating an undoable standard. But we needed to try.

I remember the legend of Ugandan commandos who failed Ranger school in the 1970s. Upon their arrival at Entebbe, at the base of the stairs to the plane, they were executed.

After a couple of days, I spoke with Captain Garcia and Captain Archie Phillips of the SOG (TTDF special operations group, primarily a counter-drug unit). They backpedaled on the idea of how tough the course should be. Both requested that standards should be enforced yet not be unrealistic. Both, nonetheless, requested a draconian application of whatever standard we chose. I recommended that some events have a dual standard. One standard would be fixed, and the other would be based on a bell-shaped curve eliminating the bottom 10 percent on certain events. All present liked that idea.

My team arrived at noon on March 17. Major Jacobson and Master Sergeant Murphy (a member of the U.S. embassy staff) were very helpful and made the move through customs and the airport quite smooth. Over lunch, the team discussed the manner in which we would handle the commandos (as we referred to our students). We agreed to go with the total "Ranger school" approach. We would do all the admin work on the first day and give them a false sense of security.

From the moment we met our students for the first time until we graduated the survivors some thirty days later, my learning curve regarding the lessons of working with another country's army over the amount of time we were in Trinidad was a nearly vertical line. In conversations with many of the prospective commandos, I discovered that all was not as it had been described in the many briefings with the Trini leadership.

Over half of our forty-two students had not volunteered. Five of them had no field equipment, only uniforms and a laundry bag. Three of them found out they were coming only two days before reporting. We were assured that all the students would have their own maps and compasses, and none of them did. Our students represented the second string; the first string had been sent to France for the French commando course. The mess hall, we were told, would be on standby to accommodate the meals at any time for the students. We discovered "any time" meant 0730, 1230, and 1700. No one expected any training to occur on Friday; three-day weekends were the standard in Trinidad. Who knew?

As part of processing, we administered the Army physical fitness test: Only five of the forty-two passed.

As fate would have it, the group adjutant, the first man I met when I signed into 3rd Group, was from Trinidad, and his family owned a bar about an hour south of where we were staying. Major M. flew down with the military transport that brought the team. He was on vacation and invited us for an evening at the family bar, the Side Door Pub in California, Trinidad. The chef had prepared true island food in the Indian tradition. We ate beans with roti dipped in pepper sauce, washing it all down with the best beer—that is, free beer. We could not finish the platters of food they brought us. Then out came a belly dancer who appeared to me somewhere between sixteen and twenty-six. I can say without qualification that hers was the most erotic performance I have ever seen. "Spellbound" is not too strong a word to describe the effect this young woman had on us. When she was finished, an older woman who identified herself as the girl's mother tapped me on the shoulder and said that she was honored her daughter could perform for the Americans. She regretted having to leave so quickly, but they had another engagement in just a few minutes. I complimented her daughter's dancing ability and asked almost as an afterthought how old our performer was. "She's fourteen." I headed back to our base with a full stomach and guilt-riddled images of a ninth-grader dancing in my head.

The following morning, we surprised the commandos by waking them up with grenade simulators, followed by a ninety-minute smoke session (hard-core calisthenics and running), followed by eight hours of classes on the basics of land navigation: how to read a map, how to use a compass, et cetera. Miles and Barber were the instructors, and they didn't feel the commandos quite grasped the lessons. We looked at the schedule and found time for retraining as necessary. Our commandos did not reflect the American sense of urgency that my team wanted to see. We were used to students in U.S. military schools acting very concerned about not achieving top honors in everything from fitness to marksmanship. The Trinis were more "don't worry; be happy," and that approach was not sitting well with my guys. This cultural disconnect manifested itself in the following week, as we nearly had a major setback in our relationship with the host nation.

The time came to take the commandos out for a practical exercise in navigating with map and compass. We used the local golf course and the surrounding jungle for the first examination. We started the test around 0900 and intended for it to be over by 2300. That way the students got a taste of both day and night navigation. At midnight, we still had one student out. At 0115 the next morning, the student was still missing, and I called Captain Garcia to apprise him of the situation. I left two SF guys on the golf course sleeping in one of our vehicles in case the guy showed up. We sent the students back to the barracks to get some sleep. At 0630, we reassembled the class and organized them into search parties. At 0930, our missing student emerged from the jungle within a few meters of the start point for the night portion. He said he had gone to sleep around 1745 and awoke at 1930. I could not understand why he had hidden while we had been searching. He had to have heard us calling for him. I didn't want to think what would have happened if we'd really lost one of their soldiers. I was so mad I threw him out of the course, instantaneous termination. Captain Garcia was noticeably relieved over the phone when I said we had found the student but less enthusiastic when I explained how I had handled the situation. When I hung up, I realized I was coming at the students as if they were from the United States. I saw our students as men trying to be like me, and I was now the gatekeeper, allowing passage only to those I felt measured up to my standard. Garcia saw the students as his children, and the lost one in need of discipline, yes, but not to be shunned or expelled. I made a note to check my temper.

After the day off, around 0200, five of us drove to the barracks housing our commandos and woke them up with the loud boom of a simulator. We smoked them for forty-five minutes and then let them go back to bed. A message was waiting for me when I got back to the SF compound. The U.S. embassy in Port-of-Spain had received a frantic call from the senior ranking general of the TTDF. Unbeknownst to me, he lived directly across the street from our commandos' barracks. The rude awakening we delivered to the students had been shared with their boss, only he thought for several minutes that it was the opening salvo of a coup. The message explained that in the future I should warn the general when we were going to use an explosion as a wakeup call.

As our training progressed, I discovered something about their field rations. The meals that the Trini mess hall delivered when we were away from the base (and we were always gone from the base during normal duty hours) didn't provide for paper plates or plastic flatware. They had to eat dinner with their fingers from metal mess kits they carried with them. Dinner was beef porridge and ice water. They never complained. The reason I was late discovering this fact is that we didn't eat with our commandos. We, the SF, brought our own food. The logistical reality I've already mentioned about rations was now the cause of my missing an important point of working with indigenous forces: If you don't share every privation, every hardship, with the men you're leading, you don't know who you're leading.

On the day of the final exam for land navigation, we woke the commandos at 0130, and they started the test at 0330. They all passed, and we didn't lose anybody. At this point, from the original forty-two, we had lost five commandos: one I dismissed; two for medical reasons; and two quit.

With land navigation behind us, our training turned to more classroom-oriented lessons, like studying tactics and writing out plans. This change gave the team more time to relax as well, and more time brought different problems for my team and me specifically. A leader, at least one born in the middle of the twentieth century and in the U.S. Army, has no credibility if he or she drinks alcohol while deployed, particularly if that leader represents the sum total of military authority over the unit. With the boss fifteen hundred miles away, anything that can be construed as compromising integrity or military decision-making will undermine the leader's authority. I learned that this was particularly true when dealing with critical thinkers (read: those with borderline criminal intelligence), like SF NCOs.

One night early in our tour in Trinidad, a member of the U.S.

embassy invited my team to the Marine House, the lodging for the Marine security detail guarding the compound in downtown Port-of-Spain. The Marine House served as a neutral zone and safe oasis, a place where State Department personnel with their degrees from Georgetown could drink beer among Marines with their degrees from public high schools. Two guys on the team were designated drivers, and the rest of us drank beer. Nobody got drunk, but that proved irrelevant. Two of my NCOs started to get into a fight. They went outside to demonstrate what they had learned during our jujitsu sessions. I immediately went out the door after them, and while my presence precluded the fight that was certainly about to ensue, one of my guys put his hand on my chest and said, "I don't want to hear your shit, sir. You been drinking, too." At that moment, confronted with irrefutable proof describing my leadership failure, I decided to restrict myself to infrequent, alcohol-free trips out for dinner and visits to the Marine House.

The days passed uneventfully as we trained and tested common soldier tasks like assembly and cleaning of a rifle, how to send a radio message, and the finer points of applying camouflage. Everyone passed. We began basic demolition training, and SFC Duran did an excellent job as primary instructor. I marveled at what he knew about blowing things up.

Demolition training marked the transition into live-fire training—not marksmanship, but how to apply marksmanship to the art of hunting other people. At its core, at the basest level, war is people hunting people.

We took the commandos to the range to practice the demolition training with real explosives. We destroyed the range, big holes everywhere, trees splintered to toothpicks, but everyone seemed to have fun. We fired a Claymore mine to show the effect it would have on troops. A thousand small steel balls impregnated into a pound of plastic explosive and housed in a green box resembling a camera without a lens, the Claymore is named for a medieval Scottish sword that could cleave a person in half. Spivey put up ten cardboard silhouettes and spaced them a few feet apart as if they were men walking on a trail. After the blast, every target had been hit multiple times. Our commandos were duly impressed.

Still, the daily routine of working out in the morning continued unabated. The physical training that we meted out withered our students. Between voluntary withdrawals and medical drops, we began live-fire training with only thirty-four commandos. Our course began to be the talk around the base. The TTDF officers and NCOs outside the course grew concerned with the number of people who were not making it. I was constantly asked about numbers.

One day we had to cancel training to allow all the commandos to go to the bank and pay their bills because it was payday. I noticed an immediate cultural connection between us and our commandos on this point. The same routine was honored in the U.S. military until the advent of electronic deposit. Even in the era of computer banking, some U.S. units will still take "payday activities" as an excuse for a long weekend.

I experienced another cultural education as I interacted with personnel in the embassy. One night I was invited to dinner. Alone with members of the staff, I observed their ritual for determining rank within their pecking order. Rather than ask me if I had a Ranger tab, a political officer casually tossed the question of where had I done my graduate work. I politely answered that since completing my undergraduate I had yet to find the time to pursue a master's degree between deployments. While my response seemed to satisfy everyone's curiosity around the table, inside I was seething. I wanted to say, "Yeah, while you were cruising bars around Adams Morgan in D.C., I was sleeping on the back deck of a tank in the Saudi desert. Glad you got your degree. Glad I could help." Instead, we discussed how the lack of a change of seasons this close to the Equator left Americans of the East Coast without a sense of time passing. Every day was the same for them. I swallowed my disgust along with the free dinner. I never did accept another offer for a night out.

Also, we continued with the midnight smoke sessions. On night, we did a two-hour road march in full kit (a term taken from the Brits to describe personal gear with a rucksack). After walking for two hours with about forty pounds on our backs, we took them straight to the pugil sticks (imagine a broom handle with a plastic cushion at each end, meant to represent a rifle with a bayonet). Even wearing football helmets, they beat the hell out of each other. From there, they went to breakfast, and we spent the rest of the day in weapons classes.

Along the way, we lost five more commandos, one to a dislocated shoulder. No one was sure how he did it. We had one commando fail the knot test. They had to tie eight of ten knots correctly, and this guy couldn't do it. I remember the pain etched on the faces of those who left this late into the training. At this stage, the guys still with us were trying so hard. I hoped everyone in the TTDF leadership who wanted a "hard course" remembered what they asked for. They wanted it hard. We gave it hard. Ground like dust in the hard training machine my team created, the commandos desperately wanted to finish with so many painful miles behind them.

We celebrated Easter weekend by conducting a shoot-fest. For Good Friday, we spent twelve hours on the rifle range. The commandos fired everything from pistols to machine guns, then cleaned weapons until 2300. My weapons specialist, SSG Takaki, knocked it out of the park, just did an excellent job as range NCOIC.

All of the events continued to inform my personal library of learning about working with other countries, especially in the developing world. I arrived in Trinidad concerned about lazy islanders living on island time while pretending to be soldiers. Instead, I found our commandos to be intelligent, motivated, and capable of great initiative. For example, most of our students had only one canteen. Some had boots four or five sizes too large. The armorers had no spare parts for broken weapons and instead cannibalized other guns. Their rations, while adequate for normal garrison activity, were not sufficient for the type of training required to sustain what we put them through. None of them complained.

Despite such individual courage, however, they continued to fail. As we entered the last week of training, we had twenty-nine of the original forty-five.

In order to find a training area with the most challenging terrain available, Spivey and I scouted around the island. We drove over to Manzanilla Beach on the east side and found some U.S. history. Merrill's Marauders had trained there for the Burma campaign in World War II, and we found the outlines of the buildings they inhabited while here. Supposedly, General Frank Merrill said that the terrain of Trinidad most closely resembled that of Burma. Very desolate, isolated beaches and mango swamps at the base of heavily vegetated steep hills, the ground should be hallowed for anyone who ever served in a Ranger unit, though most would not know their lineage began right where we were standing. The crest of the 5307 Composite Unit (Provisional)— the official name of Merrill's Marauders—is the basis for the Ranger crest today.

We opted for another location, but I will never forget standing among the ruins of a unit that so distinguished itself in a part of the global conflagration called World War II, a part mostly forgotten. Historians have noted that of the 1,200 or so men known as the Marauders, only two finished the war unscathed.

Upon return from the scouting mission, my turn came to teach some classes on mission planning. I used the same lesson plan that I had taught to my ROTC cadets at Rutgers. Without modification, I gave the exact class that I gave a year before standing on the Queen's College campus in New Brunswick, New Jersey, to a group of foreign commandos on an island two thousand miles from there. The commandos devoured it.

As the weeks passed, a new liaison officer from the TTDF headquarters was named and, with an apparent lack of any awareness of the conversations between his predecessor and me, he made clear he was not his predecessor. Captain Jack, the new guy, expressed concern over the number of failures in the course, particularly the student who had failed the knot test. The student had been given several tries but, in the end, was dropped for one knot and never the same one. He always made seven but needed eight of ten. Captain Jack informed me that the man's chain of command was considering dismissing him from the army. The dismissed student was an officer candidate, and his brief and mediocre career was about to end with a failure to tie a knot. I nodded while Captain Jack spoke. I could tell he was hoping that I would reinstate the student. I did not, and the TTDF leadership dismissed him.

Members of my team (I can't recall who) wanted to give the commandos a creed. After much discussion, we chose the Ranger Creed modified for the word "commando" I had considered writing a creed for them but questioned why I should reinvent the wheel. Where it read "Ranger," we inserted "commando."

"Recognizing that I volunteered as a commando, fully knowing the hazards of my chosen profession, I will always endeavor to uphold the prestige, honor, and high esprit de corps of my commando regiment.

"Acknowledging the fact that a commando is a more elite soldier who arrives at the cutting edge of battle by land, sea, or air, I accept the fact that as a commando my country expects me to move further, faster, and fight harder than any other soldier.

"Never shall I fail my comrades. I will always keep myself mentally alert, physically strong, and morally straight, and I will shoulder more than my share of the task whatever it may be, one hundred percent and then some.

"Gallantly will I show the world that I am a specially selected and well-trained soldier. My courtesy to superior officers, neatness of dress, and care of equipment shall set the example for others to follow.

"Energetically will I meet the enemies of my country. I shall defeat them on the field of battle for I am better trained and will fight with all my might. Surrender is not a commando word. I will never leave a fallen comrade to fall into the hands of the enemy and under no circumstances will I ever embarrass my country.

"Readily will I display the intestinal fortitude required to fight on to the commando objective and complete the mission though I be the lone survivor."

That the first letter of each part spelled "Ranger" was never mentioned. I listened to them as they learned it, discussing what it meant. When they finally had it down, the creed came from their mouths like the Lord's Prayer since they recited it with such solemnity. They seemed to be moved emotionally as they read it together.

I wanted to reward their dedication and regretted we could not give them more kit. All of them had only one uniform, and by the end of the week these got pretty ripe. They were wearing a mix of uniforms from different countries, as their quartermaster could not fit them with the standard British camouflage uniforms they were supposed to have. I couldn't help but think of all the whining in our army. Our guys didn't know how good they had it. I felt that our commandos were truly committed to what we had come to teach them.

Along with a new liaison officer, I met the new mess officer, a woman. She promised that she would give our commandos extra rations and an occasional special treat: Kool-Aid.

With two weeks to go, I began to have serious doubts concerning how we had set up the whole program of instruction. I didn't like the flavor this course was taking. Because we were running a Ranger school, we were exempt from eating and sleeping with our students all the time. While my team didn't want to eat with the students, the Trini commanders were happy to oblige us because they did not want us to eat with them either. Apparently the U.S. Navy had come here a few years ago and complained they were being overcharged for substandard food. The TTDF felt embarrassed and made sure such an accusation could not be repeated. In addition, the TTDF leaders did not want us to billet with our students because there was no room for us and our equipment in the barracks. Thus, for all the right legitimate reasons, my team played into the ugly American syndrome.

We lived apart, eating like horses. Though I felt we connected with the students, I knew there was still a gulf between us, one I discovered one night after a long day of training.

As they were sitting around in the dark, eating beef porridge with their fingers, I circled behind them and came up quietly into their group. No one was expecting me to be there. I listened as the conversation turned from the training to the trainers. Each member of my team was known among our commandos for a particular habit, usually a signature phrase. Finally they got to me. A disembodied voice bemoaned the idea that I would ever say to him, "Turn in your compass." I didn't realize that phrase had come to mean a commando was being tossed from the course. (We had issued them working compasses for the course, and without that piece of kit, navigation was impossible.) I remained silent as another voice said, "I don't see any of them living on this shit we're eating. More fucking white men come to help the Trini." I grimaced as silence ensued and listened to what I could only imagine was thoughtful chewing. I felt I needed to take the gravity from the remark.

"Well, commando," I said, attempting to shatter the stillness in what I hoped was my best authoritarian voice, "I can assure you we have not been doing any 'fucking' since we got here. We're too tired after training you guys." The startled laughter that answered my pronouncement followed me out of the circle and gave me a stronger sense that we needed to be closer to the men we were trying to make like us.

I began to consider that we should have lived with them, regardless of the complications. Both countries' armies would have been better served if we had built a base in the jungle and conducted operations out of there. Then we would have been under the constant scrutiny of our students. While that scrutiny would have forced a few changes, such as fewer nights out on the town when my guys had down time, the penny-pinching attitude of the 3rd Group staff raised its head. I could not bring myself to make my team live in the jungle, given they were all going to lose money when we got back. "Join Special Forces; go to exotic countries and live like an animal; lose money in the process."

As well as everything was going, I became concerned we were becoming tourists with rifles.

The last phase of training also incorporated water-infiltration techniques. From that training came one of our worst days, as a commando got seawater in his lungs during a scout swim. Like all the students, he was wearing a life vest, and he got the notion that he wanted to quit swimming but did not want to quit the course. (Quitting anything in the course resulted in immediate termination, just like in the U.S. Army.) These men were connected to one another by a buddy line. When our guy decided to quit swimming, he became an amazing burden to the rest of his team. Eventually, my guys hauled him into the boat. SSG Aydellot checked him out and heard water in his lungs, which wouldn't clear with coughing. Untreated, the guy would get pneumonia. We sent him to the hospital, and I glumly considered that we were about to lose another student. Fortunately, he was returned to us with a clean bill of health. We overlooked his quitting and chalked it up to momentary insanity due to water in the lungs, a convenient contrivance to keep us from losing another student.

The live-fire training created a new problem with the ammo for the commandos' rifles. The bullets we brought were too hot, too powerful for the older Trini weapons. The students carried the Galil, an Israeli weapon. We were afraid our ammo could damage them permanently. My team had brought our rifles, and I, ignorant of what I was asking, broached the subject of letting the commandos use our weapons. I regretted speaking such sacrilege immediately. Nobody shoots our rifles but us unless it's an emergency, and this was not an emergency.

We gave the students some light days and tested them on what we had trained over the previous month. These were easy days leading up to the capstone exercise, a five-day patrol. We tested them on weapons and scout swimming. We didn't have any more failures, but there were still more gates to pass.

One night during these easier days, our military liaison officer at the U.S. embassy invited us to a toga party at the Marine House. Spivey and I arrived fashionably late, attired in camouflage togas. We were the hit of the party. Around midnight we excused ourselves, explaining that we were going to the barracks to awaken our commandos. This comment brought astonished looks from the embassy personnel, who were mostly wasted and trying to see if we were wearing anything under our togas.

In an effort to convince the commandos that they are never really ever off duty, Spivey and I went to their barracks at 0130 and woke them up for a four-mile run. After the run, we went for a one-hour road march along a well-marked trail in the jungle. We handed them over to other guys on the team, who took them in small boats to the start point of a one-kilometer night swim. The commandos were smoked, but nobody quit.

As if to point up the students' dedication, one of them drove by us as we were running out the gate at the start of the run. He had been out with friends, but he went to the barracks and changed. He caught us about one mile into the run and went by me at a sprint. That level of commitment matched anything I had seen in the U.S. Army in a training environment.

Throughout the training, I routinely visited the U.S. embassy and provided updates to the staff. My visits to the embassy produced relationships that in turn produced resources that we decided to integrate into our training. One such resource came through the national museum.

One day at the embassy, I met with Gaylord Kelshaw, the island museum curator. He told me about a World War II bomber that had crashed nearby in 1942. The plane was about one hour from our base and then two hours into the jungle by foot. The team, upon hearing about it, decided to use the crash site as the objective for our first patrol and retrieve the .50-caliber machine guns that were supposedly still there. We intended to have the commandos present the relics to the museum, if we could find them. Gaylord said he would have the local press cover the presentation. He also explained, in a discreet aside to me, that our commandos, until we arrived, had most likely never qualified or even fired a real weapon with live bullets. The information was too late to change anything on the training schedule, but it did tell me that we had done a pretty good job of training our students without a mishap.

The warning I received about the lack of weapons training proved true on the range. After being assured by the TTDF leadership that our guys had shot before and could qualify without any intense instruction, we had a bad day on the weapons-qualification course. Very bad day. At first, it looked as if less than half would qualify. After a second attempt, all but three made it. With subsequent attempts these three still didn't make it. One was enthusiastic, intelligent, and very young. While there was nothing much more objective than marksmanship— you either hit the target or you don't—I hated to fail this kid. He had passed everything first try. His name was Polo, and my SF team split along the line whether to keep him or drop him. Anyone standing within a hundred feet of us would have heard the argument. The passion expressed by my guys was fanatical on both sides.

"If he can't shoot, he's not a commando."

"It doesn't matter. We're shitting on these guys' careers."

I called timeout on the debate and decided to allow the three students to try one more time the next day.

I'm sure this decision was based on the fear that Polo's career would be ruined if we failed him. I found out that the man who failed the knot test had indeed been made a civilian. What was a training exercise for us was continued employment for those we trained. I could feel my team's conflicting emotions. If we want this title *commando* to mean anything, we could not allow one of our graduates to return to his unit and not be able to hit what he shot at. Complicating the problem was a fact we didn't learn until later that night, cleaning weapons with our students. Polo was with the TTDF coast guard, not the army. They carried Uzis, a machine pistol, and not Galils, which are rifles. Failing Polo for not hitting his target with a rifle would be tantamount to failing a skier for not being able to run fast.

The next day the crisis passed, as all three qualified during the retest.

We still had the problem of shooting our ammo through their rifles. Weapons qualification required less than a hundred rounds, and we felt safe letting the students shoot our ammo. The last exercise, however, would require them to shoot hundreds of rounds. I put in a call to Fort Bragg, to the weapons committee at the schoolhouse, asking the question about our ammunition and their rifles: Were we damaging them? While waiting for the response, I discovered that the TTDF SOG had the same rifles we did and would allow our commandos to use them for the remainder of the course. Two days before we departed from the island, a person from the weapons committee called and said yes, we were right to be concerned. We could blow up their rifles with our ammo.

We devised a training plan to give our students a break before the final gate to decide if they would pass the course. Small-boat training allowed us to let the commandos rest before the final PT test. This would be the last pass-or-fail event before the final week of training, which was all patrolling. Unless they got killed or hurt during the last week, everybody who passed the PT test would graduate. In a brief exchange, I explained our approach to Captain Jack, who informed me that all our graduates would be allowed to sew a patch to their uniforms bearing the title "Commando." Each would also receive an extra ten dollars a month in pay for the rest of his career.

As I was contemplating the significance our work would have in the lives of the men who graduated, a tragedy occurred that gave all of us on the team and our students a reason to reflect. Dennis White, a member of the SOG, had volunteered to help my team during the small-boat training and was recovering one of the boats that we used. Inexplicably, he fell facefirst into the propeller of the running engine. The trauma to his throat killed him. Though our exchanges with him had been little more than pleasantries, my team passed the hat and sent a card with the money to his widow. I thought back to my training in Robin Sage when we had accidentally "killed" the wrong person. It seemed so shallow to send money for the death of a loved one. The only thing shallower was not to.

In the shadow of the death, the following morning we administered the final physical fitness test. Each man had to do forty-five pushups in two minutes, rest for no more than five minutes, do forty-five situps in two minutes, rest, and complete a two-mile run in less than sixteen minutes. I honestly thought they would all smoke it. Ten failed. I had made it clear from the beginning that the objective standards for the test would be applied. Now my guys were watching me to see if I had the guts to follow through, or if I would cave to political pressure and "make nice" with the politicos. If I did, it would destroy the credibility of the course we had busted everybody's asses to run. Ten times I uttered what I now knew to be the hated words: "Turn in your compass." Ten times, often through tears, I would hear in response simply, "Yes, sir."

The massacre to the student roster was apparently so dramatic as to shut up Captain Jack. If it had been one or two students dropped, I think he would have been flying at me, demanding to know what I thought we were doing, failing his students. But ten? The silence after the single greatest daily attrition from the TTDF was never explained, but my sense was that the leadership decided we meant business. My phone never rang.

With only seventeen commandos remaining from the original forty-five, we made preparations for the field training exercise. Spivey and I went with some guides from the museum to recon the crash site. We had enjoyed dry weather up to this point, but our guides warned us that the rainy season may begin soon. It was like someone hit a switch. As soon as we got into the jungle, it rained buckets. The trip was a gut check up a nearly vertical, vegetation-choked hill. As we continued to climb, we began to disappear into clouds. We made the top as the storm blew away and saw plane wreckage strewn from where we were standing and down the other side of the hill. The aircrew had missed clearing the hill by about a hundred feet. I'm sure they never knew what hit them. According to records at the museum, the Army Air Corps recovered the remains and left everything else. I understood why after we had finished the climb: There was no way to get the wreckage out of there. We spotted the barrel of a machine gun sticking out of the ground near one of the massive landing wheels. We marked the spot with a GPS just in case our guides forgot to show up on game day. I could just see us wandering around in the rain wearing several pounds of kit, asking if anyone had seen a plane crash.

We commenced the exercise at 0500 and moved the commandos by truck to a spot in the jungle about three kilometers from the crash site. Each man was carrying about fifty pounds, most of that ammo. Our route was going to take us along several rocky creek beds, and I did not want an accidental discharge to turn into a fatal ricochet. The students carried an empty magazine in their rifle. Miles, Robinette, and I walked with the students. Their movement technique was good: good control of the element, no problems. As we began to ascend, I heard a commotion near the front of our column. With shouts of a word I had never heard before, "*Mapapi!*" I watched the commandos dive off the creek bed and into the thick jungle on both sides. Racing down the hill, straight through the middle of us, was a snake about two feet long.

My nascent snake-eater qualities evaporated upon seeing the bared fangs. I got out of its way, but I knew we should kill it. I had no idea what a mapapi was, but I guessed from its looks it was probably poisonous. I picked up a branch and swung at it. It backed up and then struck at me. I backed up and fell flat on my ass. The students thought this was funny. I looked at one of the commandos and told him to give me his rifle. I opened one of his ammo pouches, removed a loaded magazine, and dropped the empty one from his rifle. With a move I had practiced thousands of times, I slammed the magazine into the rifle, then attempted to pull the charging handle back in order to load a round into the chamber. Of the seventeen rifles I could have grabbed, the owner of this one had sought to modify the location where the strap connected to the butt of the rifle. He had cinched it, and the water had welded it firmly behind the charging handle. I ripped the nail off my right index finger trying to remove it so I could shoot the damn snake. We watched him disappear down a hole, and part of my mystique went with him. But it left us with a crisis: It bit the guy who had stepped on him.

I threw the rifle at the hapless student and said in a loud clear voice that God should damn him.

We had not allowed for snakebites. We had no antivenom, no drugs to help until we got him to the antivenom, and no medevac to get him out of the jungle. We couldn't reach anyone by radio. I sent one of our guides and Robinette back to call the hospital, to see what we could do. They got to a pay phone, made a call to the hospital, and radioed to tell me several facts that we did not know. The island had two very modern Sikorsky helicopters on twenty-four-hour standby for aero-medevac. The hospital could send them anywhere needed. The helicopters had radios but could not talk to ours. Even if they could, we didn't have their frequency. We could have rehearsed these evacuation procedures before being faced with a life-and-death crisis. I was kicking myself for not asking questions, but the recriminations would be a lot worse if our student died.

While I'm learning all this via radio, Miles removed the commando's boot and checked the wounds. He had two sets of puncture wounds, and the snake appeared to have bitten him through the nylon top of his jungle boot. We carried him to the top of the hill, and doing so felt exactly like an event from SFAS. Even taking turns, all of us were spent by the time we got to the top. Of course, a commando weighing over two hundred pounds would be the one we had to transport. At the top, out came the machetes, and we started clearing the landing zone. We made a fire, trying to produce as much white smoke as possible, which was not hard given how wet everything was. We heard the helicopter in the distance and were cheered by the sound. Right before we had a visual of the chopper, the clouds settled on us like wet cotton. With a sense of frustration that nearly brought tears to my eyes, I listened to the helicopter circling in the valley, below the clouds. Our fire had produced white smoke, which blended perfectly with the fog enveloping us. Miles gave me the only news that I could consider good: There was no swelling around the bites. *Maybe the mapapi wasn't poisonous after all,* I thought.

I listened to the helicopter leave. We kept the fire going, and after an hour of silence, the clouds parted. It was around 1300. The commandos poured fuel on the fire, making as much smoke as possible. While wondering if the helicopter had waited around, I heard it churning toward us. It hovered over us, and the end of a rope came whipping out. I had to dive into the brush to grab it. The silhouette of a man appeared in the door of the hovering craft, and he rappelled down to us. He was wearing an orange jumpsuit and an aviation helmet with the visor down. We exchanged no pleasantries. On his belt was a clear plastic bag from which he produced the biggest papaya I had ever seen. Handing it to our commando, he yelled over the roar of the helicopter, "Eat this. Eat all of it, man. Now."

While our man dug in, the guy from the helicopter put a harness on the patient. With one boot off and his face dripping in juice, the wounded commando was hoisted into the bird, soon followed by his rescuer. The helicopter banked into the valley, and the jungle was quiet again.

The student who had rendered his rifle utterly useless in my effort to kill the snake designed a penance for himself. He fashioned a sling out of parachute cord and tied it to the .50-caliber machine gun. He carried the sixty-five-pound chunk of orange rusted metal along with the rest of his gear off the hill. He humped at least a hundred pounds back to the truck and refused all offers of assistance. He never staggered—I know, because I walked behind him. When we got to the truck, I shook his hand and told him he had done very well. I thought he needed to know that his debt had been paid.

We trucked the students straight to the museum and presented Gaylord Kelshaw, the curator, with our prize, a lump of solid rust. Everybody loved it. The press was there, and the commandos were beaming. After all the handshakes, they loaded back onto the truck and moved to the training area we would use for the rest of the FTX. They set up a patrol base for the night, and, of course, it rained like hell.

Later, I found out what a mapapi is. It's a fer-de-lance, a pit viper, and accounts for more than a few deaths every year on the island. I understood why they were diving off the trail. By the grace of God, the snake didn't try to kill our commando: The bites were dry, no venom.

In the patrol base that night, I discovered another disturbing fact, one I would have known if we had lived with the guys we had trained. I learned that more than one of our commandos did not own any socks. One was using an Ace bandage. I passed the word to my team who, without hesitation, donated a few pairs each so that all the commandos had socks. I hoped they fit.

After a night in the rain, I cleaned up and went to the embassy to report about the snakebite incident. I called back to Bragg and spoke to Major Sawyer. I learned that while we had been deployed, the battalion ran another certification exercise. I had thought this requirement was a check-the-block drill. Just go gut it out and move on. Not so. Jones decertified a team that was scheduled to go along with several others to Antigua for a three-week exercise. My team was taking their spot. I bet Sawyer could hear my grin over the phone.

That night, we conducted a raid on a deserted island, a former leper colony, which had closed in the 1960s. All the buildings were still there, including a hospital. We loaded three Zodiac boats at 1830, Duran, Barber, and me each taking a section. Duran christened us the *Nina, Pinta,* and *Santa Maria.* We got to our island at 1940. The moon was three quarters full. We were pelted by the occasional flying fish.

The bit of water we crossed is called Boca de Monos—"mouth of the dragon." As we puttered along in our little boats, I could see the faces of our Trini commandos: serious, grim war faces. During those moments in the boat, I felt utterly at peace, perfectly aligned with the universe. I was a Special Forces officer, and I was leading a group of men from another country. It may only have been training, but I would have taken those guys anywhere. The cultural division was gone, completely gone. We were a unit, a team, a lethal force, and I had helped them become that.

We disembarked on a stone pier with a gazebo. A couple of my guys had come over earlier, picked a building, and put target silhouettes inside. I traveled with the machine guns that would provide support for the assault. We set the guns on rocks and stood in knee-deep water. The target was a house set on an inlet, and we would be firing from the mouth of it across the water.

The assault element cued us via radio for the guns to begin engaging the house. The M60 machine guns began firing in perfect syncopation. For several minutes, there was a constant stream of red tracers arcing across 450 meters of black water. It was like shooting over a mirror. Once in a while a tracer would stop inside the house and light up all the windows with red light. A red flare signaled for us to stop, and I watched the assault element run into the house blasting away.

When the shooting was done, we declared success and retreated back to the pier, and I strung a hammock between two poles on the gazebo. I fell asleep listening to the ocean lap the beach where the students had put a patrol base. Thank God it didn't rain.

We repeated the raid in daylight and this time added some demo. When we finished, the house looked like a chunk of Swiss cheese.

We returned to the main island and continued the rest of the exercise. The commandos took turns leading patrols, and we did everything using live rounds and demo. Nobody got hurt, and we shot up all the ammo and blew up all the explosives. That latter point was important: Turning in live ammo after a deployment was a royal pain in the ass. Best to return with nothing but empty cartons, if that. No paperwork.

After the last raid, I walked up and told the class congratulations, they had completed the commando course. They jumped around and hugged each other. Then they formed a circle and prayed openly, thanking God that they had made it. We spent the rest of the day cleaning the equipment and preparing to travel back to Bragg. My guys kept saying they hoped the plane broke and would leave us down here. We were having that good a time with our students.

Two days before we were scheduled to leave, we had our graduation ceremony. Major Joseph spoke, and I provided an overview of the course for all the guests, who included U.S. ambassador Sally Cowal and the chief of staff for the TTDF, Brigadier General Ralph Brown. The general and I passed out the graduation certificates. The local press came by and interviewed me. It was my first experience being misquoted in the media. I had said in my remarks that with the title "Commando," most people would now expect the graduates to be able to chew nails, and that while we were good, we were not supermen. That remark was translated as my having said the commandos were now capable of chewing nails because they were supermen. This would not be the last time I was choked by my own sound bite.

The day before we loaded, I watched a man die. Spivey and I went to the SOG headquarters to give them a certificate thanking them for their support during the training. A TTDF soldier, not associated with the SOG, was nearby on an earthmover clearing a field. He was operating on steep terrain. The tires on this tractor were six feet tall. While we were having our little ceremony, the vehicle rolled past us straight for our rental car. It stopped by itself with the blade dug in about one foot from the car. The driver was nowhere to be seen. Somebody ran up the hill and then started yelling for a stretcher. Spivey and I didn't even wait to hear what was wrong. We jumped in the car and drove the mile and a half to the hooch to grab Miles and Aydellot. The whole team poured into our cars, and we were back within five minutes. We raced up the hill with all the medical gear we had, including a backboard. The SOG made a circle around us as we started administering first aid. The driver was writhing in pain. No bones were protruding through the skin, but we could see that just about every bone from his neck to his pelvis was crushed. We surmised that he had lost control of the vehicle on the steep incline, panicked, and jumped off—directly into the path of the right rear wheel. If he had just held on and ridden it down the hill, we would have laughed at how close he stopped from the rental car.

The medics performed superbly. Miles started the IV, and I got the job of administering the bags. I gave him two and a half liters of Ringer's. The rest of the team was helping however possible and cut his uniform off. For one moment, I was able to capture the scene: several Green Berets working feverishly to save someone's life whom we did not know, surrounded by Trinis who could see that we were doing all that could be done outside of a hospital. I have never been prouder to be in uniform.

After fifteen minutes, an ambulance arrived. It was a van with a stretcher and a red flashing light, what we call a "meat wagon." We transported our patient to the heliport and loaded him into the same chopper that had evacuated our snakebite victim.

While riding in the back of the ambulance, squeezing IV bags, I learned something about internal bleeding. The blood can pool in men in the scrotum sack. When we transferred him to the medevac bird, his scrotum was about the size of a regulation football. Miles said he lost the pulse at the neck during the ride. I could see Aydellot doing chest compressions on the guy as the bird lifted off.

The elation of a successful training event dissipated, and the team was grim and silent as we watched the helicopter disappear.

"I want a drink," I said. The team agreed a drink would probably be a good idea. We went to a bar about three minutes away. I knocked back a double scotch, no ice, on an empty stomach. The alcohol hit me like a train, and I just sulked until it wore off in about hour. I didn't feel very special. I didn't want to get drunk. I just wanted to be numb for a moment.

While I was numb, two guys from the team went to get Aydellot from the hospital, and we learned our patient was pronounced dead an hour after he arrived at the hospital. When my head was clear, I found and briefed Major Jacobson and members of the embassy staff on what had happened. I called back to Bragg and made sure Major Sawyer knew. Major Jacobson thought the ambassador might write a letter telling our chain of command what a good job we had done, both in the conduct of the training and in trying to save the Trini's life.

At 1300 on April 28, 1994, we loaded a C-130 and flew back to the rest of the world.

Kay. Imagine how Al Pacino looked in the movie *Scent of a Woman*, and there you have Bill Kay. He spent about two hours with me during our first meeting. We talked about his command philosophy and mine. He set out his expectations for me, and I tried to explain how I would meet them. I was making up all the answers as I went, and my biggest fear was that he would see me as a pretender to the throne. By the end of the exchange, it seemed he was willing to give me a chance but would not hesitate to pull me from the position if he thought my performance warranted it. I knew I would not have even been there had Jones not endorsed me, but I had never done the job of commanding an SF company. While past performance is a good indicator of future potential, the Peter Principle, a popular notion that all of us are promoted to the point we become incompetent, waits for all of us.

Under normal circumstances, the transition from one commander to the next would require at least two weeks where the new guy shadowed the old guy. In this instance, the old guy was already gone. He had come down on orders requiring him to move within days of receipt. There would be no ceremony as is the custom when changing commanders. I simply walked in and told everybody I was the new commander.

Transferring from Second Battalion to First Battalion was only a distance of a few hundred feet physically, but culturally, I had just moved from the Caribbean to North Africa. I left the operational area where Fun was God and partying a form of religion, where Vat 19 rum was readily available to anyone with a dollar, where women walked about attired so as to make a train of men slow down to look, to one where Allah was God and Islam was the religion, where any alcohol was forbidden, and women existed as abstract objects attired in hijabs, niqabs, and sometimes burqas. Kay could sense I needed a primer and recommended I read *Popski's Private Army*, by Vladimir Peniakoff. It is the story of British unconventional warfare efforts against the Italians in North Africa during World War II.

I devoured it, rereading it and marking it up like it was Scripture.

I sought to make my entry into the new company as inauspicious as possible. Instead of a team sergeant, I now had a sergeant major, the most senior rank an enlisted person can achieve. But he was in the hospital after neck surgery. The man running the show in the absence of the commander was the senior team leader, Captain John Cooksey. His acting sergeant major was Master Sergeant George Miller. I filled several pages with notes as they quickly explained what was going on in the company.

I, a man who had been under a green beret for a grand total of seven months, was about to assume responsibility for six Special Forces A-teams and one B-team (a group that constituted my personal staff). A sense of inadequacy bubbled within me, but I calmed my fears with a simple mantra: "I volunteered for this. I lived my whole life for this. I worked so hard to be here." The term "catastrophic success" seemed an appropriate characterization of my situation.

Again, I inventoried the equipment and was struck by how old it all was and the lack of use. Other than the vehicles (Hummers) assigned to us, the only things people seemed to use were the ruck-sacks. The Hummers ran, but they were decrepit. I discovered we had two motorcycles, both of which were nonoperational, and no one could tell me when they might be repaired. Busted equipment that no one is trying to fix is a bad indicator in any organization but particu-larly in the military.

During our initial session, Kay had told me about a training event my predecessor had left me. I was to take the company to Fort Bliss, Texas, and shoot everything in the inventory until our hearts were con-tent. We had ammunition for pistols, rifles, sniper rifles, machine guns, grenade launchers, and we even had a Stinger missile. We had over 105,000 rounds of ammo.

I asked Miller how many people we were taking. He gave me the look that I had learned a senior NCO gives when he is about to say something that he knows is true but will not be well received.

"About twenty, sir," he replied in his signature deep, gravelly voice.

I was incredulous. As my mouth was forming the obvious ques-tion of how we were going to shoot all we were taking in the month that we were to be gone, he made sure that I understood he was aware of the challenge before us by adding that we were also taking nearly

600 pounds of explosives for demo training and several cases of mortar rounds.

We had so much ammo because the entire company was supposed to go. Someone on the group staff had changed the training calendar. While the First Battalion had been told to plan training during this period, the group staff had changed the support plan, putting us on a support cycle but after everything for Fort Bliss had been coordinated. We had a training area in Texas, a plane to take us there, enough ammunition to invade a country, but not the people required to play a football game.

With my B-team and one ODA, we packed a KC-10 cargo plane and flew to Fort Bliss. We spent the next thirty days shooting as much as we could as fast as we could. We fired the sniper rifles until our shoulders ached. We melted the hand guards on the machine guns. The automatic grenade launchers began to break, and we nursed the last one in order to expend the rest of the ammunition. The Air Defense Artillery school, full of guys who train people to shoot air-defense missiles, provided a drone for our Stinger shot. Our guy hit it. We had multiple pistol competitions but even then realized that we would never shoot all the 9mm ammunition we brought. We loaded up the Uzis, that indestructible Israeli machine pistol, and literally sawed silhouettes in half.

The most important lessons I learned came from loading magazines, eating meals, and occasionally drinking a beer with my guys. After about a week, they began to open up to me. They were very concerned about the degradation of skills that they thought were important for us. One such skill was close-quarters battle, or CQB. This capability is what most folks think of when they think of Special Operations: dynamic entry into a room and the rapid, precise application of deadly force. Under the current group leadership, we were not even allowed to say "CQB." There was no support from those in higher positions for training that enhanced our capacity to run agents. Like our cousins in the CIA who actually did UW, we had a requirement to run an agent network, to handle spies. We glossed over this in the Q course and talked around it during Robin Sage.

"How do you know who to kill?"

The question is answered by our own agents (or "assets," as they are known among those who ply the trade) and by using our own analysis. We had but one school that produced about 120 graduates per year capable of creating and running an agent network necessary to conduct a UW campaign. No such training was happening within the units, at least not within 3rd Group. I was beginning to question what really made us so special aside from the hat and the tab.

One day, I heard on the news that the United Nations approved the use of force to remove the military junta from Haiti that had deposed Jean-Bertrand Aristide in 1991. Thinking this was an important development, I called back to Second Battalion and asked our operations officer if we should save any of this ammunition in case we went to Haiti. He explained that we were shooting training ammunition, that the group headquarters had access to the war stocks, and that the group staff was responsible for making sure we had what we needed. I understood what he was trying to say. The Haiti mission had been on and off for the last year. Hundreds of man-hours were wasted building pallets and canceling training only to be told to stand down at the last minute. The 3rd Group staff had lost any sense of urgency about Haiti, and rightly so. Most professional military leaders use a saying borrowed from the cavalry to describe their need to anticipate possible operations and prepare for them accordingly: Lean forward in the saddle. The common admonition associated with this phrase is something that 3rd Group had taken to heart: Yeah, but don't fall off the horse.

We returned from Fort Bliss with marvelous tans and remarkable shooting skills. I walked the hall of the company area trying to meet all of my people, asking questions, and putting my mind around this new role. My learning curve was nearly vertical. Fortunately, Kay was very approachable and entertained my new-guy questions without condescension. Still, I felt completely out of my depth.

In my absence, we had acquired a new group commander. Colonel Mark Boyatt expressed ideas that ran counter to the prevailing culture within his group staff. Where there had been complaints from the group headquarters about men on the teams wearing sunglasses with retaining straps, Boyatt made off-the-cuff remarks, such as, "If it were up to me, I wouldn't care if you guys grew ponytails." Those of us at the battalion and company level detected a sea change, but military bureaucracies adopt innovation with a speed best described as glacial. He inherited an SF organization that had spent the preponderance of its time going to developing countries in the Caribbean and Africa, training basic rifle marksmanship and small-unit tactics to indigenous troops, coming back, and then repeating the cycle. After two or three years of this routine, we were remarkably proficient at the basics and at teaching them in a foreign language. The cost of this proficiency was a lack of capability to operate in an urban environment unilaterally. Only a few teams had trained with the Air Force Special Ops aircraft, and about the same number had trained with the Special Operations Aviation Regiment 160th, those exceptional helicopters piloted by men who never worried about losing training opportunities because they had to send guys out to pick up pine cones. We were very accustomed to going to Third World countries, living in the Stone Age, and trying not to get sick on goat-butt soup. Institutionally, we had few if any of what most military professionals would consider advanced skills, such as CQB and tradecraft. Boyatt did not have the time necessary to prepare us for the operational tidal wave that was headed our way.

Within days of returning from our desert adventure, the word came down from group that the Haiti mission was a "go." The plan called for 3rd Special Forces Group to operate as part of a task force under the command of the 18th Airborne Corps. The task force included the 82nd Airborne Division, Marines, a Ranger battalion, Air Force Special Ops, and just about every C-130 cargo plane in the inventory. One way we knew we were really going this time was a function of logistics. All those planes started arriving at Pope Air Force Base, adjacent to Fort Bragg.

Colonel Boyatt called all the officers together and briefed us on the 3rd Group part of the plan. Basically, a day or two after the 18th Airborne Corps task force had clobbered the island and secured the airfields at Port-au-Prince (with the largest airborne drop for the 82nd since World War II) and Cap-Haitien, every SF team we had divided among six SF companies would hit large population centers and remove the Haitian forces as a threat. Once the companies secured the cities, we would then launch individual teams to other cities and keep everything peaceful while the State Department and White House figured out what they wanted to do.

These SF teams would each have their own town in which the team members, approximately eight to twelve guys, would be responsible for stability. When I say "town," I mean an urban area of 25,000 to 50,000 people.

In military planning, we call that the specified task. From the specified task, we determine the implied tasks, those things that we would have to do in order to achieve the specified task. To determine the implied tasks, we began to study the country's history, culture, political and physical infrastructure, and its security forces. We went into what we called a modified isolation in our team rooms and got to come and go as we pleased. The entire group, those not deployed on training missions, turned in on itself and started absorbing everything about Haiti there was to know.

Paramount among the implied tasks would be to build rapport as quickly as possible with all the actors on the island. The legitimacy of our mission would not be decided by the president who was sending us. The people held all the cards. If we weren't legit, if we could not bond with the people, we would be armed babysitters.

When we finished our analysis, I came to a general understanding of what was being asked of us. The implied tasks required a background in political science (specifically state and local government), civil engineering, advanced Special Operations skills, and fluent command of Haitian Creole and culture. Other than a minor in political science from Georgia Southern College, I was sorely lacking.

The most troubling aspect was not all the things that we would have to do after we occupied the cities. The plan called for SF to make a forced entry—that is, a deliberate assault into an urban area with multiple teams. To the best of everyone's knowledge, this one had not been done in recent memory, there was no doctrine to describe how it might be carried out even theoretically, and none of us had ever trained to do it.

There was only one way to avoid this turning into a Mogadishu redux: The people would have to be on our side. As I studied their history, I discovered a certain generational enmity between the Haitian population, descendants of slaves, and white Europeans, specifically the French. Haiti's claim to fame as the only nation to emerge from a successful slave revolt against their white masters did not indicate to me that it was fertile ground for white peacekeeping troops sent to sow the seeds of democracy and stop violence by the state security apparatus. It was an internal Haitian issue. Most police officers will tell you they do not relish answering calls for domestic violence due to the attacks against them once they pull one loving spouse off the other. I could picture us walking through town under the sullen gazes of impoverished people who did not want us there. I kept these thoughts to myself but factored them into my planning as I considered how we would secure the port town of Jacmel, on the southern coast of Haiti.

Internally, my rank once again became an issue, only this time it was because I was still a captain. My new job required a major, as that's the rank the Army requires for an SF company commander. Majors wear a gold oak leaf on their collars, and I was still nearly a year from before being able to pin it on. The SOF community is famous for its informality. Rank is typically second to competence. But normally, we did not operate in conventional-sized groups. I was to have 128 men assigned to me: nine SF teams, a civil affairs team, and the psychological operations team complete with loudspeakers. Technically, I was to command eleven separate elements. Traditionally, that's about five too many for one guy to keep up with. We would be operating in a city; I would not be able to see the teams on my left and right, only the ones along the street I was on. That reality dramatically increased the chance for fratricide. Add an adversarial population and the stage was set for a really bad day once our attack commenced. With these circumstances in mind, I saw the need (as I had been taught and trained) for strong central planning followed by intense decentralized execution. The normal informality of SF would not serve me well, as all of us were moving on unknown ground, and I knew at some point I would have to tell everybody to turn off the "good idea machines" and just listen to me. With the leadership maxim "familiarity breeds contempt" ringing in my ears, I could easily imagine nine other SF team leaders questioning every move I was about to make. There was no book to hold up and say, "But it says do it like this," nor could I go to my boss and complain, "They're questioning me." In my mind's eye, I opened the rolodex of leadership styles and found the one I was looking for under the letter A for *asshole*.

I directed my officers to address me by my rank and last name, and I afforded them the same courtesy. At our first meeting, there was rolling of eyes, but when I explained my reasoning, everybody seemed to get it.

My other concern lay in the fact that we could not train for this mission. Rehearse, yes. But rehearsals are done once the training is complete. Institutionally, we learned by training the broad concept, and then rehearsed in order to apply the training to the specific circumstances presented. We had no standard operating procedures for multi-team operations. We had never operated in a city as a unit. None of us had been to Haiti before. (Out of 128, one man had been raised in the Haitian quarter of Paris, but to my knowledge even he had never been on the island.) Worst of all, the Haitian military knew we were coming and would have weeks to prepare for our arrival.

All of these potential problems could be solved or mitigated as irrelevant if we had the people on our side. Our legitimacy would have to be unquestioned. My reading of Haitian history did not inspire me to believe the solution could be found among the indigenous people. One scholarly tome described the sentiment of Haiti's founding fathers in 1804 as they sought to write their own Declaration of Independence: "We need a white man's skin for parchment, his skull for an inkwell, his blood for ink and a bayonet for a pen." Did I mention how much a group picture of Special Ops guys resembled an Amish picnic?

Lieutenant Colonel Jones and the Second Battalion would provide the command and control for all the Green Berets who were going. The First and Third Battalion headquarters would stay at Bragg but give up nearly all of their people. Consequently, within two months of leaving Jones, I was right back with him, only now as a company commander.

His meetings with us put me at ease. We were following a force package that could flatten anything the Forces Armées d'Haïti (Armed Forces of Haiti, known by the acronym FADH, pronounced to sound like *fog*) could muster and were more concerned with facing guerrilla operations should the FADH dissolve into the population and strike as the opportunities arose. That proved to be a baseless concern, but we didn't know that sitting in North Carolina.

A few anecdotes may provide context of the mood among the Green Berets as we realized we were preparing to run the poorest country in the western hemisphere.

Brigadier General Richard Potter was going to be the overall commander for all Special Operations Forces on the island. He came on active duty in 1959, three years before I was born. There was no dimension of the SF community with which he was not intimately familiar. He called all the senior leaders into a conference room and explained that the failure to rescue the U.S. hostages from Iran in 1980 was probably the most significant factor in Jimmy Carter's defeat that year. I felt the weight of his words settle across my shoulders.

The scope and potential impact of what we were going to try was as big and broad as any military professional could hope for during a career.

With the big picture in mind, I still had to deal with the microscopic details. For example, we were taking our sniper rifles. Our snipers, one per team, requested a weapon in addition to their issue M16 rifle. They wanted something compact with a high rate of fire that could be used to break contact in the event of a close encounter. The M16 was too long to carry across the rucksack and not practical to be carried broken down inside it. They settled on a machine pistol, like an MP5. I called the weapons committee of the Q course, and after a few minutes of checking, the man who answered the phone said all the MP5s were checked out. They did, however, have many World War II–vintage Sten guns, a British weapon that fired the same 9mm bullet as the MP5. I covered the mouthpiece on the phone and explained my discovery to several snipers standing in the doorway to my office. They all nodded and said that would be okay. Our guys would be carrying museum pieces.

As soon as we were alerted, my sergeant major, Darrell Shanks, walked in from convalescent leave wearing a neck brace, his surgery less than a month old. After hearing that we were going to Cuba in order to conduct a proper isolation prior to invading Haiti, he removed the neck brace. I asked if he was cleared to travel. His response explained to me the importance he placed on a note from the doctor: "I'm not missing this."

Right before we were to leave, a warrant officer on my B-team walked into my office and placed what looked like part of a water fountain on my desk. Silver and about a foot long, it appeared to be a pump. Chief explained this was my part of the team gear to carry, a purification device designed to provide water for ten men. I asked him if we had ever used it, as it looked brand new. He told me no one even knew we had this, but we had to take everything and everybody else's ruck was full.

At the beginning of September 1994, I left Fort Bragg on what would be a totally forgettable experience for most Americans not associated with Haiti but one that consumed nearly a year of my life. We flew to Cuba with all our weapons and most of our kit aboard a chartered 747 through the worst storm that I have ever seen. We landed during a gorgeous sunrise at Guantanamo Bay Naval Base, then traveled by bus to a large open field on the leeward side of the island, where we found a stack of wooden crates. Inside each crate was a large Army tent waiting to be erected. By the end of the day, nearly a thousand Green Berets had constructed a tent city that would serve as our isolation facility. Initially we slept on the ground wearing insect repellent, as there was no way to hang our mosquito netting. Army cots appeared within a day or two. The latrine and shower facilities were about three hundred feet away, making midnight bathroom calls a reason to quit drinking liquids after 1800.

We continued our planning and began rehearsing our initial assault on one of the base's softball fields. I found an orange traffic cone to use as a bullhorn. My element would be riding into our landing zone on six Chinook helicopters, about the biggest one the Army makes. Once on the ground, we had to negotiate a mile and a half of downtown streets to get to the Haitian army barracks. We didn't expect them to be waiting inside and playing cards. We planned for the worst-case scenario: shooters hiding inside every building, the local population losing its mind, and no cavalry to come get us if things got bad. While we did not have the cavalry, we did have the next best thing: an AC-130 gunship that would loiter over us as we entered the city. We hoped that a firepower demonstration would be enough to convince the Haitian security forces that resistance was futile. We picked some targets based on a map reconnaissance; one was the building marked as the arsenal. I sent a request for information to the intelligence section supporting us for this mission, asking for confirmation that this building was still used as a weapons depot. The answer back was "Yes." I decided that if these FADH guys so much as popped a firecracker I would obliterate that building, as both a show of force and an opportunity to remove usable weapons from the area.

About half a mile from our tents, there was a little club that sold hot dogs and hamburgers. The leeward side had been blocked off for us, but the club was right on the edge and remained open. It had one thing that we all came to relish while waiting for the green light to go into Haiti: cable TV, with access to CNN. My sergeant major and I would spend a few minutes each day listening to the news and trying to reconcile what we were seeing in the images broadcast from Haiti with what we were getting in intelligence reports. On television, the Haitian army reminded us of an armed rabble occasionally wearing military uniforms. Intelligence reports painted them as less than competent, due to the lack of training, equipment, and pay, but still a force not to be discounted.

With these reports in mind, the commanders at every level went into painstaking detail to synchronize all the destructive power at our disposal. We knew the Haitian army's capacity for logistics would be a limiting factor for them in a sustained fight. And while our enemy had homefield advantage, the SF guys were very accustomed to walking into unfamiliar terrain and dominating it. Decades of training in the decaying urban areas of former European colonies made us a natural fit for the Haiti mission. One of the main reasons for this was how comfortable we were in our ability to use our weapons, which included our language capabilities. We didn't need interpreters to know what the people were thinking. And if they were thinking of harming us, we had that covered too. All those basic rifle marksmanship classes, though not the advanced skills of CQB, gave us the opportunity to shoot. A lot.

Most SF soldiers carry two weapons, a rifle and a pistol, giving us at least a sense of redundancy, though if a 9mm pistol is really going to make the difference between life and death we probably got into a situation we should never have been in to begin with. Usually, we have thirteen magazines of thirty rounds each for the rifle and four magazines for the pistol. I had my first of three giant surprises when my supply sergeant informed me there was a shortage of 9mm ammo. No one could ever explain it. I would go with one magazine. In the States, I would have bought some at a gun store. In Gitmo, there was none for us to get.

I got my second surprise when the Ranger battalion settled in near the SF tent city. I watched a support unit erect the Rangers' tents, to include one with hot showers and clothes washers and dryers. Later that day, the Rangers arrived. As we got closer to D-Day, the day the invasion would actually commence, word came down that the four-star at U.S. Special Operations Command, himself having grown up in the Rangers and a highly respected warrior in his own right, wanted to address us. Somewhere, somehow, a massive miscommunication had occurred. At the appointed day and time, with our uniforms stuck to us from two weeks of living in an outdoor sauna while planning and rehearsing a mission that no SF had ever done before (a unilateral multiteam assault on an urban area), something over 900 Green Berets made a mass formation in front of our tents near a road where the general was supposed to stop and inspire us before we launched. In typical Army fashion, we formed up fifteen minutes early and melted in the Caribbean sun waiting for him. He was about two hundred meters behind us, talking to the Rangers, who were responding to everything he said with heartfelt, bloodcurdling "hoo-ahs," their signature battle cry. Such a response to an inspirational speech underscored the difference in the cultures between Rangers and SF, between just about any unit of soldiers and SF. We don't do "hoo-ah."

The white sedan with the red plaque bearing four stars approached. The group command sergeant major called us to attention. Dirty and stinking but ramrod straight, we waited for the sedan to coast to a stop and for the general to deliver the words that were intended to carry us through the darker moments that may await us. I could tell by his face through the glass that no one had told him we were standing alongside the road just for him. If he could have known the adverse effect on our morale of his driving past, he would have no doubt stopped and spoken to us. The slight coupled with the ammunition debacle confirmed in most Green Berets' minds that we weren't so special anymore.

The last and biggest surprise occurred when President Clinton canceled the invasion within a couple of hours of the biggest parachute drop since World War II. Shanks and I were sitting in the club watching CNN when the announcement came. I will never forget watching President Clinton on a widescreen TV telling the American people that, thanks to the efforts of Colin Powell, Sam Nunn, and Jimmy Carter, the ruling junta had agreed to leave the island in preparation for the return of President Aristide. Just past the TV was a set of double doors providing a view of the road leading to the airfield and the dark Caribbean beyond. As the president spoke, a steady stream of Rangers filed past, walking back from the aircraft with engines winding down.

It felt like a giant *coitus interruptus.*

Boyatt called us together among the tents and explained that the operation was on a twenty-four-hour hold. The next day we stood around like actors on a stage waiting for direction. By the afternoon, we got the word: The Green Berets were going.

The question on everybody's mind was: "To do what?"

The 10th Mountain Division had been scheduled to follow the 82nd, and now the 10th was the main effort. I thought of the 10th Division as the "stunt" division, especially after what they had been through the year before in Mogadishu. I could picture a stereotypical Hollywood director screaming "Cut" and ordering the stunt division onto the set, which in this case was a grossly ill-defined mission in a country that 90 percent of Americans could not care less about.

None of those about to enter Haiti knew what had been negotiated. The rules of engagement, the protocol designed to tell us who we could kill, had changed three times in the last day. Basically, it came to this: If somebody had a gun and didn't look like an American GI, he was going to die. Were the FADH now our friends and did they know that all had been resolved? I made a decision to talk to my team leaders before we went in and lay down my own thoughts on how we were going to go about doing whatever it was we were going to do.

"Nothing on this island is worth any of your lives or those of your men. If there is a mistake, make sure the result is a dead Haitian, not a dead American."

I would regret those words.

We watched on the big TV as the 10th Mountain assaulted the airport. Members of the U.S. embassy staff were there to greet them. In a scene out of *Apocalypse Now*, dozens of helicopters swarmed over the runway and deposited the infantrymen who were sure this was a combat mission. They rolled out of the choppers and took up fighting positions behind their rucksacks. One squad landed directly in front of the embassy personnel, and from our view by television, the soldiers appeared to be defending themselves from a group of men and women in suits and dresses. The military attaché assigned to the embassy tried to get one of the guys behind the rucks to stand up and quit acting like they were in a firefight. The soldier shook off the attaché's entreaty and remained resolutely behind his nylon bag of kit.

The SF NCOs gathered around the screen groaned. One sergeant said what we were all thinking: "Does any motherfucker know what the fuck is going on? If so, please stand up." There was no laughter.

Jones called all the commanders together and explained that we would go in the next day by helicopter. Once we got to PAP (as we all came to call Port-au-Prince), we would flow to our cities as planned.

I waited until the meeting was over and said to Jones as quietly as possible, "Sir, I'm not trying to be a wiseass, but what is our mission?"

"Tony, that's a good question. I'm not sure, either. I just know we're going. Be hard and take charge. We'll figure out."

The next day we flew to Haiti via CH-53 Air Force helicopters. Five days later we were still sitting in PAP in a cargo warehouse, sweltering in 95-degree heat and wearing the mandatory body armor and helmet. The leadership of the 10th Mountain didn't know what all these Green Berets were going to do either. The story went around that General Potter worked nonstop for the five-day period to get us out to our sectors. We understood the risk aversion in the 10th. They had lost people in Somalia one year before. But keeping us confined on the airfield was counterintuitive to a solid security posture.

One vignette shows how the SF culture runs counter to the mainstream military mindset post—Desert Storm. One of our better French-speaking SF NCOs was standing at the fence that separated us from the main street of the city, having a lively conversation with several Haitians, when a senior officer from the 10th walked up and demanded to know what was going on. The sergeant said he was just talking to the locals, trying to find out what was going on around the airport. The officer cut him off.

"Quit talking to these people!" he said, as angrily as if he had caught the guy buying dope. "Why are you talking to them?"

"That's how we do our job, sir."

A mask of confusion covered the officer's face as he tried to make sense of what he was looking at. "Get away from the fence. Now!" he growled.

The exchange swept across the SF crew like a bad cold. I shook my head in disbelief.

Potter finally got us out of the airport. My teams would be the first to go. We would be wheels up at 0700 the next day. Jacmel waited on the southern coast like an untested safe haven, anyplace being better than the warehouse and its mind-numbing boredom and heat. Best of all, Potter had established that we could not do our jobs wearing body armor and helmets. The area wouldn't look or feel stable and secure if the guys making these claims were wearing protective gear. I called my team leaders together and told them the good news. I went to sleep that night wondering what the next day would bring. I only had to wait one hour.

At approximately one in the morning, another SF officer, Ray

Helton, a man with many years under our distinctive headgear, found me sleeping on the dock of the warehouse. He woke me to explain that General Potter wanted a briefing from me describing what I thought we were going to do when we got to Jacmel. He would be waiting for me at 0600. In Robin Sage just nine months before, I had five days and multiple information briefings to prepare for a presentation to a training cadre describing a fictitious mission in western North Carolina. I now had five hours and no briefings to prepare for a presentation to one of the most esteemed Green Beret officers there ever was and to describe a real-world operation that would have me providing security to the Southern Claw, the bottom third of the country.

Helton gave me two pieces of advice: Do not show fear or any hesitation, as Potter will smell it and tear my throat out; and know exactly how many people I was taking by rank (how many officers, warrant officers, and sergeants).

I considered repeating what Jones had told me ("Be hard; take charge.") and figured such brevity would probably get me fired. I put the outline of an orders briefing on a 3 x 5 card, no data, just the headers like terrain, enemy forces, friendly forces, et cetera. I did have the mission statement: Create a stable and secure environment for the return of democracy to Haiti. The only thing I knew for sure was that an hour from this presentation I would be joining 127 guys as we loaded up on six big helicopters to take over a city. Somehow.

My B-team decided I would brief better if I was clean. I stood on a wooden pallet below the loading dock while Shanks and two other men took turns pouring water from a five-gallon can over my head. Though I put the same stinking uniform back on, the bath relaxed me enough to let me nap before my first meeting with General Potter.

At 0630, about four hours after the bath, I walked to the part of the airport building where Potter had an office. As I headed to the briefing, the SF teams walked from the warehouse to the runway to wait for the birds. On this day more than any other, I came to rely on the man who was my second-in-command, Stephen Franzoni. It was obvious from the beginning that our responsibilities as a B-team for so much real estate and for so many people required more than the eight people I had. Franzoni and his A-team augmented my B-team so that we had twenty people, a number necessary to run twenty-four-hour operations. While I performed kabuki for Potter, Franzoni would make sure that the teams were in the right spot so when the helicopters landed the men could board quickly.

General Potter was sitting behind a desk when I walked in, and a gallery of officers whom I knew and some whom I didn't were off to my left. From the moment I saluted and said my name, I could tell that I was a bacon-flavored rubber chew toy on the nose of a Rottweiler. I described the Haitian army as "the enemy," which they had been up until a week ago, and I thought the general was going to come across the desk at me.

"They are not the enemy," he said adamantly. "You are going to have to work with them. If you treat them like the enemy you're going to screw up everything I've worked for."

I rolled with it. "Yes, sir. I should've said there is no enemy except those elements which will undermine the stability and security of the area. We will treat as enemy those people who undermine what we're trying to achieve." He spit me out and allowed me to continue to the third header. I had about fifteen to go. When I described how many people I was taking, he stopped me and asked twice who was in my element by rank. Our new group commander, Boyatt, was in the gallery and could tell Potter did not like me, that the general was looking for another reason to chomp on the chew toy. Boyatt reiterated my numbers and assured him they totaled 128. Boyatt's actions at that critical moment inspired me to continue and gave Potter a reason to let me. When I had finished my presentation, Potter revealed why he did not think much of me when I had walked in and only slightly more now that I had briefed him.

"Captain Schwalm," he said, staring into my eyes as if he wanted to grab me by the collar and pull me within an inch of his face, "you should be honored to have such responsibility at such a young age." He thought I was too young to be there as one of his company commanders.

I explained that I was honored and that I would do my best. I was sure that I sounded like a little kid asking his dad to drive the family car.

To tell me that our lovefest had come to an end, he got to the obligatory question that all good commanders ask of subordinates.

"So what do you need from me?" Translated: Is there something that I, your boss who has the power to throw your ass all the way back to Bragg on the first thing smoking out of here and who could not have possibly overlooked anything IMPORTANT, can give or do for you that will make your excellently explained and plainly obvious (to even cognitively dysfunctional people) task easier?

"Yes, sir," I said, and I watched the eyebrows arch across the faces in the gallery. "I need to be wearing a major's rank. It will make my life easier with the other officers I am leading and any Haitian officers I'm working with who cannot help but notice I'm wearing the same rank as my subordinates." The air pressure in the room went to zero.

"You want me to frock you?" he asked. "You're promotable?"

"Yes, sir."

"It makes sense to me," he said, and the air pressure in the room returned to normal as everybody exhaled at the same time. Then a grin danced across his face. "You got some rank? Can't frock you without the rank."

"Sir, I'll get some . . ." I replied, looking around the room. I watched an SF major in the crowd pull the rank from his collar and toss it to me. Thank God I caught it.

Potter took it from me and recited the officer oath from memory, pinning the gold oak leaf to my right collar.

When he finished, he shook my hand and asked, "Anything else?"

I wanted to say, "Well, sir, a mission briefing now that all the weeks of planning have been obviated by the invasion being cancelled would be nice. Also, maybe somebody can explain to me why the guerrillas are going to do the commando fight. I have just come from the school that taught me to be a Green Beret, where everything was about working by, through, and with indigenous forces, and my first mission in a hostile fire zone as a Green Beret is Ranger school meets the Peace Corps. No insurgents are waiting for me, and there are no foreign troops to instruct. I need CQB and access to the world's biggest Piggly Wiggly if our intelligence about these people's poverty is correct, but I'll go with the small-unit tactics and three days of rations. Finally, I hope my guys know how to gather intelligence from agents who don't speak English, because I don't even speak French, much less Creole."

"No, sir," I said instead and saluted. He returned the salute and I walked out. The team leaders were waiting outside the door for any last-minute changes. There were hurried congratulations at my promotion as I hoisted my 105-pound rucksack, which I discovered when it was weighed was the lightest one on my B-team. (One medic had 137 pounds and could barely walk.) We strode to the runway like lions. No changes. Still no plan.

Franzoni was at the runway, and everybody was perfectly arrayed waiting for the helicopters that were flying over from Guantanamo. At 0600, I had been a nervous SF captain, trying to convince one of the most respected and feared SF generals in the community that I knew what I was doing. "I'm going to Jacmel, and I'm going to make it safe." At 0700, I was an SF major leading 128 men into something that I could not articulate in military phrases.

Other than the birth of my children and the end of the ground war in Desert Storm, I had never been prouder than when I looked down the runway at Port-au-Prince International Airport and saw those men, my Green Berets, loading the Chinooks. We weren't going down the rabbit hole this time. We were going to another planet.

SEVENTEEN

LANDING IN JACMEL, HAITI, and the actions of the ensuing months were like something from science fiction. Intergalactic travel was the closest thing I could think of to make sense of the cultural abyss we spanned in the seventy miles we flew from the U.S. compound in Port-au-Prince to the seaside city which became my home for five months.

The citizens of the city overlooking the Caribbean began each day with thoughts consumed by what they would *not* be eating. Children walked with empty bellies to school, where they would be slapped for not staying awake during rote memorization drills. Businesses that still had merchandise to sell opened with the knowledge that most patrons would have no money to buy anything. The vendors in the city market spread their wares in hand-woven baskets as pigs rooted through the garbage that littered the street. A pile of medical waste fermented under the tropical sun near the local hospital, and the flies swarmed in clouds around the putrid mess. The advent of the screened window was still in the offing. Men in khaki uniforms lounged in front of the town's army garrison, most with hands in their pockets, rusted rifles leaning against the wall of a mustard-colored building. The jail within the garrison was full of those who thought to challenge the authority of those with the rifles. No one in the city dared to congregate. Political rallies were good opportunities for one to give his life for his country. Elected leaders were exiled to the mountains that surrounded the city. Most people existed below a standard of living that could hardly be considered acceptable by any civilization. Folks starved silently, while the aristocracy grew fat from an embargo intended to topple them, an embargo imposed by a world that gloated in the delight of good intentions.

Then, with a rush of wind and the thunder of engines, six strange machines roared over the city and landed in a field near the oppressed masses. The people's faces conveyed amazement as they raced to the noise, and many smiled nervously as they saw the machines that screamed like a hurricane. The people stared in astonishment as a ramp on the back of each craft lowered. And then the little green men began to disembark. From each ramp, heavily laden men began to emerge into the light of the sun. These men carried huge, heavy bags strapped to their backs, and their hands were full of rifles. Big rifles, little rifles, submachine guns, hand grenades, and smoke grenades hung from everything that these men carried. One of the green men walked up to one of the people and asked, "Who is your leader?" Not able to speak the language of the green men, the islander shrugged his shoulders and smiled with fear. By now thousands of hopeful people had run to the landing area, chatting nervously about this unexpected arrival. The alien man tried again, this time in the language that he heard being spoken: "Who is your leader? We are here to free you."

Upon hearing this, the people began to shout and jump and dance. The little green men shared in their enthusiasm by smiling broadly at all the happy people. The islanders ran to the men, hugged them, and wept at the promise that they thought they had heard. ("Did they say 'feed us' or 'free us'?") But not all were happy. The people who did not wake up hungry were unhappy. These aristocrats lived in fortresses surrounded by walls topped with broken glass. They owned the men in khaki with rusted rifles that kept the poor people in place. But now these aliens had landed with a promise of hope for all islanders. The aristocrats were unimpressed as they looked down from the fortresses in the mountains onto the landing area as the flying machines lifted into the air and left. They spoke on wireless phones to each other. What will happen to us? Who are these little green men? Why does our army not fight these strangers? They should kill them, no? But the army was afraid. They had never seen aliens who appeared lethal yet friendly. The whole city stopped to sing and shout for these little green men who said they would stay until the city was free for Democracy, whoever he was. No one could do anything against the will of the people on this day— the day the little green men landed in Jacmel, Haiti. And the Haitians asked, "Who are you guys?" And the men said to all who would listen, "We are U.S. Special Forces, and we're here to help."

The green men would keep getting off helicopters in Haiti in September of 1994 until 1,200 had landed. Within days, they had blanketed the island, crawling over it like bloodhounds, looking for weapons caches, cholera epidemics, and the flow of money into and out of the cities. They solved crimes ("Is this your goat? Can you prove it?"); liberated jails ("Nobody can remember what this guy did? You're free, pal."); coordinated disaster relief (feeding and housing approximately 25,000 people in one city alone); and provided books to schools. They organized work crews to repair water pipes, re-installed exiled political leaders, and arrested bad guys. The green men stood down the Haitian army (almost without a shot), organized an interim security force, and delivered babies (best count is eight, one by caesarean performed under lantern light). They performed the medical evacuation of missionaries assaulted by bandits (then caught the bandits), rebuilt schools (rarely used), and carried relief workers to places unreachable by mortal men. As this was hardly the first trip away from home for the little green men and many were on their third or fourth marriage, they called back to families in the homeland to see if they still had families back in the homeland. One A-team reported the presence of a werewolf and requested silver bullets. A helicopter brought silver bullets. The team dispatched the werewolf, and the people rejoiced. All of these actions occurred against a backdrop of the most squalid living conditions that anyone can imagine. Said another way, you can only get so poor, and then you die. The Haitians were not dead, but very close.

The little green men did all this and more over a period of two years without a written plan.

This last statement is key. No written plan existed as 1,200 Green Berets took responsibility for 5 million people, 80 percent of whom were unemployed and 90 percent were functionally illiterate, according to various sources that purport to monitor such data. There was a mission statement from the diplomats and generals in D.C. and Port-au-Prince that became a mantra: "create a stable and secure environment for the return of democracy to Haiti." Never, however, was there a detailed plan or single source document with the "how-to" for the Haiti mission. How do 1,200 guys with guns but no plan pacify and take responsibility for 5 million people?

The short answer was that the people loved us, and we worked hard to never let that rapport fade or our legitimacy diminish. The longer answer was Robin Sage. Without a plan, we went with the common experiences gained in western North Carolina. When my guys explained that a voodoo priest wanted to see me to pinpoint the location of the weapons cache, my mind immediately went to the medicine man from 10th Group who wondered if I was trainable. When Aristide returned and the people asked us for help in cleaning up the country—literally sweeping the few miles of paved road—I understood the place he held in their minds because I had been taught that empathy was required when working with indigenous people. The one difference between Robin Sage and Operation Uphold Democracy (as our mission came to be called) was the absence of a guerrilla force with which to work or a government to embrace and support. I found Haiti to be filled with amazingly resilient, hard-working people who somehow came to be living on a moonscape directly adjacent to the Dominican Republic. We did not do UW or COIN. We walked around (and around and around) making sure everybody played nice, really just trying to meet people, any people, all the people. We needed rapport with the local population, and we needed it in a big way. There was no functioning government, no police to speak of, no political or security infrastructure at all. We found just a mass of hungry people who had learned to live together without cops on every corner and to travel without traffic lights.

On one of my initial walks through Jacmel, I went by a building that had about thirty young children standing wide-eyed on the front porch. I realized it was an orphanage. When I checked my map to mark the building so I could return to it later, with rapport in mind and to maybe provide some aid, I discovered that it was the arsenal we had marked for destruction as a demonstration target had the invasion gone as planned.

I tried to imagine how such a catastrophe might be briefed. "Tell us again, Major Dumbass, why you called for fire on the orphanage. What? You thought the locals would love you when you reduced the building and the kids inside to slurry?"

Building rapport mandated that we strive to remain objective, at least appear to be fair and impartial as we tried to run the country. While we didn't let the Haitian army or the interim security force mistreat anyone, we also protected the security force from the people who really wanted to hurt somebody for a past wrong.

Or at least we tried.

In the city of Croix-des-Bouquets, one of my teams discovered that the local police had abandoned the garrison and a vigilante force had taken over. Rather than jail anyone caught stealing and conduct a trial, the vigilantes killed them by machete blows and tied the perpetrators to their life-ending prizes, staking both thief and ill-gotten gains along the road to the city as object lessons for anyone who might think Croix-des-Bouquets was an easy target.

Such was the reason behind the team's radio call requesting some quick reinforcements after discovering two dead Haitian men tied to a goat and a pig. We weren't sure how long they had been out there, but the Caribbean sun shows no mercy on corpses. The pig, an omnivore, found himself in the happy place of being tied to sun-dried meat and was digging in when the team arrived. They found someone who was ostensibly the leader of the vigilante force and told him that the corpses were a health hazard and should be buried. While this conversation was occurring, a Haitian policeman from the old guard who worked in PAP arrived and demanded to know who had killed these men and why they were tied to animals. A heated exchange ensued with about 300 local residents shouting at the cop, who drew his pistol and shot a member of the vigilante force. Regrettably, for the cop at least, the other 299 members of the volunteer security program swarmed him, killed him, and burned his car and his apartment. The team fired warning shots, but nobody was going to risk his life to save Officer Dum-Dum. I sent another SF team and calm was restored.

Another explanation for how we accomplished a little stability on the island was due to who we were within the SF community. The 3rd Special Forces Group was uniquely suited to the mission because most of us had come of age in the Caribbean and Africa, and Haiti probably more than any other country is a synthesis of those two worlds. There was a connection between many members of the SF teams and the local Haitians through language and a sense of what it means to be in a country with no resources except cheap manual labor. Many of our teams had done missions in eastern Africa, particularly Côte d'Ivoire (Ivory Coast) and Senegal, where the lingua franca was French. In Haiti, our French speakers were worth their weight in gold. Fortunately for me, the proximity to the Dominican Republic border made my Spanish (though limited by years of disuse) an effective bridge, often with surreal results. A few vignettes may shed some light on the importance that SF places on language and cross-cultural communication skills.

Our mission was intended to bring democracy back to the island, and in order to do this, one needs that most democratic process, namely elections. Soon after Aristide returned, the announcement came from PAP that elections were to be held. Who could facilitate these elections? Who could get the ballots to the most remote areas of the country and, more important, get them back? Who could tell the people how to vote, these people who could not read or write and were scattered across the country in places the Haitian election officials didn't even know existed?

In Jacmel, I was invited to a meeting of UN election observers and members of the Haitian election commission. The meeting was to take place in French and we were to discuss the conduct of the election. Fortunately for me, the UN observers were from Belgium and Germany. The Belgian gentleman spoke German and French. The German gentleman spoke German and English, but English was not a language the election commission understood. They did speak Spanish. After three years stationed in Germany, I could muster enough German to follow a conversation. The dialogue went like this.

The Haitian election official would say something in French. The Belgian would translate into German for his colleague, and I would listen. If I had a question, I would ask in Spanish. The Haitian official would translate my question into French and give the answer in Spanish and French. What would have been a two-hour meeting became three, but when we finished I understood my mission. All the SF in my sector would deliver the ballots and collect them. Delivery often included several hours up a mountain path with horses packed with ballot boxes. We determined that the ballots would be pictures and names, and that voting would be indicated by a mark on the picture. We would dip the voter's thumb in paint as proof of voting and to prevent his voting more than once. Reasonable minds prevailed in PAP, and the color of the paint was changed from deep purple (invisible on most Haitians' skin) to white.

Our connection to the people for whom we had come to bring democracy manifested the night of a tropical storm, driving a spike into my conscience. "Nothing here is worth one of our lives." Jacmel flooded badly, as we got an inch an hour for thirty hours. Around 2200 on the second night of Tropical Storm Gordon, some men from the city came to my headquarters (miraculously on high ground) to ask if we could help them evacuate some people trapped by rising water. We inflated one of the rubber boats, loaded it on a Humvee, and four Green Berets accompanied the Haitians back into the town, into the thick and steady falling rain.

Within minutes, we got a call on the radio. "We need everybody. It's bad." Out we went, soaked to the skin in minutes. They were a mile from us, and when I walked up, the scene made me forget how wet I was, how long I had been away from my kids, and the mosquitoes that were eating us through our wet uniforms. The team parked the Humvee at an intersection in town and unloaded the boat between buildings in an attempt to paddle it to a residential area. A river like a locomotive had emerged in the town and was knocking houses over. In the time it had taken us to walk the mile, the rescue team had tied the boat to the front of the Humvee with a fire hose and was attempting to evacuate about thirty people, all women and children. The team was on the third trip when we arrived. The last one to be pulled from one of the houses was an elderly woman, and her rescue story made me understand the stupidity of my "not worth our lives" comment.

She had been in the window of her home and was the last one to be plucked. She could not swim to the boat, and the fire hose was let out as far as it could go. An SF NCO, wearing a life vest and carrying a simple round preserver, jumped into the water and quickly realized he could not swim wearing the vest and carrying the preserver. He shed the vest and fought the current until he had reached her. He talked her into the floating ring and brought her back to the boat. Behind them, what had once been her house lifted from its foundations and moved smartly into a swirling mass of rain, mud, and debris.

That happened a month after we arrived, and from that night on we had a trust with the Haitian people like I would never have imagined possible. Our legitimacy was cemented in place. Our rapport with the most important actors, the people, was solid. Regardless of what I said, the people knew the SF guys thought they were worth dying for. We never wore our body armor or helmets. The people greeted us as friends, warned us of any talk about violence, and simultaneously never let us forget we were not them.

They were worth dying for. Therefore, we were worth trusting.

When we would drive by, they would smile, wave, and yell, "Le blanc." The cultural nuance of calling us white had the same meaning as calling us foreigners.

Haiti was where I learned what it meant to work with other government agencies, specifically the CIA, outside the United States. To be sure, the threat to U.S. forces was very low and it was further reduced by our rapport with the local population. The CIA, nonetheless, began sending two-person teams to check on all the SF guys at their various locations, ostensibly to help us with force protection, those measures we take to prevent someone from attacking us while we're stopped and living daily garrison life in another country. A man and woman arrived at my command post one day and said they were from the embassy and had come to help us. They were wearing comfortable clothes and had concealed sidearms.

Our first conversation went something like this (as my learning curve went back to the vertical axis):

I asked, "What can you do for us?"

"We could provide early warning."

"How?"

"Through various assets."

"You have agents working in this city? Don't you think I should know about them, just in case they do something out of the ordinary and one of my guys accidentally blows their head off?"

"Not to worry," came the response dismissively. "Are you making contact with any of the locals?"

"Uh, yes, we have teams living with locals."

This response seemed to startle them. "You mean your guys are not all staying here?"

Apparently, no one in the U.S. government (save SF) was trying to get to know the Haitian people. This behavior put us squarely in the domain of the CIA, who was accustomed to being the only critical thinkers with language skills roaming the country.

The next day, our Haitian host whose name I provided to our CIA counterparts as one of the locals we had contacted said he was going to PAP and would return soon. He said it was no problem for the team to stay in his house while he was gone. About two days later, one of his friends came by the house and said our accommodating landlord had decided to teach art to the children of Soweto, a neighborhood of Johannesburg, South Africa. One of my NCOs, a man with more than a few days working with the CIA in more countries than I would ever visit, pulled me to the side and addressed my befuddled face.

"Sir, our boy must have been a national asset," he said.

"Sorry?" I replied.

"He belongs to the CIA, and he didn't tell them he was letting a team stay with him. Rather than turn him over to us, they sent him out of the country."

"Do you really think he's teaching art to the kids of South Africa?" I asked.

"Does it matter? Bottom line is we don't get to talk to him. He must be pretty well wired into whatever the CIA had going on before we got here. So here's your lesson: The CIA takes. They don't give, ever, unless it suits their purpose."

The necessity of the CIA would raise its head later, after the SF teams had gone into Afghanistan in October 2001.

While we were gaining the equivalent of graduate degrees in political science and civil engineering, trying to establish some semblance of a functioning government at the local level and get water flowing through sewage systems, the 10th Mountain Division was making sure that they didn't lose anybody in Haiti. Mogadishu was a recent memory, and it guided their leadership into keeping the entire division behind barricades. One brigade occupied the airfield in the north at Cap-Haitien and one the airfield at PAP. Very infrequently, maybe monthly, a company- or battalion-size element would "leave the wire" and conduct a security patrol, either on foot or via helicopter. Their interaction with Haitians was nonexistent—the opposite of our SF approach. They wore body armor and walked with weapons at the ready. They looked so out of place they made me wince. The people regarded them without emotion.

It was in Haiti that I came to believe that there was a time when SOF should take the lead, where the conventional forces should answer to a guy who wasn't concerned about taking ground but was more focused on winning a place with the indigenous population. We didn't hold ground, unless you consider the people the terrain. We became entrenched in Haitian society and were asked by anyone visiting the island what we thought would help the Haitians most, while our conventional brethren became entrenched and irrelevant behind jersey barriers and razor wire. We were saving lives while they were killing time, marking the days until they could get back to Watertown, New York. I am laying no blame here. They were doing what they were trained to do: fight an enemy and win battles. Only there were no enemies, so they didn't fight. They waited until someone called them home.

We became more diplomats than warriors. We did raids early on. I participated in three. On the last one, I vowed never to do another. A walk-in (somebody who just came to the gate and offered us information) explained that a leader in the political opposition party that had helped oust Aristide in 1991 was having a meeting just half a mile from our location. The target's name was Toto Fenton. We'd never heard of him, but this guy at the gate, who spoke English and sounded credible, explained the many sins of Toto, who had many weapons and bad ideas about who to use them on.

"Let's pay him a visit," I said, and we put together an ad hoc assault package. We walked up to his place, Haitians scattering like children as we approached, and executed a no-knock entry. We cleared the house and cordoned off the area.

The house was empty. No Toto. No weapons. We started rifling through everything but found nothing.

While we were ransacking his house, Toto Fenton arrived. We greeted him by throwing him facefirst into the dirt and cuffing him with plastic zip ties, now known as flex-cuffs.

My more seasoned SF guys began interrogating him, right there as he lay in the street, while the walk-in provided the questions. While this was going on, I noticed an unusual occurrence among the people standing back and watching.

They were sullen. Unlike our initial landing, when the thousands of Haitians greeted us as conquering liberators, the crowd was quiet. Their faces were blank, if not frowning. I could hear cracks forming in the foundation of our legitimacy. I saw rapport open its wings and prepare to fly.

A woman walked from the gallery and began speaking to us in Creole. The SF interrogator, who spoke French, translated for me. Mr. Walk-in suddenly got mad and forgot how to speak English.

"She says this is her brother-in-law," my guy said, motioning to a dirty Toto. Two Green Berets lifted him to his feet and sat him on his front porch. His shirtfront and trousers were caked in white dust from the road.

"She says he hasn't done anything to anybody. He wants to run for some office and Mr. I-Got-a-Secret here doesn't like him," he said, and then he held up his hand to indicate that the woman should stop talking. She complied, and he approached to within a few inches of me, so we could talk privately.

"I think we been had on this one, sir," he said quietly.

I remembered the other time I had failed to analyze the intelligence provided. The medicine man had said that we should kill the bad guy on the bridge. So we did. The walk-in whom nobody had ever seen before said the bad guy was at the house, and we should go get him. So we did.

"This is our last raid. Cut him loose and let's start apologizing. Call back to the hooch and have some MREs brought up here. Let's give the guy something for his humiliation," I said, suddenly very tired. Then I remembered something, and my anger flared. I looked at the man who had duped us by speaking English and said to him in plainly vulgar language that he should remove himself from anywhere near me. His language abilities seemed to return and he walked hurriedly away from the crowd.

The surrounding people approached us as we spoke to Toto and listened as we apologized for our stupidity. We gave him several cases of our MREs and hoped he would understand our sincere regret for destroying his house and making him lay in the dirt in front of his friends and family. I felt frustration as I groped for purpose on this Haitian adventure.

We trained to support governments or insurgent guerrillas. We didn't have a government to support or an insurgency to fuel. All we had were 5 million people who were waiting for us to deliver all the goods and services of a modern developed country. Like a poor married couple, we only had each other. So we had to hug the people and hoped they loved us in return. On the occasion of my visit to Toto Fenton, I had sought to accomplish the goal of having the people love us by choosing citizens at random and trashing their houses and reputations.

I never forgot the mistake.

Fortunately, the net effect was positive. The people saw that we would listen to reason, and that we were trying to be open. They saw that we could be diplomatic. We had several more walk-ins after that day, and I followed my resolution to never raid a house without tangible evidence that something nefarious was going on.

Until Bosnia kicked off in the fall of 1995, Haiti was the only show in the geopolitical arena, and, at least weekly, we would receive visitors in Jacmel. Whatever my briefing skills might be, they were honed as the commander of the SF teams controlling a chunk of the country. We entertained numerous staff from USAID, the State Department, the United Nations, and more members of the press than I thought I would ever meet in my life. Immediately, I could tell that my audiences were surprised that I could speak in something other than monosyllabic grunts. Our most famous guest was the U.S. ambassador at the time to the United Nations, Madeleine Albright.

She flew by helicopter to my city by the sea and spent Thanksgiving dinner with us. My sergeant major, Darrell Shanks, donated his green beret to the cause, and I presented it to her as a memento for her coming to see us over the holiday. She walked around with the beret on for the rest of the day. Over a plate of more food than a Haitian family of six would see in a day, I asked her, rather bluntly, why we were in Haiti. She didn't miss a beat and began talking about the need for stability in the region, a UN organization called the Friends of Haiti, and the requirement for the United States to take a positive role in helping Haitians come out of decades of repression. When she was finished talking, we walked her back to her helicopter, and she flew away, back to the land where most Haitians wanted to go. (At a dinner of SF officers many years later, the guest speaker, a staffer at the UN, informed the audience that the green beret we gave her now adorns a bust of Adlai Stevenson in the U.S. Ambassador's office in the UN building.) Following my conversation with Madam Ambassador, I understood there was no plan. Whatever we were doing in Haiti was like Vietnam, only without the shooting. Monetary aid would pour into this country like water on a rock and with about the same effect.

Haiti required a hundred-year Marshall Plan with a laundry list of agenda items that needed to be started simultaneously. But this wasn't relevant. Relevant were the 1996 elections and the fight for the White House. We achieved what President Clinton needed: a foreign policy success close to the homeland. Remembering back to General Potter's comment about the tragedy of the failed Iranian hostage rescue and the debilitating effect it had on Carter's campaign in 1980, I thought we had done well. President Clinton won reelection.

I had never considered the president's reelection a metric of my success. But now I could.

One day in late May of 1995, I was summoned to the phone by a public affairs officer and told to expect a call from a *New York Times* reporter, something to do with Bradley Fighting Vehicles in Desert Storm. I scratched my head and wondered why a reporter would want to contact me in Haiti to ask about the effectiveness of the Bradley. It didn't make any sense. I was a tanker in Desert Storm, and while I had Bradleys in my unit, I was far from an expert.

The phone rang at the appointed time, and the reporter immediately asked if we were following the Oklahoma City bombing. Thanks to Ross Perot, we had televisions and a satellite link, so yes, and, yes, I saw that the guy accused had been in the First Infantry Division. His name, Timothy McVeigh, was vaguely familiar to me, but I really couldn't place him.

"He was the gunner on the platoon leader's Bradley."

Thunderbolt. The interview was short, maybe ten minutes. I confirmed the reporter's facts. He had our after-action report and knew what we had and had not done. I didn't tell him about the conspiracy to murder the lieutenant, the fratricide intended by TOW missile, or the collateral damage anticipated. I didn't tell him of my actions that possibly spared the life of the lieutenant's gunner.

I have no idea what I would have done differently. Ignore the facts? Worse, give the idiots who were planning the murder some clue I knew and didn't care? I had made a decision based on what I knew. I remembered when they pulled him from Desert Storm to go to SFAS. I told him he wasn't ready. I hope that helped him fail and then quit.

My tenure in Haiti had showed me a side of soldiering that I had never imagined before joining SF. We ran the country, plain and simple. If people wanted something done at city hall, they found the closest Green Beret and explained the situation. Judge not playing fair? He's fired. Water system busted? We'll get some money and fix it. Schools don't have books? We'll call back to the States and get some books (oh yeah, in French). Some old lady threatening to suck the souls out of all the children if you don't pay her? Okay, we'll perform an exorcism and tell her she's next on the "Who Wants to Spend the Night in Jail?" show. No electricity? No problem; just point us to the generators.

But how were we able to get away with this approach? How did we go about our business and not live by the standards of what I had told my guys upon arrival—that nothing in Haiti was worth one American life? First, despite my misguided attempt to make us behave as aloof, dispassionate, and (mostly) white people who had just inherited a plantation, the true character of the Green Berets emerged from the shared experience of Robin Sage, and the people loved us. They loved us to the point that we found graffiti asking us to stay fifty years, which is roughly the life expectancy of the average Haitian.

Second, when we were confronted with indisputable data that showed we needed to move unilaterally and forcefully, we acted like soldiers who really liked killing people when we had the chance. Whether we liked killing or not was irrelevant. It is how we acted when presented with circumstances demanding lethal force.

One man did give his life for Operation Uphold Democracy. The one killed-in-action we had in Haiti was Sergeant First Class Gregory Cardott. He and another SF sergeant, T.J. Davis, were inspecting toll booths in the northern part of the island. Two Haitian men in a car approached the booth and refused to stop. The Haitians manning the checkpoint called out to the Green Berets, who in turn stopped the car. While being forcibly removed from the car, one of the Haitian men drew a pistol and shot Davis in his right forearm, his shooting arm. With Davis down, the man then shot Cardott in the chest, inflicting a mortal wound. Davis immediately switched his rifle to his left hand and killed the guy who had shot them. A crowd formed around the car, and the local population took justice into their own hands, killing the other occupant.

Word spread across the island: These little green men will blow your head off if you give them a reason. We could act like nation builders because we walked around like we owned the place, meeting with whomever we thought could help us make some development; and whenever we were confronted with the need to act with compassion, we usually did. But on those rare occasions when we needed to bare teeth and bite down, we would.

Although my time in Haiti seemed interminable, we did leave eventually. By the time we did, I felt like a real Green Beret.

With all the fanfare of stepping off the bus on a crowded street, in June 1995, my teams and I returned to Bragg. Though we got a six-week break in the middle, we had been gone for a total of ten months. I was still learning, but the curve was flatter. In the age before ubiquitous connectivity via the Internet, I corresponded with my wife through letters while I was deployed, and she would provide details of our children's progress. My son was taller than when I had last seen him, and my daughter was becoming a young lady. Holding them when I returned, watching them play, I sensed that my body's odometer had flipped over many times in the past three years. I wanted a break.

EIGHTEEN

MY BREAK FROM THE GRINDER of deployments came in the form of the U.S. Army Command and General Staff College at Fort Leavenworth, Kansas, a year-long sabbatical from the real Army where officers once again become students and try to reintegrate with their families. While attending the classes designed to prepare us for working at increased levels of responsibility, students routinely accuse the cadre of being irrelevant, and the cadre tells the students they're ignorant. I tried to spend as much time in the gym as I could. All that I learned in Haiti, in a multinational environment with ambassadors and witch doctors, left its mark on me. I remember one take-home assignment where the students were to write an operations order for the defense of the Fulda Gap, a traditional corridor for armies passing through Germany from the time of the Huns. My writing a plan to defend central Germany from the Soviet horde and having it graded by someone who had come of age in the conventional army was about as appealing to me as being electrocuted in the bathtub. When I pointed out to the instructors, in 1996, that the Soviet Union had collapsed, I didn't win any friends.

While there, in the spring of 1997, I received a phone call from the assignment officer in D.C. I was slotted to take over part of the Q course. Specifically, I was to be the commander for the men who instructed the student officers. That would put me out of the Q course less than five years before I went back to run a significantly important piece of it. I didn't know it at the time, but the honor was a nail in the coffin of my career. I commanded for two years as a tanker, six months as an SF team leader, two years as an SF company commander, and

I was now about to take command of a training unit. I should have been asking for a staff assignment, but that kind of work repulsed me. Gleefully, I accepted the assignment and relished the thought of being responsible for the next generation of leaders in the community I had come to admire, respect, and love.

Back at Bragg, I continued my SF education working in the doctrine branch of the Special Warfare Center at Bragg for ten months reviewing manuals and waiting for my predecessor to finish his command tour at the unit I was to take. After what seemed like a decade of reading SF publications, I accepted the guidon (unit flag) from my new boss, Lieutenant Colonel Manny Diemer. I shook hands with my new first sergeant, Mack Bolan; thanked the guy ahead of me, Tim Whalen, for setting high standards that I would strive to maintain; and became for a fourth time an Army commander.

Now I was a cog in the Guerrilla Factory.

I wish I could say that my first order of business was to sit down and have a roundtable with all my cadre or check on training records to see if there were any trends emerging about passing or failing the course. Rather, I went straight to the file cabinet holding all the student folders and pulled out my record. I read the note cards with comments from other students and the cadre. I reviewed the sheet with all the objective measures such as marksmanship and PT test. What struck me was one simple fact: If I had not found my map or not walked on the road in broad daylight, if for any reason I had failed Trek, though I had passed everything else, my life would've taken a completely different turn. My file contained nothing spectacular, only that I had passed everything in accordance with the established standards. My entire career after 1993 choked down into a seventy-two-hour filter called Trek.

I sat down with my cadre to entertain their thoughts on the status of the Q course for the officers. We moved to a new style of teaching, where an SF captain recently from a team would be a small-group instructor and mentor to the officer students assigned him. On the surface, this approach seemed appropriate to the intended audience because it provided a role model for the students to observe. The NCOs, however, saw it differently.

As long as anyone could remember, SF NCOs trained the SF student officers, therefore initiating the adjustment to seeing the NCOs as subject matter experts, not just men who were to be addressed as "sir." The point was valid and equally moot. The former training group commander, my boss's boss, a full colonel by the name of Charlie King, had made the decision, and he'd altered classrooms to support the new method. Four captains with very successful team time arrived in the unit at the same time I did.

Though he had relinquished command to Remo Butler, King happened to be in the area the day after I took command and dropped by my office to make sure I understood what was expected with the small-group, officer-led approach. He impressed upon me the quality of the officers that he had recruited to be the instructors.

"All of the small-group instructors are Ranger qualified."

"Forgive me, sir, but are you just trying to make me feel like chopped liver?" I asked while glancing at my left shoulder, a Ranger tab conspicuously absent.

He smiled sheepishly and responded, "Tony, you've been to combat. You don't need a tab."

I remember thinking, *Right. Tell me another one.*

Upon meeting them, I agreed with King's assessment regarding the quality of the officers he had gathered. Mark Bartholf, Mark Seidler, Mike Bownas, and Mike Stefanchek were all top shelf. (We started a joke that you had to be named either Mark or Mike *and* be Ranger qualified to be a small-group instructor.) All had recent experience in Bosnia, and I once again became a student listening to their stories.

The same quality was true of the noncommissioned officers and the warrants. Tim Simon, Paul Nosal, and John Edmonds were among the most competent warrant officers I had ever met. The NCOs were what I call "fire and forget"—they knew what to do and did it whether you were watching or not. (Note: Special Forces warrant officers are spooky. All warrant officers live in a gray area between noncommissioned and commissioned officer. They start as NCOs, which means they know the organization from the ground up. Once they volunteer for and graduate from the warrant officer course, they now command salutes from all enlisted personnel but must in turn salute all commissioned officers. In SF, in the absence of a captain, they can command an A-team. They can stay on teams for years and, by the end of a twenty-five-year military career, become walking encyclopedias of everything that is Special Operations and how it has been or could be applied to crises throughout the world. As a group, the rare bad apple notwithstanding, they are probably the most competent soldiers across the most disciplines in the Army, conventional and Special Operations.)

I discerned a common phrase among the cadre regardless of rank as we discussed the training and the people receiving it. "These guys are going to lead a team." The comment was spoken with passion and carried the sense that no one in the training pipeline wanted to be responsible for sending an incompetent to lead a group of Green Berets. The cadre expressed a strong sense of loyalty to those who were still serving on ODAs and felt an intense commitment to send only the best to the groups.

The problem, as I saw it, was deciding what or who was "the best." Do we tell a man who grew up in a city and never swam a day in his life that, because he had no access to a pool but speaks native fluent Urdu and runs like a gazelle, he can't be one of us? Does everybody need to look, talk, and act like a European Superman even when we know that our mission is to work with indigenous forces? What would our force look like if we only promoted people who could train combat troops from other countries without the use of translators? We talked about it academically, knowing that only a general and one with lots of stars could change the culture that esteemed the commando over the guerrilla.

The immediate concern was my favorite event: Trek. Tim Simon led the team that executed Trek, and they briefed me on some changes in the five years since I had graduated.

My own Trek exercise was sixty-five kilometers over three days. The new Trek was thirty kilometers over the same period. It had been moved from Uwharrie National Forest, which was foothills, to Pisgah National Forest, which was actually in the Smoky Mountains west of Asheville. We looked at the map, and I saw all the points displayed, all the places where a man would camp waiting for the students to come in exhausted, get their next point, and move on. All the points were connected by multiple lines indicating the various lanes. These lines arbitrarily crisscrossed changes in elevation as much as a thousand feet in half a mile. Though it was over more vertical terrain, the distance was relatively short, roughly six miles of walking per day. Yet more officers were failing Trek, and, as a result, our numbers for people graduating the Q course were dropping, and that was reflected in a higher cost per graduate.

The accountants who watched over our budget were complaining that we were still in the process of weeding out candidates after SFAS was supposed to have already done that. But this critique missed the point of why Trek had been placed in the middle of the officer training course in the first place. We want people who can lead themselves, who do not rely on a feedback loop to make decisions, and Trek tested that with a nuance most people missed when they compared it to the gut checks in SFAS.

For three weeks of SFAS, we were roster numbers and a last name. We did not wear our badges, our rank, or hold any implied authority by virtue of being an officer. In Trek, in the middle of the officer Q course, here was an event where only the other officers would see you, those guys who would be your peers when you got to the group. If you failed, you weren't called out at the end of an amazing gut check, only to be told when or if you could try again. Failure meant you were recycled to the next class, your assignment to your team was delayed, and your kids might have to change schools in the middle of the year because Dad had lost his map. In SFAS you trained over long distances, but on flat terrain and not anything close to the distances covered over the three days in Trek.

Colonel King wrote a paper about Trek and described something that I thought the event did measure: unsupervised predictability. What will you do when no one is around to give you feedback? One thing I learned watching five classes go through the exercise was that the typical Army officer is accustomed to hearing instantly that what he is doing is good or bad, effective or wasteful, justified or without merit. In my mind, Trek measured whether you could lead yourself.

Everyone I knew who had finished Trek felt like they had accomplished something big, something hard, alone, with no one telling them to sleep or eat or make a fire. They had demonstrated that they could think their way through a problem in a harsh wilderness while operating under a time constraint. Trek told us who could think for himself in a place where the clock was the enemy, not a soldier with a rocket launcher.

After days of discussion, and as the next Trek loomed, my boss, Lieutenant Colonel Diemer, called me into his office to discuss an event that was killing officers whom we had thought we wanted as indicated by their passing SFAS. He had data that showed Trek was not an indicator of successful performance in Robin Sage. There were complaints that the lanes were not equal, that some were harder than others; and if you were one of those students with a hard lane, then tough luck, see you next class. Other complaints were that the distances required were unrealistic—that nobody walked that far in three days breaking brush, and that no one in cadre could really explain why we did it.

I had data from previous classes that showed every lane had been passed. No lane was the "widow maker." We would have dropped it if such existed. Diemer wanted to keep Trek, but I wasn't helping him. First, we agreed that we needed to answer the question that most people would ask from an objective view: Are students failing because Trek is physically impossible? Under the old standards of sixty-plus kilometers, I would have said "Possibly." Ten kilometers (six miles) per day for three days is too hard, even at your physical peak? That time-distance standard hardly seemed the stuff of legends.

Yet no one in the training cadre had walked this Trek. We had extrapolated and compared it to other things we had all done, even other Treks, but no one in cadre had actually done the event as a student.

I remember the words jumped out of my mouth.

"What if I do it?"

Diemer's face communicated many things at once: "Hope you know what you're doing." "Please don't try to impress me—we've all done hard things in this community." "You fail, and we're going to hear about it."

"Sir, this is a mind game that our officers should be able to handle. I haven't been under a ruck in two years, but I can still do thirty clicks in three days."

"And if you can't?" he asked.

"If I don't make it to my last point in the time allotted, we have a reason to get rid of it. Or at least modify it."

He thanked me, wished me luck, and said he hoped I made it.

I went back and told the cadre. Simon was none too pleased.

"So if you don't make it, we get rid of it?" he asked. Not spoken, but understood, was the phrase "Just like that?"

"Maybe, or we modify it, but at least we can say that cadre did this and tell everybody to shut up."

"You're the boss," he said, unconvinced.

NINETEEN

TWENTY-TWO STUDENT OFFICERS and I loaded the bus at 0200 on a clear night in June of 1998. Simon and his team had been in the Pisgah National Forest preparing for the last several days. Fort Bragg slept as we drove through it, and within minutes, the snoring chorus began on the bus. I caught short naps while resting my head on my ruck. We stopped at a deserted rest area outside of Asheville, and the students lined up for the urinals. I walked up behind them and saw that the line for the men's room was fifteen deep, snaking past the open door of the ladies' room, which revealed several clean and empty stalls.

"Hey, gents," I said. "Here's an object lesson in unconventional thinking. Probably won't go to jail if we use these," and I motioned to the unoccupied bathroom that in their minds was forbidden territory. Point made. We cut our time at the rest stop by half and continued into the mountains of western North Carolina.

Upon arrival, the students laid out their gear for inspection by a member of Simon's team. I laid out mine to confirm that I was not walking around with what we affectionately call a "Nerf ruck," named for the miniature foam football that is significantly lighter than the regulation NFL version. I lined up to have my ruck weighed, picked up my packet containing my map and first point, and then rode in the back of a truck to my start point.

Within seven and a half hours of leaving Bragg, I was sweating under a fifty-six-pound rucksack on my second Trek. Gone was the toy rifle, and I wondered what I would swing at the dogs should they appear.

I followed a creek bed through thick mountain laurel and wondered if we had snakes in North America like they had in Trinidad, snakes that like to hang out in creek beds.

I got lost leaving the creek and wandered for two hours.

Finally, I hit a road intersection that showed me I had drifted about a mile off course. I dove back into the sea of rhododendron and struggled through the waves of vegetation. Soon I smelled the fire and walked up to the point sitter.

I crossed three ridgelines to get to my second point, my legs and shoulders burning in pain by the time I got there. The second point sitter gave me my next grid, and I headed off into a beautiful afternoon. The sun was just setting when I saw the fire of the third point. I checked in, got my next grid, and then walked off to find a place to rest for the night.

On the edge of an open field, under the high canopy of a tall pine, I made a fire. I opened my ruck, spread my sleeping pad, and removed everything but my salt-stained underwear. The temperature went low enough to keep the bugs off, and the fire served as my television. Nursing a cup of hot chocolate, I heard someone crash through the dark woods. My fire seemed to be a beacon that said "Someone thinks he knows what's going on," and another student hailed me as he approached.

"How's it going, man?" he asked, utterly unaware of who I was.

"It's going good," I replied. "How are you doing?"

He recognized my voice and I heard him say "Shit!" under his breath. Students are not allowed to talk to other students on the course, and he should have just walked by me. I could potentially give him a massive ration of grief. I sought to reassure him he was safe with another question.

"Where are you coming from?" I asked.

"Down south," he replied. He stopped in the light of my fire, and I could see the steam lifting from his head in the cool night air. "I'm still getting to my second point."

"The lanes are the same distance plus or minus a kilometer," I said. "If you made a long hump today, you'll be making shorter legs tomorrow."

"Roger that, sir."

"This trail right here," I said, pointing to a darker line that ran away from my fire and across the field, "runs straight to the point sitter. You can't see his fire from here. He's tucked in the trees just enough to hide."

"I'm going to check in with him and then follow your example."

"Good idea. Good luck."

I watched him disappear, climbed into my bag, and let my fire die. I felt I had lived my whole life to be where I was, asleep in my bag under a tree in North Carolina.

I awoke with the arches of my feet cramping and my calves as tight as steel cables holding a grand piano off the ground. The sunrise was the stuff Hollywood tries to re-create. Stretching, breakfast, coffee, dress, ruck, check map, and I was on my way again, slower than the day before, but not wandering. I discovered that navigation by map and compass is a perishable skill, and I sought not to waste one step going in the wrong direction. The underbrush was light in this area, and though I made good time—about a mile per hour—my body was talking to me. It was explaining that the reason we walk all the time with rucksacks in the SF group is to prepare ourselves for the massive microtrauma that comes from walking with the weight of a child on your back. No prior training meant that my body was adjusting on the fly and was very upset with me.

I bumped into Mark Bartholf, who was traversing the woods just to be outside and among the students. He asked me how I was doing.

"Can I quit?" I said, without smiling.

"No," he said, laughing.

We walked together up to my fourth point, and there was Chief Simon, checking on the point sitter.

"How you doing, sir?" he asked. He could read the pain in my face. Being an SF guy talking to another SF guy, he followed the question with a blunt assessment. "You don't look so good."

"I wish to terminate," I said, jokingly. Terminate is what SF guys do who wish to turn in the beret and go back to being whatever they were before they joined SF.

He shook his head and made a grim face. I tried to read his mind. *Why did you do this? We think this is important. You're on the verge of ruining it. What are you trying to prove?*

The exchange was cordial, but I had broken an unspoken tenet of all elite forces: Don't let anybody see you sweat. I was busting brush voluntarily to show that I thought Trek was important, but I couldn't just quickly complete it. I had to do it well. It's not how fast you walk long. It's how well you walk long and fast. I was hurting, and I showed it.

"Good luck," he said, as I headed to my fifth point. The sun got hot, and I felt every step in the bottom of my feet.

I drank water on the move. I came to a cliff and, using the map, could tell where I was by the sheerness of the descent. The area was called Turkey Falls and appeared to be a case of God having fun with my circumstances. At one point, I dangled from tree branches trying not to have the place name describe how I had made it down the mountain. I came out of the gravity-rich environment and found myself staring at a bold stream, about fifty yards across.

I knew if I fell in the water my ruck was going to soak up about five pounds of liquid pain.

I didn't fall but was shaking my head, trying to clear some dizziness. I climbed up the far bank and fell down, repeatedly. I couldn't get my legs.

I was suffering from heat stroke. I got into shade and drank water. Immediately, I vomited. It was a repeat of SERE school. I pulled a meal from my ruck. It was vegetarian pasta primavera. My stomach did a flip at the thought of trying to eat it. I sat there taking stock of the situation. I needed time to heal my body, and time was fleeting.

I waited forty-five minutes and tried a sip of water. It stayed down. We gave the students little envelopes of rehydration salts, which I had never tried, but I broke the rule of never using anything for the first time in a crisis. I poured the powder into a canteen and shook it. I took another sip, and again it stayed down. I nursed the canteen for thirty minutes, stopping if a swallow threatened to come back up. At an hour and fifteen minutes, with the sun now sailing across the sky like a baseball on a pop fly, I tried a bite of the pasta. It too stayed down. I ate and then licked the envelope of rehydration salts clean. I devoured everything in the meal, especially the salt. After one hour and forty-five minutes, I had successfully recovered myself. It was midafternoon, and my fifth point was at the top of a 750-foot climb. I filled my canteens from the stream and started up the mountain.

I got to the top of the ridge two hours later, traveling a straight-line distance of less than a mile. I knew that part of the moisture I was feeling in my socks was blood.

I walked up to the point sitter, hoping to be told I was done.

"Here you go, sir," he said. "Ready to copy your next grid?"

"Yep," I said, trying to hide my disappointment.

I had about two and a half miles to the next one—short by any standard—but the movement was over ground that would require being able to reconcile the map to the terrain. There was a knifeback ridge running straight to where I wanted to go. If I fell off that ridge, wandered down into a draw, I would be screwed, adding distance that my body didn't want to handle.

I followed the ridge until I couldn't walk anymore due to the pain in my feet. I removed my boots and wiped the blood off the bottoms of my feet so that I could apply bandages. I then laced them back on as tightly as I could.

I stayed on the ridge, predicting terrain features from the map and finding them where they should be. I got to a point where I had to come off the ridge. If I was right, there should be a road down at the bottom, and where it crossed a creek, I should find my point.

I could hear voices as I reached the road, sliding on my butt for the last hundred feet down the hill. One of Simon's NCOs saw me come from the woods and greeted me in typical SF fashion.

"Damn, sir, what took you so long?"

I finished fifth among the students. Somewhere in my head, the

Mormon Tabernacle Choir reprised the Hallelujah Chorus for me. My body felt like it had been beaten with thin steel rods. The heel pads of each foot, that big callus, fell off in the shower.

When we got back, I went to see Diemer. Limping into his office, I waited to hear that we had put the issue to rest of Trek being too hard. But the best response he could give me was that he hoped so.

The event was dropped five years later. Nobody could remember why we were doing it.

TWENTY

FIVE OFFICER CLASSES rotated through the course during my year and a half as commander. For two months my cadre would train the officers in operational planning for the various SF missions, of which the most important part is presenting the plan in a briefing to the commander. If the plan appears solid and sounds good, the team will get a green light. If it doesn't measure up to these standards, even if it is a marvelous display of tactical acumen, the team won't receive a go. I sat in on dozens of briefings, doing for the students what Lieutenant Colonel Jones had done for me, preparing them for the day when a real battalion or group commander would listen to their pitch and give the go-ahead for an operation. One presentation in particular stood out among the others. The student officers created a reason not to do the mission, which was to jump into a denied area, recon a bunker filled with shoulder-fired air-defense missiles, and then destroy it.

The student team leader was pointing to a sand table as I tried to follow his plan. "Upon infiltration by static-line parachute, if we lose more than half the team, we will abort." I raised my hand to call a stop.

"Say that, again," I said. The captain's face indicated he felt comfortable with wherever I wanted to take him in the conversation we were about to have regarding "abort criteria."

"Yes, sir. If I don't have at least four guys after we infil, we'll call for emergency extraction or execute our evasion plan," he explained.

"We know you have to account for that," I replied, referring to his contingency plan, "but somewhere along the line you have gleaned from my cadre that you should think of reasons *not* to do what we're sending you there to do."

A look of concern dimmed his face. Whatever he was thinking, he subdued it and pressed on. "But, sir, shouldn't I as the commander be concerned that we're not going on a suicide mission or allow everyone to think that no matter what happens, we just go to the target as planned?"

We call this a teaching moment.

"Actually, what I as the commander want to hear you say is that if only one of your guys makes it to the target, he will assess the best way to execute given that the rest of you are dead or otherwise lost. Then I, as the benevolent commander, would say something like 'Excellent! That's the spirit!' and then we would talk about the various what-if paths your plan might have to follow to accomplish whatever it is we told you to do. What I as the commander do not want to hear is a list of reasons why you may decide *not* to execute." I paused for effect. The captain nodded. "Imagine if I give two teams the same mission, send them into isolation, and take their briefings. One team leader says, 'And sir, if there's only one guy left, he's going to the target and will assault it with a bayonet fixed on an empty rifle.' The other team leader explains the various abort criteria. Who do you think is going?"

"Got it, sir," he said. "We'll fix this."

Once we finished and sent the students to Robin Sage, they were the responsibility of another cadre. My role changed. As I was responsible for the UW training the officers received prior to going and had rapport with them from hours of classroom and field time, I was used to shepherding those students who started "doing it wrong" during the last phase of training. I think the Robin Sage cadre had my home number on speed dial. Each time a class of officers went to the field for the final evaluations, marrying up with their enlisted counterparts for the capstone event, I would wait for the phone to ring and hear what horrible things my officer students had done. Typically by Day Seven of Robin Sage, always a Sunday, I would have to drive an hour and a half west from Bragg, meet with an SF NCO who thought he had a seriously afflicted student officer, and listen to the sins the officer had committed. Through numerous runs during my tenure, I learned that Robin Sage is a human-behavior laboratory, which brought out both the best and the worst in SF candidates. The vast majority of those who face the challenge rise to the occasion. Some of the more noteworthy failures will stay with me the rest of my life.

Once I stood with my mouth agape as the sergeant explained how he had observed the captain hiding behind a tree, watching his team die when the enemy had discovered the guerrilla base.

"Sir, he didn't just sit there, hiding. You could see he was scared," the sergeant said.

Stunned, I replied, "Let's see what he has to say."

The young infantry officer sat on a log with me, informally, and I asked him how it was going. He said pretty good. I reminded him that the only reason I visited the officers in Robin Sage was if things were not going well. He nodded and remained quiet.

"I heard you guys had a contact the other day. Whole team died," I said, trying to prompt him. He took the bait but not in the direction I had expected.

"Yes, sir," he replied. "I was the only one that made it."

"The cadre says you hid behind a tree and watched. Is that true?" This is where he was supposed to say something about how his gun jammed, or how he was out of ammo or had a seizure—something to mitigate the indictment of what the court-martial manual calls "misbehavior in the face of the enemy," which is punishable by death.

"Sir, I experienced uncharacteristic nonproactive behavior."

"Say that again," I responded, unable to hide my rising anger.

"It was uncharacteristic nonproactive behavior—"

I cut him off and congratulated him on his excellent command of the English language and then delivered my apoplectic invective of this behavior and concluded with the promise that I would launch him out of the Q course like a Polaris missile out of a submarine if he didn't get his head out of his ass.

He didn't graduate.

Another officer, while sitting with his team around a fire, admitted that he wanted to be an astronaut. Behind him, beyond the circle of light, two NCOs listened surreptitiously as the officer explained how being SF qualified would enhance his chances of being selected for the Army space program. Their concern, which I shared, was that an officer worried more about his promotion than his team could make really dumb decisions, like *not* conducting realistic live-fire training for fear of injury. His sins would be crimes of omission, his team would languish while he fretted over his annual efficiency report, and he might help several good NCOs find their way out of the SF community or get them killed.

The blood drained from his face when he realized I was there to see him. We discussed why an officer who was using SF as a stepping-stone might not be allowed to graduate.

"But, sir, I was always taught that you're supposed to be looking for your next job . . ."

"I would agree, except this isn't a job. SF is a like a priesthood. We don't want to hear that someone has joined to be a priest in order to be a pharmaceutical salesman. We don't see ourselves as a means to an end. We think we *are* an end. Like if you die as a Green Beret, that would be sad but cool. You want to be an astronaut? Go be one. Just don't do it on the backs of guys who have committed heart and soul to being what you perceive as a way to get to where you really want to go." He listened and nodded.

He didn't graduate.

The most spectacular leadership failure I observed came at the end of one Robin Sage, the captain within days of getting his beret. One of the dilemmas that some of the Robin Sage cadre like to present is the idea that the guerrilla chief has authority over the SF guys he's working with. The captain in charge has to balance maintaining rapport with the reality that no one but the U.S. military has authority to punish an American soldier unless an arrangement has been made through a treaty. In one instance, a captain surrendered his authority to the chief, with adverse consequences for the captain.

The guerrilla chief told the captain that one of the SF guys had offended him and needed to be taught to respect the chief. The captain agreed and asked what the chief thought would be a fitting punishment.

"Throw the offending soldier in the creek without his clothes," he said. "Do it today at four o'clock this afternoon." The captain said okay. The chief left the base, and his guerrillas were huddled around the fire (as it was late December and frigid in the North Carolina hills), with no one paying particular attention to the SF guys when punishment time rolled around. The captain looked at his watch and announced they needed to head to the creek if they were going to "get this over with before the chief came back." Astonished but compliant, the team followed the captain to the creek, watched their man disrobe, and then threw him into running water with a temperature of fifty-five degrees.

As the officer stood before us—Diemer was present, as this was considered a serious leadership failure—and recounted what he had done and why, I tried to imagine how the offending soldier must have felt, standing naked next to a creek, in front of his team, about to be punished for an offense that no one could prove, and wondering if such humiliation was worth it all.

We decided to let the officer try again, but I could not let him go without making him feel part of the embarrassment his teammate felt. I told him to stand at the position of attention and then I got about two inches from his face. After three minutes of continuous verbal assault in which I described his despicable and reprehensible conduct, I concluded my diatribe (delivered as loudly as I could muster without screeching) with a question.

"Do you feel like shit?" My words bounced off his face and filled the room behind me.

"Yes, sir."

"Good! Now get the fuck out of here!"

Between visits to Pineland, I would sit in on lessons the student officers received from the sergeants they might lead one day. Right before I left my job at the Q course, I walked into a classroom where the officers were receiving a class on communications. At the front of the room, talking about a radio the students would have to master in order to do their job on an A-team, was T.J. Davis, himself lately from 3rd Group. I took a seat discreetly at the back of the class and nodded to signal to him that I was just there to listen—all was good. He nodded back and continued. We knew each other but not as teammates. He finished his class, and, before he let the students go on break, he acknowledged my presence at the back by asking if I had anything I would like to say to my student officers. An object lesson sprung into my head.

"Yes," I said, as I walked to the front. "Does anyone know how many SF died in Haiti?" No one moved or had a clue. I saw Davis watching me out of the corner of my eye.

"One," I said. "SFC Greg Cardott took a round through his chest. He was a 3rdGroup guy. The guy that was with him is right there," and I pointed at Davis. "SFC Davis was shot in his shooting arm, switched hands, and killed the guy that had killed his team sergeant." Davis started looking at the floor, obviously embarrassed.

"What'd you get for that, T.J.?" I asked.

"Purple Heart, sir."

"No valor award? No combat patch? Nothing to tell the world that, given about two seconds to figure out what was going on, you killed a guy when we hadn't shot anybody for months?" The students now beheld their instructor with overt amazement, their faces aglow with the realization that they were sitting with someone who didn't start his class with a war story that was worth telling over and over.

"Welcome, to SF, men. That's the kind of guy you have to lead," I said, and I walked toward the door, leaving the NCO to fill in the blanks.

"Thanks, sir," he shouted sarcastically.

I left my assignment as the commander of the officer training company after a year and a half of immersion in the doctrine, history, practice, and planning for unconventional warfare. I had read Che and Mao. I had talked to my cadre and listened as the stories poured out.

I had tried to learn everything there was on UW.

Then I found out that nobody cared.

TWENTY-ONE

IN JULY 1999, I left Pineland, the Special Warfare Center, and Fort Bragg. I had fifteen years in the Army at that point. Except for my time in school as a student or instructor, I had stayed at the tactical level, that is—"where the rubber meets the road," as the saying goes. My men gave me a muzzle-loader rifle as a going-away gift.

After thirty days of leave, I walked into U.S. Special Operations Command (SOCOM), the four-star headquarters in Tampa, Florida, the mother ship of all Special Operations Forces worldwide. If I thought I had lived in the shadow of Olympus at the tactical level, now I was about to be supping with the gods. I imagined that SOCOM would be full of people like me, only better, with more experience, and many more combat operations, with racks of valor awards filed away in a restricted file because they had been earned on covert missions. I had asked to come to SOCOM because I wanted to see the universe of America's elite from the top. I wanted to immerse myself in the company of the really high-speed SOF.

Most people don't know this about the mother ship in Tampa. SOCOM was established mainly to buy and supply the things the commandos need to do their job. Congress created the headquarters as a result of the failed hostage-rescue attempt in 1980, which brought about the realization that, without a dedicated funding stream and a group of amazing armed athletes, the United States did not possess the capability to surgically strike an opponent. (Politically, a cruise missile is surgical. Tactically, a cruise missile is about as surgical as a chain saw.) While I watched and learned how my cousins in the highly classified special mission units or SMU's (pronounced *smooz*) were equipped, I remembered a short story from the eighth grade.

In Franz Kafka's "A Hunger Artist," a man makes a living fasting and sitting in a cage. He sits for days in his cage while people come and admire him for many various reasons, mostly for his ability to sit for days and be hungry. By the end of the story, he is working for a circus. Then, tastes change. A hungry guy no longer draws the crowd, and the circus replaces him with a panther, which is all the rage.

I began attending meetings and hearing very powerful military decision-makers, both in uniform and civilians, make a comment that stunned me. "Unconventional warfare is no longer a viable political mission. This is 1999." Then I saw the result of such thinking in the allocation of funds.

I watched the budget process. The commando didn't just get a lion's share; he got his before and at the expense of the guerrillas. The concept of several football players traveling toward a target in a black helicopter, doing great violence to those who needed it, and leaving before the press could get wind of it was much more appealing than Green Berets walking (possibly riding pack animals) with a group of people nobody really trusted anyway and hoping that in a few months a political objective would be achieved.

Traumatic amputation, unilaterally administered and measured in hours, was much preferred by the leadership (not just at SOCOM, but at the Department of Defense writ large) over the introduction of cancer-causing agents, administered by, through, and with indigenous people, measured by several months.

I began to see SF as the hunger artist. We spent months and years training men to do a mission that took months and years to accomplish. Based on conversations in the Pentagon and among members of Congress, the leadership within SOF (all the services) began to suspect that the days of Green Berets taking insurgents to blow up the bridge in support of the allied attack had passed. Fortunately, they didn't have the heart to tell us, the SF, that all that rucking and slapping and learning foreign languages was unnecessary, that we'd never get to do that which we claimed to be experts in: unconventional warfare.

Within months of my arrival at SOCOM, I confirmed the dichotomy I had suspected within the world of SOF, a disparity in the allocation of resources to SOF that always acted unilaterally versus the SF guys. The commandos really did get top priority for everything. The retort to any complaint about this disparity was the same: "Just what advanced technology does SF need to do UW anyway?" In the minds of many military decision-makers, the big Army had already given the Green Berets everything required to hang out in some forlorn backwater, gnawing on fire-roasted iguana, and delivering babies for women in a developing country. And, oh, by the way, our precious UW mission was not politically viable. The thinking went that there would never again be the political will to send Green Berets to a country and act out Robin Sage in real life.

UW became an albatross for SF. The primary reason for our existence became the excuse to lower our funding priority. Given the choice to buy a half-billion-dollar mini-sub or pay for more language instructors at Bragg, SOCOM usually pointed the nozzle of the money machine at the requests for something that sounded cooler than the image conjured by a group of men sitting in a classroom and learning to ask where the library was in Spanish.

I took the realization in stride. My daily routine at SOCOM looked boring on the outside, but it gave me access to the dialogue about how funding decisions were being made. In the months leading up to the attacks of 9/11, I became one of the gatekeepers for all the procurement of new toys for the ground side of all SOF that took place at SOCOM, one of the first stops for anyone buying new kit. If a Navy SEAL unit requested a new ground vehicle, the validation process began with me. The same was true of night-vision devices, weapons, explosives, clothing—any kit associated with ground operations. I quickly realized that "the boys" seldom included my Green Berets. The Army had crafted us in the image of Daniel Boone, and Daniel Boone did not require much to get by in his wilderness. The commando was priority one. Army SF, not so much.

I had a good life, despite daily episodes of cognitive dissonance: "What do you mean, UW is politically nonviable? Why the hell did I kill myself to join the second string?" From September 1999 to September 2001, I worked out every day for two and a half hours at lunch, started work on a master's degree at night, and chaired meetings where I tried to help the Q course get more funding to improve the way we made new SF soldiers. During this period, I decided I would retire when I reached twenty years in service, take my pension, and begin life anew.

Then, like most of America, I watched on CNN as the World Trade Center collapsed. I tried to make sense of the airplane tail sticking out of the world's largest office building. I looked up the names of friends who I knew were assigned to the Pentagon.

Overnight, my job in Tampa went from "off to the gym" to one of the most visible in SOCOM. The fight was in Afghanistan, a landlocked nation six hundred nautical miles from international water. Probably going to be a ground fight, probably going to be SOF led—something favoring our mission skills set.

Dov Zakheim talked to the SOCOM comptroller, Elaine Kingston. Basically he asked her how fast she could obligate something north of a billion dollars. She became one of the most important women in the Department of Defense, as her staff began cranking out paperwork that would turn America's wealth into combat power ten thousand miles away. I got the task to create the ad hoc group of guerrillas and commandos and prioritize a $1.8 billion budget that would prepare all Special Operations Forces for action in Afghanistan. No more two-hour lunches. Meetings at SOCOM lasted until two o'clock in the morning. Again, I felt like I had lived my whole life for that moment. In no small way, I had my hands on the money spigot and could significantly influence who got what and when. With the round table of SF officers and Navy SEALs, we started spending money aerobically.

At the time, we didn't know which approach would take priority: counterterrorism or unconventional warfare. Who was in the lead, commando or guerrilla? Unilateral or indigenous coalition? There are military people who would say it was never "either or." There was to be a synchronization of the two approaches. I would offer that while a husband and wife may say they share decision-making responsibilities in the home, we have a phrase "who wears the pants" for a reason: Somebody is going to be the lead.

Finally, the Joint Staff sent the memo. We were to conduct a doctrinally correct U.S.-sponsored insurgency, a classic UW campaign. It was to be a seven-phase effort taken right from the SF doctrine manual and pasted as notes to a war plan. The A-teams would link up with the Northern Alliance and provide the operational focus and necessary cohesion such that the United States could displace the Taliban and destroy the safe haven of Al Qaeda. Legitimacy and rapport would be the foundation for everything about to happen, and the SF guys would make the sky fall on America's enemies in the form of bombs.

The guerrillas had the lead.

In the midst of my euphoria, my heart broke when I saw that the teams would not, and could not, provide lethal aid. I was stunned. Until that moment in October of 2001, none of us in SF knew that what we had taught in the Q course was fiction: There was no mechanism allowing the Green Berets to provide guns and ammo to the guerrillas whom they sought to train, advise, and equip. The CIA had to do it for us. My time with Paddy and the access he provided to the black market during Robin Sage was just bad acting. The teams were to link up and wait while the bureaucrats sorted through the legal wickets that would bring the guns to the Afghan shooters who needed them.

Nonetheless, the plan called for SF to do UW. I decided that somehow, perhaps by miracle, the lethal aid would flow. Lethal aid costs money. I brought the issue to my ad hoc group and asked how much we thought it would cost to fund the UW campaign in Afghanistan. The SEALs sat and listened while the SF guys started talking from the Robin Sage playbook. We discussed buying transportation, paying agents for information, providing food for the Northern Alliance troops. We talked about cold-weather clothing for the indig and where we could find supplies. We talked about how much combat power would have to be mustered to be an effective counter to the Taliban and Al Qaeda. We decided the Taliban and Al Qaeda represented a U.S. infantry division's worth of combat power. Doctrine taught us that for every one of them, we needed three of us to win an attack. Ergo, we needed three divisions of Afghan guerrilla fighters. That's about 45,000 dudes. Figuring that most would bring their own AK-47, we focused on the need for ammo and magazines, maybe new turbans. When we finished, we estimated the cost for the UW campaign around $307 million.

The guys in the comptroller's office at the OSD said, "Sounds good. Check's in the mail."

That was early October 2001, and my education as an SF officer came to bear in a way that I would have never anticipated. Pictures of the fight began to trickle in, of Green Berets riding horses into battle with Afghans on either side. I was proud to say I was one of them.

But the temporal reality of UW began to raise its head. By late October, complaints were coming from CENTCOM staff, the guys at Central Command who were actually running the war. (Remember: SOCOM was an automatic-teller machine with a directional money-spraying nozzle—an important role, to be sure, but without any operational control.) The chief complaint was "What's taking so long?" Across the street at SOCOM, we, the worker bees with a background in UW, were flabbergasted.

Apparently, word of CENTCOM's frustration at the slow pace of the UW effort made it all the way back to the battlefield of Afghanistan. One of the SF team leaders addressed the concern in a situation report that found its way to SOCOM. In it, the young captain wished to inform all of us sitting in Tampa, ten thousand miles from a full-blown guerrilla war and the daily dying, that his men, his guerrillas, were killing Taliban every day. That his guerrillas were going into battle with as little as ten rounds of ammunition apiece, and they were killing and dying without complaint. He explained they were doing the best they could with what they got, and what they got was guys laying it all on the line so America doesn't try something stupid like a conventional ground war.

I am told by a first-person witness to the reading of the message to the CENTCOM leadership during a daily update that the ensuing silence would have made that team leader proud. The complaints ended there.

Then, to everyone's surprise, the UW effort started delivering results the first week of November, when Mazar-i-Sharif fell. By late December, elation at what the hunger artists had achieved was palpable. The SOF commandos, the panthers, were tearing the heart out of the people who needed it, no doubt. But the SF had just delivered a historical and resounding victory for the guerrilla approach, an approach that demanded attention.

In the midst of spending more money than I could imagine, I received a phone call from my assignment officer. He asked if I would go to Honduras to be the operations officer for Joint Task Force Bravo, a Cold War holdover unit based on a 5,000-foot runway north of Tegucigalpa. President Reagan had established it to fight communist guerrillas in El Salvador and Nicaragua, and nobody had closed it down since peace had broken out. I had thirty minutes to decide. If I said yes, I would have to leave before Christmas. I accepted, understanding that SOCOM was no longer releasing officers on staff to go to Afghanistan as augmentation for the forces over there. Here was a last chance, I reasoned, to find an operational billet.

By the end of 2001, I was in Honduras, serving as the director of operations for JTF Bravo. I was in the small, secure office that served as our operations center when the media reported that Kandahar had fallen.

The expulsion of the Taliban and Al Qaeda from Afghanistan in the opening months of Operation Enduring Freedom was the ultimate validation of the approach we taught at the schoolhouse. The selection process and training were close to the mark. The SF soldiers who grew beards and the leaders who let them demonstrated the importance of building rapport. You have more respect from Afghan men if you have a decent beard. Respect feeds legitimacy. Legitimacy breeds rapport.

With fewer than two hundred SF soldiers on the ground (and many, many combat missions by jet fighters and bombers), the Green Berets had carried the day and became the nerve center of a lethal force that destroyed the most critical asset Al Qaeda had: a safe haven. The fact that another was waiting just across the Durand Line, a border that is observed more by Westerners than the people it ostensibly divides, was not apparent to us in 2002.

The SF effort in the opening months of Afghanistan validated nearly fifty years of training. Here was a group of soldiers utterly wedded to the notion of acting legitimately in the eyes of the people they came to live among, to fight beside, and to die with. Cross-cultural communication was not something academic—it was the cornerstone for victory. With the demonstrated success of the SF communication skills came an understanding that no other approach would serve U.S. interests well in the region. A U.S. unilateral effort would ultimately fail.

The same reports—from the news, from official traffic, from everywhere—that had informed my sense that we were legitimate in our efforts began to indicate that something was amiss. Around the middle of 2005, the reports coming from Afghanistan suggested that the United States was beginning to experience institutional Alzheimer's (to paraphrase Sarah Chayes in her book *The Punishment of Virtue*). We seemed to have forgotten what we did right. The Swiss Army knives were no longer in the lead, and neither were the scalpels. The bayonets, the big conventional forces, were in the lead. By design, the conventional formations have little regard for the people as a whole. Their mission is to destroy the enemy. When the enemy looks like the local population, collateral damage becomes more than acceptable. It becomes anticipated and then irrelevant in the planning of operations.

Collateral damage, wounded and dead noncombatants, loses its significance when there is a cultural divide, such as exists between most Western military personnel and the Afghan people. This is not to say that conventional soldiers lack compassion for noncombatants; far from it. But I watched through my telescope as the United States and its Western allies used a bayonet to build schools. By design, the bayonet is not meant to do the things required to maintain rapport. If conventional forces are threatened while trying to do something in the humanitarian arena, their capacity to act with restraint is limited by an organizational design that comes from being an amazing killing machine.

No one should have gotten upset because the tanks destroyed the apricot orchards in Kandahar when driving through them. That's what tanks do. No one should have been surprised when 500-pound bombs hit the houses of noncombatants during a fire fight. That's what planes dropping bombs do when answering the call from guys who are listening to the boomlets of bullets breaking over their heads.

With such accidents, another crack formed in the bedrock of our legitimacy. Each death of a child, the killing of an Afghan family during a case of mistaken identity, and even the destruction of vineyards by tanks from NATO countries chipped away at the legitimacy of our mission. Such a loss of rapport will be difficult to mend when living behind blast walls and razor wire.

At the time of this writing, I imagine that leaving, whenever we do leave, will be victory. It will be almost as if the United States had taken a page from our experiences in Vietnam and said, "Hey, this isn't so bad."

But in 2001, a relatively small group of guys with green berets (supported by the most powerful Air Force and Navy in the world) showed how to bridge cross-cultural divides, to liberate a people while causing harm to an amorphous enemy and with a microscopic cost for a tremendous, history-changing return on the investment. I fear that feat may be forgotten as we declare victory and one day leave.

The Army Special Forces like to tout ourselves as warrior-diplomats, but we are not politicians. We are warriors who know how to learn the ways of people from other countries, to find a place at their tables, to earn their trust, and fight and kill beside their warriors in pursuit of a shared cause. For that, people living in these countries often like us and help us to clean up the politicians' messes, messes often made decades before. Sometimes we succeed. Sometimes we fail.

But we will die trying. *De oppresso liber.*

Acknowledgments

My writing this book was possible only through the kindness of Ron and Cindy Schiff, who opened their home and allowed me to live with them as if I was family.

To George Getschow ("Tony, come to Mayborn . . ."), Sarah Whyman ("Tony, there's an agent I want you to meet . . ."), and the writers and readers of the Mayborn tribe of the University of North Texas, thank you for your affirmation and the opportunity you presented to me. George, you were my portal into a world I had only read about. Sarah, you facilitated a meeting that started a journey I have wanted to take since I learned to write as a child.

To my agent, Jim Hornfischer, thank you for taking a chance on me.

To Dominick Anfuso and Sydney Tanigawa of Free Press, thank you for believing Jim and all the attention you have shown me.

To the men and women with whom I served during twenty years, please accept my heartfelt thanks. In the Big Red One, Dave Holcomb, Mark Wald, and the men of the Ironhorse will always be my brothers-in-arms.

To Gregory J. McMillan, Darrell Shanks, Steve Franzoni, John Cooksey, John Humphreys, Mack Bolan, Chuck Jenkins, and the men of the Green Berets, I count myself truly fortunate to have the honor of having served with you. The world may not know how much has been given to wear that distinctive hat, and I hope this book helps explain the sacrifice.

To my parents, Faye and Horace, and my sister, Stephanie, thank you for your encouragement as I rode a rocket sled on a roller-coaster track during the years it took to craft this book.

To my daughter, Amanda, thank you for your time and expertise in reviewing the drafts. The memory of our sitting together and reading aloud is an indelible and delightful image I will carry the rest of my days.

To Stephanie, my partner, thank you for believing in me. Without your love, trust, and support, this book could not have happened.

Index

About the Author

TONY SCHWALM is a retired lieutenant colonel with the U.S. Army Special Forces.

In more than twenty years in the Army, his assignments around the globe included leadership positions in combat operations, humanitarian assistance missions, and counter-drug operations. Since the attacks of September 11, 2001, he served with U.S. Special Operations Command and has supported Special Operations Command Central and Joint Special Operations Command, creating state-of-the-art technology architectures to support Special Operations Forces. As a tank company commander in Operation Desert Storm, he was awarded the Bronze Star for Valor.

He is currently assigned to the Combined Joint Special Operations Task Force–Afghanistan, as a Department of the Army civilian leading a group of social scientists supporting special operations forces in that war-torn country.